MW01598656

TRAEGER GRILL & SMOKER COOKBOOK

The Complete Guide for Beginners to Master Your Wood Pellet Grill, With 300+ Healty and Tasty Recipes for the Perfect BBQ

Grill Academy

Table of Contents

Introduction

The Traeger Grill is a pellet grill that allows you to cook anything, anywhere. The grill is specifically designed to make grilling easy and allows you to cook food with ease. The Traeger Grill is also perfect for anyone who has limited space, and it is easy to store when not in use.

The Traeger grill is a great product for people who love to grill but don't have the time or space to deal with charcoal or gas. It's a high-quality grill that's designed to use wood pellets as fuel for the fire. It is neighboring a great way to smoke meat and also grill food. It can be used as an outdoor grill or indoors with the included stand for the unit and it has a very sleek design. The best thing about this grill is that it offers different types of cooking options, so you don't have to just do one type of grilling process. It also uses a patented pellet system, which ensures even grilling every time and doubles as an auger that drops wood pellets on the flame if they catch fire.

A Traeger grill uses direct-heat convection technology to evenly cook your food. The grill was designed to cook foods faster and at lower temperatures, but can get hotter than a standard smoker or oven. This saves you time and money! They take about an hour to smoke meats such as pork shoulder, brisket, ribs, chicken breasts or wings.

It also has a thermostat control system that monitors internal temperature automatically, which makes for much more precise cooking than most other units out there on the market today.

The Traeger grill can cook at temperatures as low as 150 degrees Fahrenheit and as high as 450 degrees. It is easy to use and will please any meat-eating enthusiast, whether amateur or professional.

The smoker's design helps you to cook for a larger group of people while spending less time tending to the barbecue. The taste is incredible!

Temperatures as small as 150 degrees Fahrenheit in addition as high as 450 degrees Fahrenheit can be cooked on the Traeger grill. It's easy to use and will please any meat-eater, whether they're a novice or a pro.

Traeger is also known for its high-quality wood pellets, which ensure that all of its items remain durable even when exposed to harsh weather for extended periods of time. These pellets are made entirely of natural hardwood (no fillers) and have a clear smoke flavor during the cooking process. Owing to the improved airflow control valve, they often burn hotter than conventional wood pellets. The food is flavored with wood pellets which gives the food a nice smoky taste. The Traeger Grill works by taking the smoke from wood pellets and then using the convection system to warm it up and infuse it with your food. The process of cooking on the Traeger is pretty simple: you fill the hopper with pellets, close the lid, set the temperature, and let it cook.

One of the popular features of the Traeger wood pellet grill is the result of its smoke from the wood pellet. Many customers are amazed by the wood pellet smoker. There are hundreds of positive and amazing testimonials about the grill. The Traeger grill allows users to smoke and grill their food and the meat can be smoked for up to 15 hours. The grill is easy to use, functional, and reliable. The Traeger grill is also very durable because of its body. The body of the grill is made of cast iron. The BBQ grill is easy to install and is easy to maintain. The grill can create smoke by using wood pellets and it can be adjusted to a temperature of about 225 degrees Fahrenheit. The food cooked on the grill has a consistent smoky flavor because of the wood pellets. The grill is an automatic cooker, meaning it conserves the heat that it produces, and it doesn't lose heat.

CHAPTER 1:
What Is The Trager Wood Pellet Grill

Traeger Wood Pellet Grills are electric grills that use wood pellets as their fuel source. The specially designed wood pellets can also be used as flavor enhancers to give food an excellent smoky taste. With his grill, Joe Traeger revolutionized barbecuing and made it convenient and straightforward. Traeger Wood Pellet Grill and Smoker does not require constant monitoring and can be left to regulate itself while cooking. It differs from other smoker grills such as the Traeger electric smoker and the pellet grills that use a digital control to adjust the temperature. The grill uses a wood pellet fuel that causes it to smoke. The different types of wood pellets that the grill uses to smoke food are Applewood pellets, Hickory wood pellets, Mesquite wood pellets, Cherry wood pellets, and Alder wood pellets. The wood pellets can be used to smoke chicken, turkey, fish, oysters, cow beef, and many other types of poultry. The wood pellets can be used to smoke other foods such as pizza, vegetables, and other foods. The wood pellets are made using recycled wood materials. The wood pellet grill can also be used to grill food and bake food.

The grill is easy to use because it's made of a simple design and it doesn't have any complicated elements. The Traeger wood pellet grill is easy to use and can be used indoors as well as outdoors. The user can check the temperature to make sure that the food is cooked perfectly. Most types of grills can be used both as gas grills and charcoal grills.

There are five models of Traeger Pellet Grills available, depending on the size and capabilities. The models include:

- Pro Series

- Ironwood Series

- Timberline Series

- Portable Grill Series

- Commercial Grill Series

Some of the components featured in the models are:

Pellet Hopper: This is the part of the grill that stores the wood pellets. It's recommended to keep it filled to prevent the interruption of cooking activities. The number of pellets used depends on the time and temperature required for cooking a particular meal.

Porcelain-Coated Grill Grate: This holds the food to be prepared. It is coated with porcelain to prevent the sticking of meals. The grate is also very easy to clean.

Cast Iron Grate: This grate allows for an even distribution of heat when grilling. It creates a perfect sear when used.

Steel Construction: Made from cold-rolled steels, they are durable and reliable as a cover for the Traeger grill. It helps with the regulation of temperature and can be cleaned easily because of its non-stick surface.

Convection Blower: This is important to the grill as it is responsible for maintaining a constant flow of air to keep the pellets in the Firepot aflame.

Auger: This conveys the pellets from the hopper to the Firepot.

Auto Start Firepot: This is where the wood pellets are ignited for cooking. It is controlled by the Thermostat and does not require any external firing methods.

Hot Rod Ignitor: When turned on, it causes the pellets in the Firepot to ignite and rise to the temperature selected on the Thermostat Controller.

Fire Baffle Plate: It is positioned around the Firepot and serves as a deflector shield to retain heat. The plate ensures that the heat produced is absorbed and spread evenly to the cooking grates.

Thermostat Controller: This is used to set the temperature of the wood pellet grill. It controls the Hot Rod Ignitor and ensures that the selected temperature is maintained throughout cooking.

Grease Drain Pan and Bucket: Used during indirect grilling, baking, roasting, and smoking. The Grease Drain Pan collects the grease produced during cooking and transports it to the Grease Bucket through the Grease Drain Tube.

Smoke Exhaust: This is used to control the flow of air out of the grill. It is essential for maintaining the temperature of the cooking chamber.

Some special aspects of the Traeger Grills are:

1. **The fuel**

Most other types of grills make use of charcoal, natural gas, or propane as a source of fuel. In the case of these fuel sources, the user needs to have a bit of knowledge of the grill type and be present to 'babysit' the grill.

On the other hand, Traeger grills use wood pellets that are all-natural and all-wood. These pellets can burn well in a controlled environment and provide flavorful food. Additionally, these pellets are FDA-approved and safe for home and outdoor use.The pellets are available in 14 distinct flavors. They can be used to create a new range of individual flavors and do not harm the environment when burned.

2. **Flavor**

Traeger pellets are available in 14 different types of pellets like pecan, apple, mesquite, hickory, etc. Apart from infusing delicious flavor to the meat, you can also use them for baking sweets like pie and cookies.

3. **No flare-up**

There are no flare-ups in roasting, baking, smoking, or grilling when you are using indirect electric heat, not gas. This is because electric heat (indirect) does not lead to flare-ups. The appliances are also not exposed to dripping temperatures.

4. **Control of the temperature**

One of the best aspects of the Traeger Grill is total control of the temperature. Once you set it, the grill is capable of maintaining consistent heat, even if the weather may not look favorable.

The Traeger grills can be set in 5-degree increments, which is a feature not seen in many grills, especially charcoal and gas ones. All you need to do is cook the food using the recipe and not worry about the appliance dropping down the temperature.

Additionally, since pellets are essentially electric, you are not tied to your grill like a gas grill. For instance, you do not have to keep checking the grill from time to time to ensure that the food has not burned.

5. **Environmentally-friendly**

Grills manufactured by Traeger make use of all-natural and real wood pellets that can burn within a controlled system, thereby offering flavor, ease of use, and convenience.

These grills are also approved by the FDA and the flavors of the pellets can be blended to create a mix of flavors. Additionally, burning these pellets will not cause any harm to the environment, as mentioned before.

Traeger Wood Pellet Grill Vs. Charcoal and Wood Grills

Traeger wood pallets have numerous benefits that other charcoal and gas grills cannot provide. Barbecuing is a great gathering excuse and outdoor activity, but it is a hassle to set. In this day and age where everything is becoming more convenient, this activity should also become easier to deal with as well.

It is easy to start:

Getting a charcoal or gas grill to ignite is a hassle, but the fire inside the firepot is easy to turn on. It also is much safer as you don't have to stick your hands inside the grill to start the fire.

It's versatile:

This grill is not only used for grilling but can be used for different processes of cooking as well. You can bake, roast, smoke, and braise using this device. This also increases the menu at your barbecue gathering.

No burnt areas

Because the cooking process happens by convection mechanism, the entire piece of meat, or whatever your cooking gets cooked evenly. There is also no need to flip around the meat constantly. Also, the drip tray prevents direct fire from hitting your food, so no charring occurs.

More flavor in your dishes

In grilling, nothing beats all-natural hardwood flavor. Professional chefs use them, and now, with ease, so could you. It is not hard to produce a much more delicious juicy meat steak at your home anymore.

Pellets to Use

The dark charcoal type of wood pellets is used for cooking food. They are burned to cook food inside it. It is made of a variety of woods like beech, maple, and cherry that has a composition of 15 - 20 percent mesquite, it burns at 1400 degrees. The process of burning wood pellets is very simple. You need to pour it into a box, add in the grill and light it with a matchstick, then it will burn to give you the best flavor.

The burning wood pellets will provide you the warmth and keep you surrounded with the great and the best natural flavor. This is the burning pellets or the logs that make the grills unique.

How It Works

Many people try to grill using real firewood methods while grilling in the Traeger grill. But they do not know how to use the Traeger grill with wood pellets. Let's first see how the Traeger pellet grill works.

To start with the Traeger grill, the user has to open the lid and set the temperature at 250 and make the grill smoke by turning it on. It has to be set as 250 for the first 30 mins. The user also has to turn on the heat of the grill and grill meat or food, which you want to use. The smoke has to be essential for cooking with pellets. If the Traeger grill is not important to work with, then the user can also set the smoker for working with the Traeger pellets.

It will not work without smoke. So, the first thing to do is get the griller hot and the smoker working. The temperature will rise up to 260. The grill grates are placed on the grill so as to let the smoke pass through the meat while cooking. The temperature will rise up to 260; if one is not able to control it, be sure to turn off the barbecue grill. The Traeger grill is very simple to use and it is quite easy to control the temperature.

Once you want to know how to use the Traeger grill and smoke, you will be able to find it quite easy and all you need to do is to open the lid and then set the temperature. Switch on the smoke for the first time so that smoke can come out and cook the food.

It is the same as the way how to use Traeger pellet grill for smoking

So, if you want to do BBQs for your family, then the Traeger grill is the best choice to use. It has the capacity to hold about seventeen burgers. So, one can easily do a party or BBQ night for quite a large crowd. The food will be very tasty, once it is ready with the Traeger pellet grill.

CHAPTER 2:
The Tips and Tricks for Making the Best Use of The Traeger Grill

If you are looking for some tips and tricks that can help you better utilize your Traeger grill, they are listed for you. If you already have the appliance, you are already on the sweet side of life. Whether you are a grill newbie or a master, there are always things that you can learn to become the ultimate grill and smoker master.

Some of the top tricks, tips, and hacks that can make your barbequing, smoking, and grilling experience better include:

1. **Always use disposable drip bucket liners**

If you get tired of cleaning up that slimy residue every time you decide to grill or smoke some steak or are prone to bumping the bucket off accidentally when putting on the cover, it is recommended that you look for bucket liners disposable ones of course. With the help of these disposable drip bucket liners, cleaning will become much easier.

2. **Grill lights to light the way**

If you plan to cook at night or are always bumping around the grill in the dark, you can look for some grill lights. If you are a serious smoker but are busy dealing with the headlamp or flashlight, these grill lights will come in very handy.

No wonder this device is one of the top sellers on several online shopping sites. The grill lights are fitted with a magnetic base and can clamp and bend according to the shape of the grill.

3. **Drip tray liners for easier cleaning**

If you want to get serious, then it is time to dump the aluminum foil. Once you have the drip tray liners, you will not have to deal with wadded-up, oily, blackened, or small tears in the foil.

The overall idea here is to make the cleaning process easier so that you can redirect your focus to the more important things, such as smoking and grilling.

4. **Meat temperature and meat smoking magnets to measure the temperature accurately**

One of the worst that can happen while grilling and smoking meat is guessing the cooking temperature. With the help of meat smoking and temperature magnets, you can now leave all frantic web searches behind.

With these devices, you will know the internal temperature that you need to cook meat safely. Then, you will always have perfectly cooked pieces of meat all the time.

5. **Wireless thermometer or Tappecue for the perfect temperature**

You spent hundreds of dollars on a perfect grill already. However, you can still end up spending tens and thousands of dollars more each time you decide to cook on it.

If you want to protect your important investment from harm, you need to ensure that you do not have to 'peek' while cooking. With the Tappecue, you will get the internal temperature that you are looking for.

6. **Swap out pellets with bucket head vacuum**

Imagine that you need to move from the apple to the hickory flavor. However, you see that the grill is more than half-full of apple pellets. What can you do in this scenario? Of course, you can choose to wait until the pellets cool down and then remove them. Another solution to this issue is using a bucket head vacuum.

Once done, you will be left with storage that you can use at any time. Additionally, you do not even need a specialized bucket for this purpose; you can use a simple bucket and storage lid kit that is fitted with a filter.

7. **Add extra smoke on any type of cooking with an A-maze-n Smoker Tube**

If you love smoking, you should definitely buy a dedicated smoker tube – like the A-maze-n Smoker Tube. Known for its great simplicity, this tube is one of the best tools for a seasoned smoker. All you need to do is to add some pellets and light them at just one end. Then, leave it on the grates.

A smoker tube is a great option for cold-smoking fish, nuts, and cheese; of course, it can also be used for some extra smoke on meats, like brisket, pulled pork, etc.

CHAPTER 3:
How To Clean The
Traeger Grill After Use

Traeger grills are easy to clean compare to similar grills. You would need to clean it every five uses, which is wonderful. Traditional grills can be a chore to clean and can get pretty grimy quickly. Luckily, the Traeger's design allows you to get your grill ready for the next cook-out in few simple steps.

1. Open the grill lid and wipe the grates with a paper towel or damp cloth. If your grates have more residue, you can use a grill mark brush instead. Use a scraper to remove debris at the back wall of the grill then let all the dirt fall on the bottom of the drip tray.

2. Brush or wipe the inside of the smoke exhaust and empty the grease bucket.

3. Take out the drip pan and replace it with fresh aluminum foil.

4. Siphon the ash beneath the heat deflector and on the inside of the fire pot using a vacuum.

5. Use a grease cleaner or soapy water on a spray bottle to clean the exterior of the grill. Spray it while carefully avoiding the electronic controls. Leave it on for 1 minute, then wipe it down with a clean cloth.

More Tips:

- Make sure that the grill has completely cooled down before cleaning.

- Take the opportunity to visually inspect the parts when cleaning to have them in excellent working order.

- Follow the top to bottom cleaning method.

- Empty the Traeger hopper and vacuum the insides to get any ash or dust.

- You may need to clean the temperature probes when they get grubby. Do these gently by using a clean damp cloth.

- Be careful when drawing out the grate since you may damage or scrape the temperature probe.

- Always replace the foil every cook cycle to keep the smoke flavors pristine and avoid getting any particulates from preceding cooks sticking to what you are currently grilling.

- Use grease liners or aluminum foil for the grease bucket for easy cleanup. Never pour the grease down the drain since this will clog your pipes.

Cooking Temperatures, Times, and Doneness

As a general guide, below are different temperatures and the time required for the following food items.

Fish and Seafood:

- Whitefish and Salmon can be grilled at 400-450° F for 5-8 minutes on each side or until flaky

- Steamed lobster can be cooked at 200-225° F for 15 minutes per pound of lobster.

- Scallops cook at 190° F for 1-1.5 hours

- Shrimps require 400-450° F for 3-5 minutes on each side

Pork:

- Pork ribs may be smoked at 275° F for 3-6 hours

- Pork loin cooks at 400° F until the internal temperature reaches 145-150° F

- Pulled pork butt may be cooked at 225-250° F and until the internal temperature reaches 205° F

- Bacon and sausages cook at 425° F for 7 minutes on each side or until cooked

Beef:

- Beef short ribs cook at 225-250° F for 4-6 hours until the meat easily pulls off from the bone

- Beef brisket cooks at 250° F for 4 hours then covered with foil to cook for another 4 hours or more

- Medium rare beef tenderloin cooks at 225-250° F for 3 hours

- Beef jerky requires a low heat setting for 4-5 hours

Poultry:

- The whole chicken cooks at 400° F until internal temperature reaches 165° F

- Chicken breast requires 400° F and 15 minutes on each side

- Pheasant cooks at 200° F for 2-3 hours until internal temperature reaches 160° F

- A smoked turkey requires a temperature of 180-225° F for 10-12 hours or until the internal temperature is 165° F The air fryer is a cooking device that was invented in 2010. It is a small countertop kitchen appliance that looks like a convection oven. It cooks food using the process of hot air circulation with the use of a mechanical fan.

CHAPTER 4:
Beef Recipes

1. Simple Smoked Pulled Beef

Preparation Time: 15 minutes

Cooking Time: 9 hours

Servings: 10

Ingredients:

- 1 6-pound chuck roast
- 2 ½ tablespoons salt
- 2 ½ tablespoons black pepper
- 2 ½ tablespoons garlic powder
- ½ cup chopped onion
- 3 cups beef broth

Directions:

1. Preheat the smoker to 225°F (107°C). Let the lid closed and wait for 15 minutes.
2. Mix garlic powder with black pepper and salt until combined.
3. Rub the chuck roast with the spice mixture then using your hand massage the roast until it is thoroughly seasoned.
4. Place the seasoned roast on the grill then cook the roast for 3 hours. Spray the roast with beef broth once every hour.

5. After 3 hours, sprinkle chopped onion on the bottom of a pan then pours the remaining beef broth over the onion—about 2 cups.

6. Transfer the cooked roast to the pan then place the pan on the grill.

7. Increase the smoker's temperature to 250°F (121°C) then cooks for 3 hours more.

8. After 3 hours, cover the pan with aluminum foil then lower the temperature to 165°F (74°C).

9. Cook the roast for another 3 hours until done.

10. Once it is done, transfer the smoked beef to a flat surface and let it cool.

11. Once it is cold, using a fork shred the beef then place on a serving dish.

12. Serve and enjoy!

Nutrition:

- Calories: 104
- Carbs: 6g
- Fat: 2g
- Protein: 16g

2. Smoked Beef Churl Barbecue

Preparation Time: 20 minutes

Cooking Time: 4 hours

Servings: 10

Ingredients:

- 1 5 pound-beef chuck rolls
- 5 tablespoons ground black peppercorns –
- ¼ cup kosher salt

Directions:

1. Combine salt and black peppercorns in a bowl. Mix until combined.
2. Rub the beef chuck with the spice mixture then set aside.
3. Preheat a grill over medium heat for about 10 minutes.
4. Place the charcoal on the grill then waits until the grill reaches 275°F (135°C).
5. Wrap the beef with aluminum foil then place on the grill. Keep the grill's temperature to 275°F (135°C)
6. Cook the beef chuck for 5 hours.
7. When the smoked beef is done, take the smoked beef out of the grill then let it cool for a few minutes.
8. Cut the smoked beef into thin slices then serves with any kind of roasted vegetables, as you desired.

Nutrition:

- Calories: 230
- Carbs: 22g
- Fat: 9g
- Protein: 15g

3. Honey Glazed Smoked Beef

Preparation Time: 10 minutes

Cooking Time: 8 hours

Servings: 10

Ingredients:

- 1 6-pound beef brisket
- 2 ½ tablespoons salt
- 2 ½ tablespoons pepper
- ¾ cup barbecue sauce
- 3 tablespoons red wine
- 3 tablespoons raw honey

Directions:

1. Preheat the smoker to 225°F (107°C). Spread the charcoal on one side.
2. Meanwhile, rub the beef brisket with salt, pepper, and barbecue sauce.
3. When the smoker has reached the desired temperature, place the brisket on the grill with the fat side up. Splash red wine over beef brisket.
4. Smoke the beef brisket for 8 hours. Check the smoker every 2 hours and add more charcoal if it is necessary.
5. Once it is done, take the smoked beef brisket from the smoker then transfers to a serving dish.
6. Drizzle raw honey over the beef and let it sit for about an hour before slicing.
7. Serve with roasted or sautéed vegetables according to your desire.

Nutrition:

Calories: 90   Carbs: 8g   Fat: 1g   Protein: 11g

4. Spiced Smoked Beef with Oregano

Preparation Time: 10 minutes

Cooking Time: 8 hours

Servings: 10

Ingredients:

- 1 8-pounduntrimmed brisket; 6 tablespoons paprika
- ¼ cup salt; 3 tablespoons garlic powder
- 2 tablespoons onion powder; 1 ½ tablespoons black pepper
- 1 ½ tablespoons dried parsley; 2 ½ teaspoons cayenne pepper
- 2 ½ teaspoons cumin; 1 ½ teaspoons coriander
- 2 teaspoons oregano; ½ teaspoon hot chili powder
- Preheat the smoker prior to smoking.
- Add woodchips during the smoking time.

Directions:

1. Cook the brisket for 6 hours.
2. After 6 hours, usually the smoker temperature decreases to 170°F (77°C).
3. Take the brisket out from the smoker then wrap with aluminum foil.
4. Return the brisket to the smoker then cooks again for 2 hours—this will increase the tenderness of the smoked beef.
5. Once it is done, remove the smoked beef from the smoker then place in a serving dish.
6. Cut the smoked beef into slices then enjoy!

Nutrition:

Calories: 267 Carbs: 0g

Fat: 21g Protein: 20g

5. BBQ Sweet Pepper Meatloaf

Preparation Time: 20 minutes

Cooking Time: 3 hours and 15 minutes

Servings: 8

Ingredients:

- 1 cup chopped red sweet peppers; 5 pounds ground beef
- 1 cup chopped green onion; 1 tablespoon salt; 2 eggs
- 1 tablespoon ground black pepper; 1 cup panko breadcrumbs
- 2 tablespoon BBQ rub and more as needed; 1 cup ketchup

Directions:

1. Switch on the Traeger grill, fill the grill hopper with Texas beef blend flavored Traeger's, power the grill on by using the control panel, select 'smoke' on the temperature dial, or set the temperature to 225 degrees F and let it preheat for a minimum of 5 minutes.

2. Meanwhile, take a large bowl, place all the ingredients in it except for ketchup and then stir until well combined.

3. Shape the mixture into meatloaf and then sprinkle with some BBQ rub.

4. When the grill has preheated, open the lid, place meatloaf on the grill grate, shut the grill, and smoke for 2 hours and 15 minutes.

5. Then change the smoking temperature to 375 degrees F, insert a food thermometer into the meatloaf and cook for 45 minutes or more until the internal temperature of meatloaf reaches 155 degrees F.

6. Brush the top of meatloaf with ketchup and then continue cooking for 15 minutes until glazed.

7. When done, transfer food to a dish, let it rest for 10 minutes, then cut it into slices and serve.

Nutrition: Calories: 160.5 Fat: 2.8g Carbs: 13.2g Protein: 17.2g Fiber: 1g

6. Blackened Steak

Preparation Time: 10 minutes

Cooking Time: 60 minutes

Servings: 4

Ingredients:

- 2 steaks, each about 40 ounces
- 4 tablespoons blackened rub
- 4 tablespoons butter, unsalted

Directions:

1. Switch on the Traeger grill, fill the grill hopper with hickory flavored Traeger's, power the grill on by using the control panel, select 'smoke' on the temperature dial, or set the temperature to 225 degrees F and let it preheat for a minimum of 15 minutes.

2. Transfer steaks to a dish and then repeat with the remaining steak.

3. Let seared steaks rest for 10 minutes, then slice each steak across the grain and serve.

Nutrition:

- Calories: 184.4 Cal
- Fat: 8.8 g
- Carbs: 0 g
- Protein: 23.5 g

7. BBQ Brisket

Preparation Time: 12 hours

Cooking Time: 10 hours

Servings: 8

Ingredients:

- 1 beef brisket, about 12 pounds
- Beef rub as needed

Directions:

1. Season beef brisket with beef rub until well coated, place it in a large plastic bag, seal it and let it marinate for a minimum of 12 hours in the refrigerator.

2. When ready to cook, switch on the Traeger grill, fill the grill hopper with hickory flavored Traeger's, power the grill on by using the control panel, select 'smoke' on the temperature dial, or set the temperature to 225 degrees F and let it preheat for a minimum of 15 minutes.

3. When the grill has preheated, open the lid, place marinated brisket on the grill grate fat-side down, shut the grill, and smoke for 6 hours until the internal temperature reaches 160 degrees F.

4. Then wrap the brisket in foil, return it back to the grill grate and cook for 4 hours until the internal temperature reaches 204 degrees F.

5. When done, transfer brisket to a cutting board, let it rest for 30 minutes, then cut it into slices and serve.

Nutrition:

- Calories: 328 Cal
- Fat: 21 g
- Protein: 32 g

8. Prime Rib Roast

Preparation Time: 24 hours

Cooking Time: 4 hours and 30 minutes

Servings: 8

Ingredients:

- 1 prime rib roast, containing 5 to 7 bones
- Rib rub as needed

Directions:

1. Season rib roast with rib rub until well coated, place it in a large plastic bag, seal it and let it marinate for a minimum of 24 hours in the refrigerator.

2. When ready to cook, switch on the Traeger grill, fill the grill hopper with cherry flavored Traeger's, power the grill on by using the control panel, select 'smoke' on the temperature dial, or set the temperature to 225 degrees F and let it preheat for a minimum of 15 minutes.

3. When the grill has preheated, open the lid, place rib roast on the grill grate fat-side up, change the smoking temperature to 425 degrees F, shut the grill, and smoke for 30 minutes.

4. Then change the smoking temperature to 325 degrees F and continue cooking for 3 to 4 hours until roast has cooked to the desired level, rare at 120 degrees F, medium rare at 130 degrees F, medium at 140 degrees F, and well done at 150 degrees F.

5. When done, transfer roast rib to a cutting board, let it rest for 15 minutes, then cut it into slices and serve.

Nutrition:

- Calories: 248 Cal
- Fat: 21.2 g
- Protein: 28 g

9. Thai Beef Skewers

Preparation Time: 15 minutes

Cooking Time: 8 minutes

Servings: 6

Ingredients:

- ½ of medium red bell pepper, destemmed, cored, cut into a ¼-inch piece
- ½ of beef sirloin, fat trimmed
- 1 teaspoon minced garlic
- ½ cup salted peanuts, roasted, chopped
- 1 tablespoon grated ginger
- 1 lime, juiced
- 1 teaspoon ground black pepper
- 1 tablespoon sugar
- 1/4 cup soy sauce
- 1/4 cup olive oil

Directions:

1. Prepare the marinade and for this, take a small bowl, place all of its ingredients in it, whisk until combined, and then pour it into a large plastic bag.

2. Cut into beef sirloin 1-1/4-inch dice, add to the plastic bag containing marinade, seal the bag, turn it upside down to coat beef pieces with the marinade and let it marinate for a minimum of 2 hours in the refrigerator.

3. When ready to cook, switch on the Traeger grill, fill the grill hopper with cherry flavored Traeger's, power the grill on by using the control panel, select 'smoke' on the temperature dial, or set the temperature to 425 degrees F and let it preheat for a minimum of 5 minutes.

4. Meanwhile, remove beef pieces from the marinade and then thread onto skewers.

5. When the grill has preheated, open the lid, place prepared skewers on the grill grate, shut the grill, and smoke for 4 minutes per side until done.

6. When done, transfer skewers to a dish, sprinkle with peanuts and red pepper, and then serve.

Nutrition:

- Calories: 124 Cal
- Fat: 5.5 g
- Carbs: 1.7 g
- Protein: 15.6 g
- Fiber: 0 g

10. Cowboy Cut Steak

Preparation Time: 10 minutes

Cooking Time: 1 hour and 15 minutes

Servings: 4

Ingredients:

- 2 cowboy cut steak, each about 2 ½ pounds
- Salt as needed; Beef rub as needed

For the Gremolata:

- 2 tablespoons chopped mint; 1 bunch of parsley, leaves separated
- 1 lemon, juiced; 1 tablespoon lemon zest
- ½ teaspoon minced garlic; ¼ teaspoon salt
- 1/8 teaspoon ground black pepper
- 1/4 cup olive oil

Directions:

1. Switch on the Traeger grill, fill the grill hopper with mesquite flavored Traeger's, power the grill on by using the control panel, select 'smoke' on the temperature dial, or set the temperature to 225 degrees F and let it preheat for a minimum of 5 minutes.

2. When done, transfer steaks to a dish, let rest for 15 minutes, and meanwhile, change the smoking temperature of the grill to 450 degrees F and let it preheat for a minimum of 10 minutes.

3. Then return steaks to the grill grate and cook for 7 minutes per side until the internal temperature reaches 130 degrees F.

Nutrition:

Calories: 361 Cal   Fat: 31 g

Carbs: 1 g   Protein: 19 g   Fiber: 0.2 g

11. Grilled Butter Basted Steak

Preparation Time: 10 minutes

Cooking Time: 40 minutes

Servings: 2

Ingredients:

- 2 steaks, each about 16 ounces, 1 ½-inch thick
- Rib rub as needed
- 2 teaspoon Dijon mustard
- 2 tablespoons Worcestershire sauce
- 4 tablespoons butter, unsalted, melted

Directions:

1. Switch on the Traeger grill, fill the grill hopper with hickory Traeger's, power the grill on by using the control panel, select 'smoke' on the temperature dial, or set the temperature to 225 degrees F and let it preheat for a minimum of 15 minutes.

2. Then return steaks to the grill grate and cook for 3 minutes per side until the internal temperature reaches 140 degrees F.

3. Transfer steaks to a dish, let rest for 5 minutes and then serve.

Nutrition:

- Calories: 409.8 Cal
- Fat: 30.8 g
- Carbs: 3.1 g
- Protein: 29.7 g
- Fiber: 0.4 g

12. Chili Rib Eye Steaks

Preparation Time: 10 minutes

Cooking Time: 1 hour

Servings: 4

Ingredients:

- 4 rib-eye steaks, each about 12 ounces
- 1 tablespoon minced garlic
- 1 teaspoon salt
- 1 teaspoon brown sugar
- 2 tablespoons red chili powder
- 1 teaspoon ground cumin
- 2 tablespoons Worcestershire sauce
- 2 tablespoons olive oil

Directions:

1. Prepare the rub and for this, take a small bowl, place all of its ingredients in it and then stir until mixed.

2. Brush the paste on all sides of the steak, rub well, then place steaks into a plastic bag and let it marinate for a minimum of 4 hours.

3. Then return steaks to the grill grate and cook for 3 minutes per side until the internal temperature reaches 140 degrees F.

4. Transfer steaks to a dish, let rest for 5 minutes and then serve.

Nutrition:

- Calories: 293 Cal
- Fat: 0 g
- Protein: 32 g

13. BBQ Beef Short Ribs

Preparation Time: 15 minutes

Cooking Time: 10 hours

Servings: 8

Ingredients:

- 4 beef short rib racks, membrane removed, containing 4 bones
- 1/2 cup beef rub
- 1 cup apple juice

Directions:

1. Switch on the Traeger grill, fill the grill hopper with apple-flavored Traeger's, power the grill on by using the control panel, select 'smoke' on the temperature dial, or set the temperature to 225 degrees F and let it preheat for a minimum of 15 minutes.

2. Meanwhile, prepare the ribs, and for this, sprinkle beef rub on both sides until well coated.

3. When the grill has preheated, open the lid, place ribs on the grill grate bone-side down, shut the grill, and smoke for 10 hours until internal temperature reaches 205 degrees F, spritzing with apple juice every hour.

4. When done, transfer ribs to a cutting board, let rest for 10 minutes, then cut into slices and serve.

Nutrition:

- Calories: 280 Cal
- Fat: 15 g
- Carbs: 17 g
- Protein: 20 g
- Fiber: 1 g

14. Thai Beef Salad

Preparation Time: 10 minutes

Cooking Time: 10 minutes

Servings: 4

Ingredients:

- 1 ½ pound skirt steak; 1 ½ teaspoon salt
- 1 teaspoon ground white pepper; 4 jalapeño peppers, minced
- ½ teaspoon minced garlic; 4 tablespoons Thai fish sauce
- 4 tablespoons lime juice; 1 tablespoon brown sugar
- 1 small red onion, peeled, thinly sliced; 6 cherry tomatoes, halved
- 2 green onions, ¼-inch diced; 1 cucumber, deseeded, thinly sliced
- 1 heart of romaine lettuce, chopped; ½ cup chopped mint
- 2 tablespoons cilantro; ½ teaspoon red pepper flakes
- 1 tablespoon lime juice; 2 tablespoons fish sauce

Directions:

1. Switch on the Traeger grill, fill the grill hopper with cherry flavored Traeger's, power the grill on by using the control panel, select 'smoke' on the temperature dial, or set the temperature to 450 degrees F and let it preheat for a minimum of 15 minutes.

2. Take a large salad, place all the ingredients for the salad in it, drizzle with dressing and toss until well coated and mixed.

3. When done, transfer steak to a cutting board, let it rest for 10 minutes and then cut it into slices.

4. Add steak slices into the salad, toss until mixed, and then serve.

Nutrition:

Calories: 128 Cal   Fat: 6 g   Carbs: 6 g   Protein: 12 g   Fiber: 1 g

15. Traeger Smoked Beef Jerky

Preparation Time: 15 minutes

Cooking Time: 5 hours

Servings: 10

Ingredients:

- 3 lb. sirloin steaks, sliced into 1/4-inch thickness
- 2 cups soy sauce; 1/2 cup brown sugar
- 1 cup pineapple juice; 2 Tablespoon sriracha
- 2 Tablespoon red pepper flake; 2 Tablespoon hoisin
- 2 Tablespoon onion powder
- 2 Tablespoon rice wine vinegar
- 2 Tablespoon garlic, minced

Direction:

1. Mix all the ingredients in a zip lock bag. Seal the bag and mix until the beef is well coated. Ensure you get as much air as possible from the zip lock bag.
2. Put the bag in the fridge overnight to let marinate. Remove the bag from the fridge 1 hour prior to cooking.
3. Startup your wood pallet grill and set it to smoke setting. Layout the meat on the grill with half-inch space between them.
4. Let them cook for 5 hours while turning after every 2-1/2 hours.
5. Transfer from the grill and let cool for 30 minutes before serving.

Nutrition:

Calories 80   Total fat 1g   Protein 14g

Sugar 5g   Fiber 0g   Sodium: 650mg

16. Grilled Butter Basted Porterhouse Steak

Preparation Time: 15 minutes

Cooking Time: 40 minutes

Servings: 4

Ingredients:

- 4 Tablespoon butter, melted
- 2 Tablespoon Worcestershire sauce
- 2 Tablespoon Dijon mustard
- Traeger Prime rib rub

Direction:

1. Set your Traeger grill to 225°F with the lid closed for 15 minutes.
2. In a mixing bowl, mix butter, sauce, Dijon mustard until smooth. brush the mixture on the meat then season with the rub.
3. Arrange the meat on the grill grate and cook for 30 minutes.
4. Use tongs to transfer the meat to a patter then increase the heat to high.
5. Return the meat to the grill grate to grill until your desired doneness is achieved.
6. Baste with the butter mixture again if you desire and let rest for 3 minutes before serving. Enjoy.

Nutrition:

Calories 726   Total fat 62g

Protein 36g   Sugar 1g

Fiber 1g   Sodium: 97mg

17. Traeger Grill Prime Rib Roast

Preparation Time: 5 minutes

Cooking Time: 4 hours

Servings: 10

Ingredients:

- 7 lb. bone prime rib roast
- Traeger prime rib rub

Direction:

1. Coat the roast generously with the rub then wrap in a plastic wrap. let sit in the fridge for 24 hours to marinate.

2. Set the temperatures to 500°F.to to preheat with the lid closed for 15 minutes.

3. Place the rib directly on the grill fat side up and cook for 30 minutes.

4. Reduce the temperature to 300°F and cook for 4 hours or until the internal temperature is 120°F- rare, 130°F-medium rare, 140°F-medium and 150°F-well done.

5. Remove from the grill and let rest for 30 minutes then serve and enjoy.

Nutrition:

- Calories 290
- Total fat 23g
- Protein 19g
- Sugar 0g
- Fiber 0g
- Sodium: 54mg

18. Traeger Grill Teriyaki Beef Jerky

Preparation Time: 15 minutes

Cooking Time: 5 hours

Servings: 10

Ingredients:

- 3 cups soy sauce
- 2 cups brown sugar
- 3 garlic cloves
- 2-inch ginger knob, peeled and chopped
- 1 Tablespoon sesame oil
- 4 lb. beef, skirt steak

Direction:

1. Place all the ingredients except the meat in a food processor. Pulse until well mixed.

2. Trim any excess fat from the meat and slice into 1/4-inch slices. Add the steak with the marinade into a zip lock bag and let marinate for 12-24 hours in a fridge.

3. Set the Traeger grill to smoke and let preheat for 5 minutes.

4. Arrange the steaks on the grill leaving a space between each. Let smoke for 5 hours.

5. Remove the steak from grill and serve when warm.

Nutrition:

Calories 80   Total fat 1g,

Protein 11g   Sugar 6g,

Fiber 0g   Sodium: 390mg

19. Traeger smoked Brisket

Preparation Time: 20 minutes

Cooking Time: 9 hours

Servings: 6

Ingredients:

- 2 Tablespoon garlic powder
- 2 Tablespoon onion powder
- 2 Tablespoon paprika
- 2 Tablespoon chili powder
- 1/3 cup salt; 1/3 cup black pepper
- 12 lb. whole packer brisket, trimmed
- 1-1/2 cup beef broth

Direction:

1. Set your Traeger temperature to 225°F. Let preheat for 15 minutes with the lid closed.
2. Meanwhile, mix garlic, onion, paprika, chili, salt, and pepper in a mixing bowl.
3. Season the brisket generously on all sides.
4. Place the meat on the grill with the fat side down and let it cool until the internal temperature reaches 160°F.
5. Remove the meat from the grill and double wrap it with foil. Return it to the grill and cook until the internal temperature reaches 204°F.
6. Remove from grill, unwrap the brisket and let rest for 15 minutes.
7. Slice and serve.

Nutrition:

Calories 270 Total fat 20g Protein 20g Sugar 1g Fiber 0g Sodium: 1220mg

20. Traeger Smoked Rib-eye Steaks

Preparation Time: 15 minutes

Cooking Time: 35 minutes

Servings: 1

Ingredients:

- 2-inch-thick rib-eye steaks
- Steak rub of choice

Direction:

1. Preheat your Traeger grill to low smoke.

2. Sprinkle the steak with your favorite steak rub and place it on the grill. Let it smoke for 25 minutes.

3. Remove the steak from the grill and set the temperature to 400°F.

4. Return the steak to the grill and sear it for 5 minutes on each side.

5. Cook until the desired temperature is achieved; 125°F-rare, 145°F-Medium, and 165°F.-Well done.

6. Wrap the steak with foil and let rest for 10 minutes before serving. Enjoy.

Nutrition:

- Calories 225
- Total fat 10.4g
- Protein 32.5g
- Sugar 0g
- Fiber 0g
- Sodium: 63mg

21. Traeger Grill Deli-Style Roast Beef

Preparation Time: 15 minutes

Cooking Time: 4 hours

Servings: 2

Ingredients:

- 4lb round-bottomed roast
- 1 Tablespoon coconut oil
- 1/4 Tablespoon garlic powder; 1/4 Tablespoon onion powder
- 1/4 Tablespoon thyme; 1/4 Tablespoon oregano
- 1/2 Tablespoon paprika; 1/2 Tablespoon salt
- 1/2 Tablespoon black pepper

Direction:

1. Combine all the dry hubs to get a dry rub.
2. Roll the roast in oil then coat with the rub.
3. Set your grill to 185°F and place the roast on the grill.
4. Smoke for 4 hours or until the internal temperature reaches 140°F.
5. Remove the roast from the grill and let rest for 10 minutes.
6. Slice thinly and serve.

Nutrition:

- Calories 90
- Total fat 3g
- Protein 14g
- Sugar 0g
- Fiber 0g
- Sodium: 420mg

22. Traeger Beef Jerky

Preparation Time: 15 minutes

Cooking Time: 5 hours

Servings: 10

Ingredients:

- 3 lb. sirloin steaks;
- 2 cups soy sauce
- 1 cup pineapple juice;
- 1/2 cup brown sugar
- 2 tbsp sriracha; 2 tbsp hoisin
- 2 tbsp red pepper flake
- 2 tbsp rice wine vinegar
- 2 tbsp onion powder

Directions:

1. Mix the marinade in a zip lock bag and add the beef. Mix until well coated and remove as much air as possible.

2. Place the bag in a fridge and let marinate overnight or for 6 hours. Remove the bag from the fridge an hour prior to cooking

3. Startup the Traeger and set it on the smoking settings or at 190F.

4. Lay the meat on the grill leaving a half-inch space between the pieces. Let cool for 5 hours and turn after 2 hours.

5. Remove from the grill and let cool. Serve or refrigerate

Nutrition:

Calories 309   Total fat 7g   Saturated fat 3g

Total carbs 20g   Net carbs 19g   Protein 34g

Sugars 15g   Fiber 1g   Sodium 2832mg

23. Traeger Smoked Beef Roast

Preparation Time: 10 minutes

Cooking Time: 6 hours

Servings: 6

Ingredients:

- 1-3/4 lb. beef sirloin tip roast
- 1/2 cup BBQ rub
- 2 bottles amber beer
- 1 bottle BBQ sauce

Directions:

1. Turn the Traeger onto the smoke setting.
2. Rub the beef with BBQ rub until well coated then place on the grill. Let smoke for 4 hours while flipping every 1 hour.
3. Transfer the beef to a pan and add the beer. The beef should be 1/2 way covered.
4. Braise the beef until fork tender. It will take 3 hours on the stovetop and 60 minutes on the instant pot.
5. Remove the beef from the ban and reserve 1 cup of the cooking liquid.
6. Use 2 forks to shred the beef into small pieces then return to the pan with the reserved braising liquid.
7. Add BBQ sauce and stir well then keep warm until serving. You can also reheat if it gets cold.

Nutrition:

Calories 829   Total fat 46g   Saturated fat 18g

Total carbs 4g   Net carbs 4g   Protein 86g

Sugars 0g   Fiber 0g   Sodium 181mmg

24. Traeger Beef Tenderloin

Preparation Time: 10 minutes

Cooking Time: 45 minutes

Servings: 6

Ingredients:

- 4 lb. beef tenderloin
- 3 tbsp steak rub
- 1 tbsp kosher salt

Directions:

1. Preheat the Traeger to high heat.
2. Meanwhile, trim excess fat from the beef and cut it into 3 pieces.
3. Coat the steak with rub and kosher salt. Place it on the grill.
4. Close the lid and cook for 10 minutes. Open the lid, flip the beef and cook for 10 more minutes.
5. Reduce the temperature of the grill until 225F and smoke the beef until the internal temperature reaches 130F.
6. Remove the beef from the grill and let rest for 15 minutes before slicing and serving.

Nutrition:

Calories 999   Total fat 76g   Saturated fat 30g

Total carbs 0g   Net carbs 0g   Protein 74g

Sugars 0g   Fiber 0g   Sodium 1234mmg

25. Trager New York Strip

Preparation Time: 5 minutes

Cooking Time: 15 minutes

Servings: 6

Ingredients:

- 3 New York strips
- Salt and pepper

Directions:

1. If the steak is in the fridge, remove it 30 minutes prior to cooking.

2. Preheat the Traeger to 450F.

3. Meanwhile, season the steak generously with salt and pepper. Place it on the grill and let it cook for 5 minutes per side or until the internal temperature reaches 128F.

4. Remove the steak from the grill and let it rest for 10 minutes.

Nutrition:

- Calories 198
- Total fat 14g
- Saturated fat 6g
- Total carbs 0g
- Net carbs 0g
- Protein 17g
- Sugars 0g
- Fiber 0g
- Sodium 115mg

26. Traeger Stuffed Peppers

Preparation Time: 20 minutes

Cooking Time: 5 hours

Servings: 6

Ingredients:

- 3 bell peppers, sliced in halves ; 1 lb. ground beef, lean
- 1 onion, chopped; 1/2 tbsp red pepper flakes
- 1/2 tbsp salt; 1/4 tbsp pepper
- 1/2 tbsp garlic powder; 1/2 tbsp onion powder
- 1/2 cup white rice; 15 oz stewed tomatoes
- 8 oz tomato sauce; cups cabbage, shredded
- 1-1/2 cup water; 2 cups cheddar cheese

Directions:

1. Arrange the pepper halves on a baking tray and set aside.
2. Preheat your grill to 325F.
3. Brown the meat in a large skillet. Add onions, pepper flakes, salt, pepper garlic, and onion and cook until the meat is well cooked.
4. Add rice, stewed tomatoes, tomato sauce, cabbage, and water. Cover and simmer until the rice is well cooked, the cabbage is tender and there is no water in the rice.
5. Place the cooked beef mixture in the pepper halves and top with cheese. Place in the grill and cook for 30 minutes.
6. Serve immediately and enjoy it.

Nutrition:

Calories 422   Total fat 22g   Saturated fat 11g   Total carbs 24g

Net carbs 19g   Protein 34g   Sugars 11g   Fiber 5g   Sodium 855mg

27. Traeger Prime Rib Roast

Preparation Time: 10 minutes

Cooking Time: 2 hours

Servings: 8

Ingredients:

- lb. rib roast, boneless; 4 tbsp salt; 1 tbsp black pepper
- 1-1/2 tbsp onion powder; 1 tbsp granulated garlic; 1 tbsp rosemary
- 1 cup chopped onion; 1/2 cup carrots, chopped
- 1/2 cup celery, chopped; 2 cups beef broth

Directions:

1. Remove the beef from the fridge 1 hour prior to cooking.
2. Preheat the Traeger to 250F.
3. In a small mixing bowl, mix salt, pepper, onion, garlic, and rosemary to create your rub.
4. Generously coat the roast with the rub and set it aside.
5. Combine chopped onions, carrots, and celery in a cake pan then place the bee on top.
6. Place the cake pan in the middle of the Traeger and cook for 1 hour.
7. Pour the beef broth at the bottom of the cake pan and cook until the internal temperature reaches 120F.
8. Remove the cake pan from the Traeger and let rest for 20 minutes before slicing the meat.
9. Pour the cooking juice through a strainer, then skim off any fat at the top. Serve the roast with the cooking juices.

Nutrition:

Calories 721   Total fat 60g   Saturated fat 18g   Total carbs 3g

Net carbs 2g   Protein 43g   Sugars 1g   Fiber 1g   Sodium 2450mmg

28. Traeger Kalbi Beef short Ribs

Preparation Time: 10 minutes

Cooking Time: 6 hours

Servings: 6

Ingredients:

- 1/2 cup soy sauce
- 1/2 cup brown sugar
- 1/8 cup rice wine
- 2 tbsp minced garlic
- 1 tbsp sesame oil
- 1/8 cup onion, finely grated
- 2-1/2 lb. beef short ribs, thinly sliced

Directions:

1. Mix soy sauce, sugar, rice wine, garlic, sesame oil and onion in a medium mixing bowl.
2. Add the beef in the bowl and cover it in the marinade. Cover the bowl with a plastic wrap and refrigerate for 6 hours.
3. Heat your Traeger to high and ensure the grill is well heated.
4. Place the marinated meat on the grill and close the lid ensuring you don't lose any heat.
5. Cook for 4 minutes, flip, and cook for 4 more minutes on the other side.
6. Remove the meat and serve with rice and veggies of choice. Enjoy.

Nutrition:

Calories 355   Total fat 10g   Saturated fat 6g   Total carbs 22g

Net carbs 22g   Protein 28g   Sugars 19g   Fiber 0g   Sodium 1213mg

29. Traeger Beef Short Rib Lollipop

Preparation Time: 15 minutes

Cooking Time: 3 hours

Servings: 4

Ingredients:

- 4 beef short rib lollipops
- BBQ Rub
- BBQ Sauce

Directions:

1. Preheat your Traeger to 275F.
2. Season the short ribs with BBQ rub and place them on the grill.
3. Cook for 4 hours while turning occasionally until the meat is tender.
4. Apply the sauce on the meat in the last 30 minutes of cooking.
5. Serve and enjoy.

Nutrition:

- Calories 265
- Total fat 19g
- Saturated fat 9g
- Total carbs 1g
- Net carbs 0g
- Protein 22g
- Sugars 1g
- Fiber 0g
- Sodium 60mmg

30. Traeger Tri-Tip

Preparation Time: 10 minutes

Cooking Time: 1 hour 30 minutes

Servings: 6

Ingredients:

- 3 lb. tri-tip
- 1-1/2 tbsp kosher salt
- 1 tbsp black pepper
- 1 tbsp paprika
- 1/2 tbsp cayenne
- 1 tbsp onion powder
- 1 tbsp garlic powder

Directions:

1. Preheat your Traeger to 250F.
2. Mix the seasoning ingredients and generously season the tri-tip.
3. Place it in the Traeger and cook for 30 minutes. Flip the tri-tip and cook for an additional 30 minutes.
4. Turn up the Traeger and coo for additional 30 minutes. Pull out the meat at 125F for medium-rare and 135F for medium.
5. Let the meat rest for 10 minutes before slicing and serving.

Nutrition:

Calories 484   Total fat 25g   Saturated fat 0g   Total carbs 1g

Net carbs 1g   Protein 59g   Sugars 0g   Fiber 0g   Sodium 650mmg

31. Bacon-Swiss Cheesesteak Meatloaf

Preparation Time: 15 minutes

Cooking Time: 2 hours

Servings: 8-10

Ingredients:

- 1 tablespoon canola oil; 2 garlic cloves, finely chopped
- 1 medium onion, finely chopped; 2 pounds extra-lean ground beef
- 1 poblano chile, stemmed, seeded, and finely chopped
- 2 pounds extra-lean ground beef; 2 cups shredded Swiss cheese
- 2 tablespoons Montreal steak seasoning; 1 tablespoon A.1. Steak Sauce
- ½ pound bacon, cooked and crumbled; 2 cups shredded Swiss cheese
- 1 egg, beaten; 2 cups breadcrumbs; ½ cup Tiger Sauce

Directions:

1. On your stove top, heat the canola oil in a medium sauté pan over medium-high heat. Add the garlic, onion, and poblano, and sauté for 3 to 5 minutes, or until the onion is just barely translucent.

2. Supply your smoker with wood pellets and follow the manufacturer's specific start-up procedure. Preheat, with the lid closed, to 225°F.

3. In a large bowl, combine the sautéed vegetables, ground beef, steak seasoning, steak sauce, bacon, Swiss cheese, egg, and breadcrumbs. Mix with your hands until well incorporated, then shape into a loaf.

4. Put the meatloaf in a cast iron skillet and place it on the grill. Insert meat thermometer inserted in the loaf reads 165°F.

5. Top with the meatloaf with the Tiger Sauce, remove from the grill, and let rest for about 10 minutes before serving.

Nutrition:

Calories: 120 Cal Fat: 2 g Carbohydrates: 0 g Protein: 23 g Fiber: 0 g

32. London Broil

Preparation Time: 20 minutes

Cooking Time: 12-16 minutes

Servings: 3-4

Ingredients:

- 1 (1½- to 2-pound) London broil or top round steak
- ¼ cup soy sauce; 2 tablespoons white wine
- 2 tablespoons extra-virgin olive oil; ¼ cup chopped scallions
- 2 tablespoons packed brown sugar; 2 garlic cloves, minced
- 2 teaspoons red pepper flakes; 1 teaspoon freshly ground black pepper

Directions:

1. Using a meat mallet, pound the steak lightly all over on both sides to break down its fibers and tenderize. You are not trying to pound down the thickness.

2. In a medium bowl, make the marinade by combining the soy sauce, white wine, olive oil, scallions, brown sugar, garlic, red pepper flakes, and black pepper.

3. Put the steak in a shallow plastic container with a lid and pour the marinade over the meat. Cover and refrigerate for 4 hours.

4. Supply your smoker with wood pellets and follow the manufacturer's specific start-up procedure. Preheat, with the lid closed, to 350°F.

5. Place the steak directly on the grill, close the lid, and smoke for 6 minutes. Flip, then smoke with the lid closed for 6 to 10 minutes more, or until a meat thermometer inserted in the meat reads 130°F for medium-rare.

6. The meat's temperature will rise by about 5 degrees while it rests.

Nutrition: Calories: 316 Cal   Fat: 3 g   Carbohydrates: 0 g   Protein: 54 g

33. French Onion Burgers

Preparation Time: 35 minutes

Cooking Time: 20-25 minutes

Servings: 4

Ingredients:

- 1-pound lean ground beef
- 1 tablespoon minced garlic
- 1 teaspoon Better Than Bouillon Beef Base
- 1 teaspoon dried chives
- 1 teaspoon freshly ground black pepper
- 8 slices Gruyere cheese, divided
- ½ cup soy sauce
- 1 tablespoon extra-virgin olive oil
- 1 teaspoon liquid smoke
- 3 medium onions, cut into thick slices (do not separate the rings)
- 1 loaf French bread, cut into 8 slices
- 4 slices provolone cheese

Directions:

1. In a large bowl, mix together the ground beef, minced garlic, beef base, chives, and pepper until well blended.

2. Divide the meat mixture and shape into 8 thin burger patties.

3. Top each of 4 patties with one slice of Gruyere, then top with the remaining 4 patties to create 4 stuffed burgers.

4. Supply your smoker with wood pellets and follow the manufacturer's specific start-up procedure. Preheat, with the lid closed, to 425°F.

5. Arrange the burgers directly on one side of the grill, close the lid, and smoke for 10 minutes. Flip and smoke with the lid closed for 10 to 15 minutes more, or until a meat thermometer inserted in the burgers reads 160°F. Add another Gruyere slice to the burgers during the last 5 minutes of smoking to melt.

6. Meanwhile, in a small bowl, combine the soy sauce, olive oil, and liquid smoke.

7. Arrange the onion slices on the grill and paste on both sides with the soy sauce mixture. Smoke with the lid closed for 20 minutes, flipping halfway through.

8. Lightly toast the French bread slices on the grill. Layer each of 4 slices with a burger patty, a slice of provolone cheese, and some of the smoked onions. Top each with another slice of toasted French bread. Serve immediately.

Nutrition:

- Calories: 704 Cal
- Fat: 43 g
- Carbohydrates: 28 g
- Protein: 49 g
- Fiber: 2 g

34. Beef Shoulder Clod

Preparation Time: 10 minutes

Cooking Time: 12-16 hours

Servings: 16-20

Ingredients:

- ½ cup sea salt
- ½ cup freshly ground black pepper
- 1 tablespoon red pepper flakes
- 1 tablespoon minced garlic
- 1 tablespoon cayenne pepper
- 1 tablespoon smoked paprika
- 1 (13- to 15-pound) beef shoulder clod

Directions:

1. Combine spices
2. Generously apply it to the beef shoulder.
3. Supply your smoker with wood pellets and follow the manufacturer's specific start-up procedure. Preheat, with the lid closed, to 250°F.
4. Put the meat on the grill grate, close the lid, and smoke for 12 to 16 hours, or until a meat thermometer inserted deeply into the beef reads 195°F. You may need to cover the clod with aluminum foil toward the end of smoking to prevent overbrowning.
5. Let the meat rest and serve

Nutrition:

Calories: 290 Cal   Fat: 22 g

Carbohydrates: 0 g   Protein: 20 g

35. Corned Beef and Cabbage

Preparation Time: 30 minutes

Cooking Time: 4-5 hours

Servings: 6-8

Ingredients:

- 1-gallon water
- 1 (3- to 4-pound) point cut corned beef brisket with pickling spice packet
- 1 tablespoon freshly ground black pepper
- 1 tablespoon garlic powder
- ½ cup molasses
- 1 teaspoon ground mustard
- 1 head green cabbage
- 4 tablespoons (½ stick) butter
- 2 tablespoons rendered bacon fat
- 1 chicken bouillon cube, crushed

Directions:

1. Refrigerate overnight, changing the water as often as you remember to do so—ideally, every 3 hours while you're awake—to soak out some of the curing salt initially added.

2. Supply your smoker with wood pellets and follow the manufacturer's specific start-up procedure. Preheat, with the lid closed, to 275°F.

3. Remove the meat from the brining liquid, pat it dry, and generously rub with the black pepper and garlic powder.

4. Put the seasoned corned beef directly on the grill, fat-side up, close the lid, and grill for 2 hours. Remove from the grill when done.

5. In a small bowl, combine the molasses and ground mustard and pour half of this mixture into the bottom of a disposable aluminum pan.

6. Transfer the meat to the pan, fat-side up, and pour the remaining molasses mixture on top, spreading it evenly over the meat. Cover tightly with aluminum foil.

7. Transfer the pan to the grill, close the lid, and continue smoking the corned beef for 2 to 3 hours, or until a meat thermometer inserted in the thickest part reads 185°F.

8. Rest meat, serve.

Nutrition:

- Calories: 295 Cal
- Fat: 17 g
- Carbohydrates: 19 g
- Protein: 18 g
- Fiber: 6 g

36. Cheeseburger Hand Pies

Preparation Time: 35 minutes

Cooking Time: 10 minutes

Servings: 6

Ingredients:

- ½ pound lean ground beef; 1 tablespoon minced onion
- 1 tablespoon steak seasoning; 1 cup cheese
- 8 slices white American cheese, divided; 2 eggs
- 2 (14-ounce) refrigerated prepared pizza dough sheets, divided
- 24 hamburger dill pickle chips; 2 tablespoons sesame seeds
- 6 slices tomato, for garnish; Ketchup and mustard, for serving

Directions:

1. Supply your smoker with wood pellets and follow the manufacturer's specific start-up procedure. Preheat, with the lid closed, to 325°F.

2. On your stove top, in a medium sauté pan over medium-high heat, brown the ground beef for 4 to 5 minutes, or until cooked through. Add the minced onion and steak seasoning.

3. Toss in the shredded cheese blend and 2 slices of American cheese and stir until melted and fully incorporated.

4. Remove the cheeseburger mixture from the heat and set aside.

5. Make sure the dough is well chilled for easier handling. Working quickly, roll out one prepared pizza crust on parchment paper and brush with half of the egg wash.

6. Arrange the remaining 6 slices of American cheese on the dough to outline 6 hand pies.

Nutrition:

Calories: 325 Cal   Fat: 21 g   Carbohydrates: 11 g   Protein: 23 g   Fiber: 0 g

37. Pastrami

Preparation Time: 10 minutes

Cooking Time: 4-5 hours

Servings: 12

Ingredients:

- 1-gallon water, plus ½ cup; ½ cup packed light brown sugar
- 1 (3- to 4-pound) point cut corned beef brisket with brine mix packet
- 2 tablespoons freshly ground black pepper; ¼ cup ground coriander

Directions:

1. Cover and refrigerate overnight, changing the water as often as you remember to do so—ideally, every 3 hours while you're awake—to soak out some of the curing salt originally added.

2. Supply your smoker with wood pellets and follow the manufacturer's specific start-up procedure. Preheat, with the lid closed, to 275°F.

3. In a small bowl, combine the black pepper and ground coriander to form a rub.

4. Drain the meat, pat it dry, and generously coat on all sides with the rub.

5. Place the corned beef directly on the grill, fat-side up, close the lid, and smoke for 3 hours to 3 hours 30 minutes, or until a meat thermometer inserted in the thickest part reads 175°F to 185°F.

6. Add the corned beef, cover tightly with aluminum foil, and smoke on the grill with the lid closed for an additional 30 minutes to 1 hour.

7. Remove the meat, refrigerate

Nutrition:

Calories: 123 Cal   Fat: 4 g

Carbohydrates: 3 g   Protein: 16 g

38. Smoked and Pulled Beef

Preparation Time: 10 Minutes

Cooking Time: 6 Hours

Servings: 6

Ingredients:

- 4 lb. beef sirloin tip roast
- 1/2 cup BBQ rub
- Two bottles of amber beer
- One bottle barbecues sauce

Directions:

1. Turn your wood pellet grill onto smoke setting, then trim excess fat from the steak.
2. Coat the steak with BBQ rub and let it smoke on the grill for 1 hour.
3. Continue cooking and flipping the steak for the next 3 hours. Transfer the steak to a braising vessel. Add the beers.
4. Braise the beef until tender, then transfer to a platter reserving 2 cups of cooking liquid.
5. Use a pair of forks to shred the beef and return it to the pan. Add the reserved liquid and barbecue sauce. Stir well and keep warm before serving. Enjoy.

Nutrition:

- Calories 829
- Total fat 46g
- Total carbs 4g
- Protein 86g
- Sodium: 181mg

39. Wood Pellet Smoked Beef Jerky

Preparation Time: 15 Minutes

Cooking Time: 5 Hours

Servings: 10

Ingredients:

- 3 lb. sirloin steaks, sliced into 1/4-inch thickness
- 2 cups soy sauce; 1/2 cup brown sugar
- 1 cup pineapple juice; 2 tbsp sriracha
- 2 tbsp red pepper flake; 2 tbsp hoisin
- 2 tbsp onion powder; 2 tbsp rice wine vinegar
- 2 tbsp garlic, minced

Directions:

1. Mix all the fixings in a Ziplock bag.
2. Seal the bag and mix until the beef is well coated.
3. Put the bag in the fridge overnight to let marinate. Remove the bag from the fridge 1 hour before cooking.
4. Startup your wood pallet grill and set it to smoke setting. You need to layout the meat on the grill with a half-inch space between them.
5. Let them cook for 5 hours while turning after every 2-1/2 hours.
6. Transfer from the grill and let cool for 30 minutes before serving.
7. Enjoy.

Nutrition:

Calories 80   Total fat 1g

Total carbs 5g   Protein 14g

Sugar 5g   Sodium: 650mg

40. Reverse Seared Flank Steak

Preparation Time: 10 Minutes

Cooking Time: 10 Minutes

Servings: 2

Ingredients:

- 1.5 lb. Flank's steak
- 1 tbsp salt
- 1/2 onion powder
- 1/4 tbsp garlic powder
- 1/2 black pepper, coarsely ground

Directions:

1. Preheat your wood pellet grill to 225°F.

2. In a mixing bowl, mix salt, onion powder, garlic powder, and pepper. Generously rub the steak with the mixture.

3. Place the steaks on the preheated grill, close the lid, and let the steak cook.

4. Crank up the grill to high, then let it heat. The steak should be off the grill and tented with foil to keep it warm.

5. Once the grill is heated up to 450°F, place the steak back and grill for 3 minutes per side.

6. Remove from heat, pat with butter, and serve. Enjoy.

Nutrition:

Calories 112   Total fat 5g

Total carbs 1g   Protein 16g

Sodium: 737mg

41. Smoked Midnight Brisket

Preparation Time: 15 Minutes

Cooking Time: 12 Minutes

Servings: 6

Ingredients:

- 1 tbsp Worcestershire sauce
- 1 tbsp Traeger beef Rub
- 1 tbsp Traeger Chicken rub
- 1 tbsp Traeger Blackened Saskatchewan rub
- 5 lb. flat cut brisket
- 1 cup beef broth

Directions:

1. Rub the sauce and rubs in a mixing bowl, then rub the mixture on the meat.
2. Preheat your grill to 180°F with the lid closed for 15 minutes. You can use super smoke if you desire.
3. Place the meat on the grill and grill for 6 hours or until the internal temperature reaches 160°F.
4. Remove the meat from the grill and double wrap it with foil.
5. Add beef broth and return to grill, with the temperature increased to 225°F. Cook for 4 hours or until the internal temperature reaches 204°F.
6. Remove from grill and let rest for 30 minutes. Serve and enjoy with your favorite BBQ sauce.

Nutrition:

Calories 200   Total fat 14g   Total carbs 3g   Protein 14g   Sodium: 680mg

42. Cocoa Crusted Grilled Flank Steak

Preparation Time: 15 Minutes

Cooking Time: 6 Minutes

Servings: 7

Ingredients:

- 1 tbsp cocoa powder; 2 tbsp chili powder
- 1 tbsp chipotle chili powder; 1/2 tbsp garlic powder
- 1/2 tbsp onion powder; 1-1/2 tbsp brown sugar
- 1 tbsp cumin; 1 tbsp smoked paprika
- 1 tbsp kosher salt; 1/2 tbsp black pepper
- Olive oil; 4 lb. Flank steak

Directions:

1. Whisk together cocoa, chili powder, garlic powder, onion powder, sugar, cumin, paprika, salt, and pepper in a mixing bowl.
2. Drizzle the steak with oil, then rub with the cocoa mixture on both sides.
3. Preheat your wood pellet grill for 15 minutes with the lid closed.
4. Cook the meat on the grill grate for 5 minutes or until the internal temperature reaches 135°F.
5. Remove the meat from the grill and cool for 15 minutes to allow the juices to redistribute.
6. Slice the meat against the grain and on a sharp diagonal.
7. Serve and enjoy.

Nutrition:

Calories 420   Total fat 26g   Total carbs 21g

Protein 3g   Sugar 7g   Fiber 8g   Sodium: 2410mg

43. Wood Pellet Grill Prime Rib Roast

Preparation Time: 5 Minutes

Cooking Time: 4 Hours

Servings: 10

Ingredients:

- 7 lb. bone prime rib roast
- Traeger prime rib rub

Directions:

1. Coat the roast generously with the rub, then wrap in a plastic wrap. Let sit in the fridge for 24 hours to marinate.

2. Set the temperatures to 500°F.to to preheat with the lid closed for 15 minutes.

3. Place the rib directly on the grill fat side up and cook for 30 minutes.

4. Decrease the temperature to 300°F and cook for 4 hours or until the internal temperature is 120°F- rare, 130°F-medium rare, 140°F-medium and 150°F-well done.

5. Remove from the grill and let rest for 30 minutes, then serve and enjoy.

Nutrition:

- Calories 290
- Total fat 23g
- Total carbs 0g
- Protein 19g
- Sodium: 54mg
- Potassium 275mg

44. Smoked Longhorn Cowboy Tri-Tip

Preparation Time: 15 Minutes

Cooking Time: 4 Hours

Servings: 7

Ingredients:

- 3 lb. tri-tip roast
- 1/8 cup coffee, ground
- 1/4 cup Traeger beef rub

Directions:

1. Preheat the grill to 180°F with the lid closed for 15 minutes.
2. Meanwhile, rub the roast with coffee and beef rub. Place the roast on the grill grate and smoke for 3 hours.
3. Remove the roast from the grill and double wrap it with foil. Increase the temperature to 275°F.
4. Return the meat to the grill and cook for 90 minutes or until the internal temperature reaches 135°F.
5. Remove from the grill, unwrap it and let rest for 10 minutes before serving.
6. Enjoy.

Nutrition:

- Calories 245
- Total fat 14g
- Total Carbs 0g
- Protein 23g
- Sodium: 80mg

45. Wood Pellet Grill Teriyaki Beef Jerky

Preparation Time: 15 Minutes

Cooking Time: 5 Hours

Servings: 10

Ingredients:

- 3 cups soy sauce
- 2 cups brown sugar
- Three garlic cloves
- 2-inch ginger knob, peeled and chopped
- 1 tbsp sesame oil
- 4 lb. beef, skirt steak

Directions:

1. Place all the fixings except the meat in a food processor. Pulse until well mixed.
2. Trim any extra fat from the meat and slice into 1/4-inch slices. Add the steak with the marinade into a zip lock bag and let marinate for 12-24 hours in a fridge.
3. Set the wood pellet grill to smoke and let preheat for 5 minutes.
4. Arrange the steaks on the grill, leaving a space between each. Let smoke for 5 hours.
5. Remove the steak from the grill and serve when warm.

Nutrition:

Calories 80   Total fat 1g

Total Carbs 7g   Protein 11g

Sugar 6g   Sodium: 390mg

46. Grilled Butter Basted Rib-eye

Preparation Time: 20 Minutes

Cooking Time: 20 Minutes

Servings: 4

Ingredients:

- Two rib-eye steaks, bone-in
- Salt to taste
- Pepper to taste
- 4 tbsp butter, unsalted

Directions:

1. Mix steak, salt, and pepper in a Ziplock bag. Seal the bag and mix until the beef is well coated. Ensure you get as much air as possible from the Ziplock bag.

2. Set the wood pellet grill temperature to high with a closed lid for 15 minutes. Place a cast-iron into the grill.

3. Place the steaks on the grill's hottest spot and cook for 5 minutes with the lid closed.

4. Open the lid and add butter to the skillet. When it's almost melted, place the steak on the skillet with the grilled side up.

5. Cook for 5 minutes while busting the meat with butter. Close the lid and cook until the temperature is 130°F.

6. Remove the steak from the skillet and let rest for 10 minutes before enjoying with the reserved butter.

Nutrition:

Calories 745   Total fat 65g

Total Carbs 5g   Net Carbs 5g

Protein 35g

47. Wood Pellet Smoked Ribeye Steaks

Preparation Time: 15 Minutes

Cooking Time: 35 Minutes

Servings: 1

Ingredients:

- 2-inch-thick ribeye steaks
- Steak rub of choice

Directions:

1. Preheat your pellet grill to low smoke.
2. Sprinkle the steak with your favorite steak rub and place it on the grill. Let it smoke for 25 minutes.
3. Remove the steak from the grill and set the temperature to 400°F.
4. Return the steak to the grill and sear it for 5 minutes on each side.
5. Cook until the desired temperature is achieved; 125°F-rare, 145°F-Medium, and 165°F.-Well done.
6. Wrap the steak with foil and let rest for 10 minutes before serving.
7. Enjoy.

Nutrition:

- Calories 225
- Total fat 10.4g
- Total Carbs 0.2g
- Protein 32.5g
- Sodium: 63mg,
- Potassium 463mg

48. Smoked Trip Tip with Java Chophouse

Preparation Time: 10 Minutes

Cooking Time: 90 Minutes

Servings: 4

Ingredients:

- 2 tbsp olive oil
- 2 tbsp java chophouse seasoning
- 3 lb. trip tip roast, fat cap, and silver skin removed

Directions:

1. Startup your wood pellet grill and smoker and set the temperature to 225°F.
2. Rub the roast with olive oil and seasoning, then place it on the smoker rack.
3. Smoke until the internal temperature is 140°F.
4. Remove the tri-tip from the smoker and let rest for 10 minutes before serving. Enjoy.

Nutrition:

- Calories 270
- Total fat 7g
- Total Carbs 0g
- Protein 23g
- Sodium: 47mg
- Potassium 289mg

49. Supper Beef Roast

Preparation Time: 5 Minutes

Cooking Time: 3 Hours

Servings: 7

Ingredients:

- 3-1/2 beef top round; 3 tbsp vegetable oil
- Prime rib rub; 2 cups beef broth
- One russet potato, peeled and sliced
- Two carrots, peeled and sliced
- Two celery stalks, chopped
- One onion, sliced; Two thyme sprigs

Directions:

1. Rub the roast with vegetable oil and place it on the roasting fat side up. Season with prime rib rub, then pours the beef broth.

2. Set the temperature to 500°F and preheat the wood pellet grill for 15 minutes with the lid closed.

3. Cook for 30 minutes or until the roast is well seared.

4. Reduce temperature to 225°F. Add the veggies and thyme and cover with foil. Cook for three more hours or until the internal temperature reaches 135°F.

5. Remove from the grill and let rest for 10 minutes. Slice against the grain and serve with vegetables and the pan drippings.

6. Enjoy.

Nutrition:

Calories 697   Total fat 10g   Total Carbs 127g   Protein 34g

Sugar 14g   Fiber 22g   Sodium: 3466mg   Potassium 2329mg

50. Wood Pellet Grill Deli-Style Roast Beef

Preparation Time: 15 Minutes

Cooking Time: 4 Hours

Servings: 2

Ingredients:

- 4lb round-bottomed roast
- 1 tbsp coconut oil
- 1/4 tbsp garlic powder
- 1/4 tbsp onion powder
- 1/4 tbsp thyme
- 1/4 tbsp oregano
- 1/2 tbsp paprika
- 1/2 tbsp salt
- 1/2 tbsp black pepper

Directions:

1. Combine all the dry hubs to get a dry rub.
2. Roll the roast in oil, then coat with the rub.
3. Set your grill to 185°F and place the roast on the grill.
4. Smoke for 4 hours or until the internal temperature reaches 140°F.
5. Remove the roast from the grill and let rest for 10 minutes.
6. Slice thinly and serve.

Nutrition:

Calories 90   Total fat 3g

Total Carbs 0g   Protein 14g

Sodium: 420mg

CHAPTER 5:
Pork Recipes

51. Maple Baby Backs

Preparation Time: 25 minutes

Cooking Time: 4 hours

Servings: 4-6

Ingredients:

- 2 (2- or 3-pound) racks baby back ribs
- 2 tablespoons yellow mustard
- 1 batch Sweet Brown Sugar Rub
- ½ cup plus 2 tablespoons maple syrup, divided
- 2 tablespoons light brown sugar
- 1 cup Pepsi or other non-diet cola
- ¼ cup Bill's Best BBQ Sauce

Directions:

1. Supply your smoker with wood pellets and follow the manufacturer's specific start-up procedure. Preheat the grill

2. Eradicate the membrane. This can be done by cutting just through the membrane in an X pattern and working a paper towel between the membrane and the ribs to pull it off.

3. Coat the ribs on both sides with mustard and season them with the rub. Rub into meat.

4. Grill ribs and smoke for 3 hours.

5. Remove grill and place bone-side up, on enough aluminum foil to wrap the ribs completely. Add maple syrup over the ribs and sprinkle them with 1 tablespoon of brown sugar. Flip the ribs and repeat the maple syrup and brown sugar application on the meat side.

6. Increase the grill's temperature to 300°F.

7. Fold in three sides of the foil around the ribs and add the cola. Fold in the last side, completely enclosing the ribs and liquid. Place ribs back to the grill for 30 to 45 minutes.

8. Remove the ribs from the grill and unwrap them from the foil.

9. In a small bowl, stir together the barbecue sauce and remaining 6 tablespoons of maple syrup. Use this to baste the ribs. Return the ribs to the grill, without the foil, and cook for 15 minutes to caramelize the sauce.

10. Cut into individual ribs and serve immediately.

Nutrition:

- Calories: 330 Cal
- Fat: 24 g
- Carbohydrates: 11 g
- Protein: 17 g
- Fiber: 0 g

52. Simple Smoked Baby Backs

Preparation Time: 25 minutes

Cooking Time: 4-6 hours

Servings: 4-8

Ingredients:

- 2 (2- or 3-pound) racks baby back ribs
- 2 tablespoons yellow mustard
- 1 batch Not-Just-for-Pork Rub

Directions:

1. Supply your smoker with wood pellets and follow the manufacturer's specific start-up procedure. Preheat grill

2. Eradicate the membrane from the backside of the ribs. This can be done by cutting just through the membrane in an X pattern and working a paper towel between the membrane and the ribs to pull it off.

3. Coat the ribs on both sides with mustard and season them with the rub. Work rubs onto meat.

4. smoke until their internal temperature reaches between 190°F and 200°F.

5. Remove the racks from the grill and cut into individual ribs. Serve immediately.

Nutrition:

- Calories: 245 Cal
- Fat: 12 g
- Carbohydrates: 10 g
- Protein: 22 g
- Fiber: 0 g

53. Sweet Smoked Country Ribs

Preparation Time: 25 minutes

Cooking Time: 4hours

Servings: 2-4

Ingredients:

- 2 pounds country-style ribs; 1 batch Sweet Brown Sugar Rub
- 2 tablespoons light brown sugar; 1 cup Pepsi or other cola
- ¼ cup Bill's Best BBQ Sauce

Directions:

1. Supply your smoker with wood pellets and follow the manufacturer's specific start-up procedure. With the lid closed, preheat the grill until the temperature is 180 degrees

2. Sprinkle the ribs with the rub and use your hands to work the rub into the meat.

3. Place the ribs directly on the grill grate and smoke for 3 hours.

4. Remove the ribs from the grill and place them on enough aluminum foil to wrap them completely. Dust the brown sugar over the ribs.

5. Increase the grill's temperature to 300°F.

6. Fold in three sides of the foil around the ribs and add the cola. Fold in the last side, completely enclosing the ribs and liquid. Return the ribs to the grill and cook for 45 minutes.

7. Remove the ribs from the foil and place them on the grill grate. Baste all sides of the ribs with barbecue sauce. Cook for 15 minutes more to caramelize the sauce.

8. Remove the ribs from the grill and serve immediately.

Nutrition:

Calories: 230 Cal   Fat: 17 g   Carbohydrates: 0 g   Protein: 20 g   Fiber: 0 g

54. Classic Pulled Pork

Preparation Time: 15 minutes

Cooking Time: 16-20 hours

Servings: 8-12

Ingredients:

- 1 (6- to 8-pound) bone-in pork shoulder
- 2 tablespoons yellow mustard
- 1 batch Not-Just-for-Pork Rub

Directions:

1. Supply your smoker with wood pellets and follow the manufacturer's specific start-up procedure.

2. Coat the pork shoulder all over with mustard and season it with the rub.

3. Place the shoulder on the grill grate and smoke until its internal temperature reaches 195°F.

4. Pull the shoulder from the grill and wrap it completely in aluminum foil or butcher paper. Place it in a cooler, cover the cooler, and let it rest for 1 or 2 hours.

5. Remove the pork shoulder from the cooler and unwrap it. Remove the shoulder bone and pull the pork apart using just your fingers. Serve immediately as desired. Leftovers are encouraged.

Nutrition:

- Calories: 414 Cal
- Fat: 29 g
- Carbohydrates: 1 g
- Protein: 38 g
- Fiber: 0 g

55. Maple-Smoked Pork Chops

Preparation Time: 10 minutes

Cooking Time: 55 minutes

Servings: 4

Ingredients:

- 4 (8-ounce) pork chops, bone-in or boneless (I use boneless)
- Salt
- Freshly ground black pepper

Directions:

1. Supply your smoker with wood pellets and follow the manufacturer's specific start-up procedure.
2. Drizzle pork chop with salt and pepper to season.
3. Place the chops directly on the grill grate and smoke for 30 minutes.
4. Increase the grill's temperature to 350°F. Continue to cook the chops until their internal temperature reaches 145°F.
5. Remove the pork chops from the grill and let them rest for 5 minutes before serving.

Nutrition:

- Calories: 130 Cal
- Fat: 12 g
- Carbohydrates: 3 g
- Protein: 20 g
- Fiber: 0 g

56. Apple-Smoked Pork Tenderloin

Preparation Time: 15 minutes

Cooking Time: 4-5 hours

Servings: 4-6

Ingredients:

- 2 (1-pound) pork tenderloins
- 1 batch Not-Just-for-Pork Rub

Directions:

1. Supply your smoker with wood pellets and follow the manufacturer's specific start-up procedure. Preheat the grill

2. Generously season the tenderloins with the rub. W

3. Put tenderloins on the grill and smoke for 4 or 5 hours, until their internal temperature reaches 145°F.

4. The tenderloins must be put out of the grill and let it rest for 5-10 minutes then begin slicing into thin pieces before serving

Nutrition:

- Calories: 180 Cal
- Fat: 8 g
- Carbohydrates: 3 g
- Protein: 24 g
- Fiber: 0 g

57. Barbecued Tenderloin

Preparation Time: 5 minutes

Cooking Time: 30 minutes

Servings: 4-6

Ingredients:

- 2 (1-pound) pork tenderloins
- 1 batch Sweet and Spicy Cinnamon Rub

Directions:

1. Supply your smoker with wood pellets and follow the manufacturer's specific start-up procedure. Preheat the grill
2. Generously season the tenderloins with the rub. Work rubs onto meat.
3. Place the tenderloins and smoke internal temperature reaches 145°F.
4. As you put out the tenderloins from the grill, let it cool down for 5-10 minutes before slicing it up and serving it

Nutrition:

- Calories: 186 Cal
- Fat: 4 g
- Carbohydrates: 8 g
- Protein: 29 g
- Fiber: 1 g

58. Lovable Pork Belly

Preparation Time: 15 Minutes

Cooking Time: 4 Hours and 30 Minutes

Servings: 4

Ingredients:

- 5 pounds of pork belly; 1 cup dry rub
- 3 tablespoons olive oil

For Sauce

- Two tablespoons honey
- Three tablespoons butter
- 1 cup BBQ sauce

Directions:

1. Take your drip pan and add water. Cover with aluminum foil.
2. Pre-heat your smoker to 250 degrees F
3. Add pork cubes, dry rub, olive oil into a bowl and mix well
4. Use water fill water pan halfway through and place it over drip pan.
5. Add wood chips to the side tray
6. Transfer pork cubes to your smoker and smoke for 3 hours (covered)
7. Remove pork cubes from the smoker and transfer to foil pan, add honey, butter, BBQ sauce, and stir
8. Cover the pan with foil and move back to a smoker, smoke for 90 minutes more
9. Remove foil and smoke for 15 minutes more until the sauce thickens
10. Serve and enjoy!

Nutrition:

Calories: 1164   Fat: 68g   Carbohydrates: 12g   Protein: 104g

59. County Ribs

Preparation Time: 15 Minutes

Cooking Time: 3 Hours

Servings: 4

Ingredients:

- 4 pounds country-style ribs
- Pork rub to taste; 2 cups apple juice
- ½ stick butter, melted
- 18 ounces BBQ sauce

Directions:

1. Take your drip pan and add water. Cover with aluminum foil.
2. Pre-heat your smoker to 275 degrees F
3. Season country style ribs from all sides
4. Use water fill water pan halfway through and place it over drip pan.
5. Add wood chips to the side tray.
6. Transfer the ribs to your smoker and smoke for 1 hour and 15 minutes until the internal temperature reaches 160 degrees F
7. Take foil pan and mix melted butter, apple juice, 15 ounces BBQ sauce and put ribs back in the pan, cover with foil
8. Transfer back to smoker and smoke for 1 hour 15 minutes more until the internal temperature reaches 195 degrees F
9. Take ribs out from liquid and place them on racks, glaze ribs with more BBQ sauce, and smoke for 10 minutes more
10. Take them out and let them rest for 10 minutes, serve and enjoy!

Nutrition:

Calories: 251   Fat: 25g   Carbohydrates: 35g   Protein: 76g

60. Wow-Pork Tenderloin

Preparation Time: 15 Minutes

Cooking Time: 3 Hours

Servings: 4

Ingredients:

- One pork tenderloin
- ¼ cup BBQ sauce
- Three tablespoons dry rub

Directions:

1. Take your drip pan and add water. Cover with aluminum foil.
2. Pre-heat your smoker to 225 degrees F
3. Rub the spice blend all finished the pork tenderloin
4. Use water fill water pan halfway through and place it over drip pan.
5. Add wood chips to the side tray
6. Transfer pork meat to your smoker and smoke for 3 hours until the internal temperature reaches 145 degrees F
7. Brush the BBQ sauce over pork and let it rest
8. Serve and enjoy!

Nutrition:

- Calories: 405
- Fat: 9g
- Carbohydrates: 15g
- Protein: 59g

61. Awesome Pork Shoulder

Preparation Time: 15 Minutes + 24 Hours

Cooking Time: 12 Hours

Servings: 4

Ingredients:

- 8 pounds of pork shoulder

For Rub

- One teaspoon dry mustard; One teaspoon black pepper
- One teaspoon cumin; One teaspoon oregano
- One teaspoon cayenne pepper; 1/3 cup salt
- ¼ cup garlic powder; ½ cup paprika
- 1/3 cup brown sugar; 2/3 cup sugar

Directions:

1. Bring your pork under salted water for 18 hours
2. Pull the pork out from the brine and let it sit for 1 hour
3. Rub mustard all over the pork
4. Take a bowl and mix all rub ingredients. Rub mixture all over the meat
5. Wrap meat and leave it overnight
6. Take your drip pan and add water. Cover with aluminum foil. Pre-heat your smoker to 250 degrees F
7. Use water fill water pan halfway through and place it over drip pan. Add wood chips to the side tray.
8. Transfer meat to smoker and smoke for 6 hours
9. Take the pork out and wrap in foil, smoke for 6 hours more at 195 degrees F. Shred and serve. Enjoy!

Nutrition: Calories: 965 Fat: 65g Carbohydrates: 19g Protein: 71g

62. Herbed Prime Rib

Preparation Time: 15 Minutes

Cooking Time: 4 Hours

Servings: 4

Ingredients:

- 5 pounds prime rib; Two tablespoons black pepper
- ¼ cup olive oil; Two tablespoons salt

Herb Paste

- ¼ cup olive oil
- One tablespoon fresh sage
- One tablespoon fresh thyme
- One tablespoon fresh rosemary
- Three garlic cloves

Directions:

1. Take a blender and add herbs, blend until thoroughly combined
2. Take your drip pan and add water. Cover with aluminum foil.
3. Pre-heat your smoker to 225 degrees F
4. Use water fill water pan halfway through and place it over drip pan.
5. Add wood chips to the side tray
6. Coat rib with olive oil and season it well with salt and pepper
7. Transfer seasoned rib to your smoker and smoke for 4 hours
8. Remove rib from the smoker and keep it on the side. Let it cool for 30 minutes. Cut into slices and serve. Enjoy!

Nutrition:

Calories: 936   Fat: 81g   Carbohydrates: 2g   Protein: 46g

63. Premium Sausage Hash

Preparation Time: 30 Minutes

Cooking Time: 45 Minutes

Servings: 4

Ingredients:

- Nonstick cooking spray; Two finely minced garlic cloves
- One teaspoon basil, dried; One teaspoon oregano, dried
- One teaspoon onion powder; One teaspoon of salt
- 4-6 cooked smoker Italian Sausage (Sliced)
- One large-sized bell pepper, diced; One large onion, diced
- Three potatoes, cut into 1-inch cubes
- Three tablespoons of olive oil; French bread for serving

Directions:

1. Pre-heat your smoker to 225 degrees Fahrenheit using your desired wood chips
2. Cover the smoker grill rack with foil and coat with cooking spray
3. Take a small bowl and add garlic, oregano, basil, onion powder, and season the mix with salt and pepper
4. Take a large bowl and add sausage slices, bell pepper, potatoes, onion, olive oil, and spice mix
5. Mix well and spread the mixture on your foil-covered rack
6. Place the rack in your smoker and smoke for 45 minutes
7. Serve with your French bread. Enjoy!

Nutrition:

Calories: 193   Fats: 10g

Carbs: 15g   Fiber: 2g

64. Explosive Smoky Bacon

Preparation Time: 20 Minutes

Cooking Time: 2 Hours and 10 Minutes

Servings: 10

Ingredients:

- 1 pound thick-cut bacon
- One tablespoon BBQ spice rub
- 2 pounds bulk pork sausage
- 1 cup cheddar cheese, shredded
- Four garlic cloves, minced
- 18 ounces BBQ sauce

Directions:

1. Take your drip pan and add water; cover with aluminum foil.
2. Pre-heat your smoker to 225 degrees F
3. Use water fill water pan halfway through and place it over drip pan.
4. Add wood chips to the side tray
5. Reserve about ½ a pound of your bacon for cooking later on
6. Lay 2 strips of your remaining bacon on a clean surface in an X formation
7. Alternate the horizontal and vertical bacon strips by waving them tightly in an over and under to create a lattice-like pattern
8. Sprinkle one teaspoon of BBQ rub over the woven bacon
9. Arrange ½ a pound of your bacon in a large-sized skillet and cook them for 10 minutes over medium-high heat
10. Drain the cooked slices on a kitchen towel and crumble them
11. Place your sausages in a large-sized re-sealable bag

12. While the sausages are still in the bag, roll them out to a square that has the same sized as the woven bacon

13. Cut off the bag from the sausage and arrange them sausage over the woven bacon

14. Toss away the bag

15. Sprinkle some crumbled bacon, green onions, cheddar cheese, and garlic over the rolled sausages

16. Pour about ¾ bottle of your BBQ sauce over the sausage and season with some more BBQ rub

17. Roll up the woven bacon tightly all around the sausage, forming a loaf

18. Cook the bacon-sausage loaf in your smoker for about one and a ½ hour

19. Brush up the woven bacon with remaining BBQ sauce and keep smoking for about 30 minutes until the center of the loaf is no longer pink

20. Use an instant thermometer to check if the internal temperature is at least 165 degrees Fahrenheit

21. If yes, then take it out and let it rest for 30 minutes

22. Slice and serve!

Nutrition:

- Calories: 507
- Fats: 36g
- Carbs: 20g
- Fiber: 2g

65. Alabama Pulled Pig Pork

Preparation Time: 1 Hour

Cooking Time: 12 Hours

Servings: 8

Ingredients:

- 2 cups of soy sauce
- 1 cup of Worcestershire sauce
- 1 cup of cranberry grape juice
- 1 cup of teriyaki sauce
- One tablespoon of hot pepper sauce
- Two tablespoons of steak sauce
- 1 cup of light brown sugar
- ½ a teaspoon of ground black pepper
- 2 pound of flank steak cut up into ¼ inch slices

Directions:

1. Take a non-reactive saucepan and add cider, salt, vinegar, brown sugar, cayenne pepper, black pepper, and butter
2. Bring the mix to a boil over medium-high heat
3. Add in water and return the mixture to a boil
4. Carefully rub the pork with the sauce
5. Take your drip pan and add water. Cover with aluminum foil.
6. Pre-heat your smoker to 225 degrees F
7. Use water fill water pan halfway through and place it over drip pan.
8. Add wood chips to the side tray
9. Smoke meat for about 6-10 hours. Make sure to keep basting it with the sauce every hour or so

10. After the first smoking is done, take an aluminum foil and wrap up the meat forming a watertight seal

11. Place the meat in the middle of your foil and bring the edges to the top, cupping up the meat complete

12. Pour 1 cup of sauce over the beef and tight it up

13. Place the package back into your smoker and smoke for 2 hours until the meat quickly pulls off from the bone

14. Once done, remove it from the smoker and pull off the pork, discarding the bone and fat

15. Place the meat chunks in a pan and pour 1 cup of sauce for every4 pound of meat

16. Heat until simmering and serve immediately!

Nutrition:

- Calories: 1098
- Fats: 86g
- Carbs: 38g
- Fiber: 3g

CHAPTER 6:

Lamb Recipes

66. Lamb Chops

Preparation Time: 10 minutes

Cooking Time: 12 minutes

Servings: 6

Ingredients:

- 6 (6-ounce) lamb chops
- 3 tablespoons olive oil
- Ground black pepper

Directions:

1. Preheat the pallet grill to 450 degrees F.
2. Coat the lamb chops with oil and then, season with salt and black pepper evenly.
3. Arrange the chops in pallet grill grate and cook for about 4-6 minutes per side.

Nutrition:

Calories: 376 Cal   Fat: 19.5 g

Carbohydrates: 0 g   Protein: 47.8 g

Fiber: 0 g

67. Lamb Ribs Rack

Preparation Time: 10 minutes

Cooking Time: 2 hours

Servings: 2

Ingredients:

- 2 tablespoons fresh sage
- 2 tablespoons fresh rosemary
- 2 tablespoons fresh thyme
- 2 peeled garlic cloves
- 1 tablespoon honey
- Black pepper; ¼ cup olive oil
- 1 (1½-pound) trimmed rack lamb ribs

Directions:

1. Combine all ingredients
2. While motor is running, slowly add oil and pulse till a smooth paste is formed.
3. Coat the rib rack with paste generously and refrigerate for about 2 hours.
4. Preheat the pallet grill to 225 degrees F.
5. Arrange the rib rack in pallet grill and cook for about 2 hours.
6. Remove the rib rack from pallet grill and transfer onto a cutting board for about 10-15 minutes before slicing.
7. With a sharp knife, cut the rib rack into equal sized individual ribs and serve.

Nutrition:

Calories: 826 Cal Fat: 44.1 g Carbohydrates: 5.4 g Protein: 96.3 g Fiber: 1 g

68. Lamb Shank

Preparation Time: 10 minutes

Cooking Time: 4 hours

Servings: 6

Ingredients:

- 8-ounce red wine
- 2-ounce whiskey
- 2 tablespoons minced fresh rosemary
- 1 tablespoon minced garlic
- Black pepper
- 6 (1¼-pound) lamb shanks

Directions:

1. In a bowl, add all ingredients except lamb shank and mix till well combined.
2. In a large resealable bag, add marinade and lamb shank.
3. Seal the bag and shake to coat completely.
4. Refrigerate for about 24 hours.
5. Preheat the pallet grill to 225 degrees F.
6. Arrange the leg of lamb in pallet grill and cook for about 4 hours.

Nutrition:

- Calories: 1507 Cal
- Fat: 62 g
- Carbohydrates: 68.7 g
- Protein:163.3 g
- Fiber: 6 g

69. Leg of a Lamb

Preparation Time: 10 minutes

Cooking Time: 2 hours and 30 minutes

Servings: 10

Ingredients:

- 1 (8-ounce) package softened cream cheese
- ¼ cup cooked and crumbled bacon
- 1 seeded and chopped jalapeño pepper
- 1 tablespoon crushed dried rosemary; 2 teaspoons garlic powder
- 1 teaspoon onion powder; 1 teaspoon paprika
- 1 teaspoon cayenne pepper; Salt, to taste
- 1 (4-5-pound) butterflied leg of lamb; 2-3 tablespoons olive oil

Directions:

1. For filling in a bowl, add all ingredients and mix till well combined.
2. For spice mixture in another small bowl, mix together all ingredients.
3. Place the leg of lamb onto a smooth surface. Sprinkle the inside of leg with some spice mixture.
4. Place filling mixture over the inside surface evenly. Roll the leg of lamb tightly and with a butcher's twine, tie the roll to secure the filling
5. Coat the outer side of roll with olive oil evenly and then sprinkle with spice mixture. Preheat the pallet grill to 225-240 degrees F.
6. Arrange the leg of lamb in pallet grill and cook for about 2-2½ hours. Remove the leg of lamb from pallet grill and transfer onto a cutting board. With a piece of foil, cover leg loosely and transfer onto a cutting board for about 20-25 minutes before slicing.
7. With a sharp knife, cut the leg of lamb in desired sized slices and serve.

Nutrition: Calories: 715Cal Fat: 38.9g Carbohydrates: 2.2g Protein: 84.6 g

70. Lamb Breast

Preparation Time: 10 minutes

Cooking Time: 2 hours and 40 minutes

Servings: 2

Ingredients:

- 1 (2-pound) trimmed bone-in lamb breast
- ½ cup white vinegar
- ¼ cup yellow mustard
- ½ cup BBQ rub

Directions:

1. Preheat the pallet grill to 225 degrees F.
2. Rinse the lamb breast with vinegar evenly.
3. Coat lamb breast with mustard and the, season with BBQ rub evenly.
4. Arrange lamb breast in pallet grill and cook for about 2-2½ hours.
5. Remove the lamb breast from the pallet grill and transfer onto a cutting board for about 10 minutes before slicing.
6. With a sharp knife, cut the lamb breast in desired sized slices and serve.

Nutrition:

- Calories: 877 Cal
- Fat: 34.5 g
- Carbohydrates: 2.2 g
- Protein: 128.7 g
- Fiber: 0 g

71. Smoked Lamb Shoulder Chops

Preparation Time: 4 hours

Cooking Time: 25-30 minutes

Servings: 4

Ingredients:

- 4 lamb shoulder chops
- 4 cups buttermilk
- 1 cup cold water
- ¼ cup kosher salt
- 2 tablespoons olive oil
- 1 tablespoon Texas style rub

Directions:

1. In a large bowl, add buttermilk, water and salt and stir till salt is dissolved.
2. Add chops and coat with mixture evenly.
3. Refrigerate for at least 4 hours. Remove the chops from bowl and rinse under cold water.
4. Coat the chops with olive oil and then sprinkle with rub evenly. Preheat the pallet grill to 240 degrees F.
5. Arrange the chops in pallet grill grate and cook for about 25-30 minute or till desired doneness.
6. Meanwhile preheat the broiler of oven.
7. Cook the chops under broiler till browned.

Nutrition:

Calories: 328 Cal   Fat: 18.2 g

Carbohydrates:11.7 g   Protein: 30.1 g

72. Lamb Skewers

Preparation Time: 5 minutes

Cooking Time: 8-12 minutes

Servings: 6

Ingredients:

- One lemon, juiced; Two crushed garlic cloves
- Two chopped red onions; One t. chopped thyme
- Pepper; Salt
- One t. oregano; 1/3 c. oil
- ½ t. cumin; Two pounds cubed lamb leg

Directions:

1. Refrigerate the chunked lamb.
2. The remaining ingredients should be mixed together. Add in the meat. Refrigerate overnight.
3. Pat the meat dry and thread onto some metal or wooden skewers. Wooden skewers should be soaked in water.
4. Add wood pellets to your smoker and follow your cooker's startup procedure. Preheat your smoker, with your lid closed, until it reaches 450.
5. Grill, covered, for 4-6 minutes on each side. Serve.

Nutrition:

- Calories: 201 Cal
- Fat: 9 g
- Carbohydrates: 3 g
- Protein: 24 g
- Fiber: 1 g

73. Brown Sugar Lamb Chops

Preparation Time: 2 hours

Cooking Time: 10-15 minutes

Servings: 4

Ingredients:

- Pepper; Salt
- One t. garlic powder
- Two t. tarragon
- One t. cinnamon
- ¼ c. brown sugar
- 4 lamb chops
- Two t. ginger

Directions:

1. Combine the salt, garlic powder, pepper, cinnamon, tarragon, ginger, and sugar. Coat the lamb chops in the mixture and chill for two hours.

2. Add wood pellets to your smoker and follow your cooker's startup procedure. Preheat your smoker, with your lid closed, until it reaches 450.

3. Place the chops on the grill, cover, and smoke for 10-15 minutes per side. Serve.

Nutrition:

- Calories: 210 Cal
- Fat: 11 g
- Carbohydrates: 3 g
- Protein: 25 g
- Fiber: 1 g

74. Traeger Smoked Lamb Chops

Preparation Time: 10 Minutes

Cooking Time: 50 Minutes

Servings: 4

Ingredients:

- One rack lamb; 2 tbsp rosemary, fresh
- 2 tbsp sage, fresh; 1 tbsp thyme, fresh
- Two garlic cloves, roughly chopped; 1 tbsp honey
- 2 tbsp shallots, roughly chopped; 1/2 tbsp salt
- 1/2 tbsp ground pepper; 1/4 cup olive oil

Directions:

1. Preheat the Traeger to 225F
2. Trim any excess fat and silver skin from the lamb.
3. Combine the rest of the ingredients in the food processor and generously rub the lamb with the seasoning.
4. Place the seasoned lamb on the Traeger and cook for 45 minutes or until the internal temperature reaches 120F.
5. Sear the lamb on the Traeger for 2 minutes per side or until the internal temperature reaches 125F for medium-rare or 1450F for medium.
6. Let rest for 5 minutes beforehand slicing it. Enjoy

Nutrition:

Calories 916   Total fat 78.3g

Total carbs 2.7g   Protein 47g

Sugars 0.1g   Fiber 0.5g

Sodium 1324mmg

75. Traeger Smoked Lamb Shoulder

Preparation Time: 20 Minutes

Cooking Time: 3 Hours

Servings: 7

Ingredients:

- 5 lb. lamb shoulder; 1 cup cider vinegar
- 2 tbsp. oil; 2 tbsp. kosher salt
- 2 tbsp. black pepper, freshly ground
- 1 tbsp. dried rosemary

For the Spritz

- 1 cup apple cider vinegar
- 1 cup apple juice

Directions:

1. Preheat the Traeger to 225F with a pan of water for moisture.
2. Trim any extra fat from the lamb and rinse the meat in cold water. Pat dry with a paper towel.
3. Inject the cider vinegar in the meat, then pat dry with a clean paper towel.
4. Rub the meat with oil, salt, black pepper, and dried rosemary. Tie the lamb shoulder with a twine.
5. Place in the smoker for an hour, then spritz after every 15 minutes until the internal temperature reaches 165F.
6. Remove from the Traeger and let rest for 1 hour before shredding and serving.

Nutrition:

Calories 472   Total Fat 37g   Total carbs 3g   Protein 31g   Sodium 458mg

76. Traeger Smoked Pulled Lamb Sliders

Preparation Time: 10 Minutes

Cooking Time: 9 Hours

Servings: 7

Ingredients:

- 5 lb. lamb shoulder, boneless
- 1/2 cup olive oil; 1/3 cup kosher salt
- 1/3 cup pepper, coarsely ground
- 1/3 cup granulated garlic

For the spritz

- 4 oz Worcestershire sauce
- 6 oz apple cider vinegar

Directions:

1. Preheat the Traeger to 225F with a pan of water for moisture.
2. Trim any excess fat from the lamb, then pat it dry with some paper towel. Rub with oil, salt, pepper, and garlic.
3. Place the lamb in the Traeger smoker for 90 minutes, then spritz every 30 minutes until the internal temperature reaches 165F.
4. Transfer the lamb to a foil pan, then add the remaining spritz liquid. Cover with a foil and place back in the Traeger.
5. Smoke until the internal temperature reaches 205F.
6. Remove from the smoker and let rest in a cooler without ice for 30 minutes before pulling it. Serve with slaw or bun and enjoy.

Nutrition:

Calories 235   Total Fat 6g   Total Carbs 22g   Protein 20g

Sugars 7g   Fiber 1g   Sodium 592mg   Potassium 318mg

77. Traeger Smoked Lamb Meatballs

Preparation Time: 10 Minutes

Cooking Time: 1 Hour

Servings: 20 Meatballs

Ingredients:

- 1 lb. lamb shoulder, ground
- Three garlic cloves, finely diced
- 3 tbsp. shallot, diced
- 1 tbsp. salt; One egg
- 1/2 tbsp. pepper; 1/2 tbsp. cumin
- 1/2 tbsp. smoked paprika
- 1/4 tbsp. red pepper flakes
- 1/4 tbsp. cinnamon
- 1/4 cup panko breadcrumbs

Directions:

1. Set your Traeger to 250F.
2. Combine all the fixings in a small bowl, then mix thoroughly using your hands.
3. Form golf ball-sized meatballs and place them on a baking sheet.
4. Place the baking sheet in the smoker and smoke until the internal temperature reaches 160F.
5. Remove the meatballs from the smoker and serve when hot.

Nutrition:

Calories 93   Total fat 5.9g   Total carbs 4.8g

Protein 5g   Sugars 0.3g   Fiber 0.3g

Sodium 174.1mg   Potassium 82.8mg

78. Traeger Crown Rack of Lamb

Preparation Time: 30 Minutes

Cooking Time: 30 Minutes

Servings: 6

Ingredients:

- Two racks of lamb. Frenched
- 1 tbsp garlic, crushed; 1 tbsp rosemary
- 1/2 cup olive oil; Kitchen twine

Directions:

1. Preheat your Traeger to 450F.
2. Rinse the lab with clean cold water, then pat it dry with a paper towel.
3. Lay the lamb even on a chopping board and score a ¼ inch down between the bones. Repeat the process between the bones on each lamb rack. Set aside.
4. In a small mixing bowl, combine garlic, rosemary, and oil. Brush the lamb rack generously with the mixture.
5. Bend the lamb rack into a semicircle, then place the racks together such that the bones will be up and will form a crown shape.
6. Wrap around four times, starting from the base moving upward. Tie tightly to keep the racks together.
7. Place the lambs on a baking sheet and set in the Traeger. Cook on high heat for 10 minutes. Reduce the temperature to 300F and cook for 20 more minutes or until the internal temperature reaches 130F.
8. Remove the lamb rack from the Traeger and let rest while wrapped in a foil for 15 minutes. Serve when hot.

Nutrition:

Calories 390   Total fat 35g   Total carbs 0g   Protein 17g   Sodium 65mg

79. Traeger Smoked Leg

Preparation Time: 15 Minutes

Cooking Time: 3 Hours

Servings: 6

Ingredients:

- One leg of lamb, boneless
- 2 tbsp oil
- Four garlic cloves, minced
- 2 tbsp oregano
- 1 tbsp thyme
- 2 tbsp salt
- 1 tbsp black pepper, freshly ground

Directions:

1. Trim excess fat from the lamb, ensuring you keep the meat in an even thickness for even cooking.

2. In a mixing bowl, mix oil, garlic, and all spices. Rub the mixture all over the lamb, then cover with a plastic wrap.

3. Place the lamb in a fridge and let marinate for an hour.

4. Transfer the lamb on a smoker rack and set the Traeger to smoke at 250F.

5. Smoke the meat for 4 hours or until the internal temperature reaches 145F

6. Remove from the Traeger and serve immediately.

Nutrition:

Calories 356 Total fat 16g Total carbs 3g Protein 49g

Sugars 1g   Fiber 1g   Sodium 2474mg

80. Traeger Grilled Aussie Leg of Lamb

Preparation Time: 30 Minutes

Cooking Time: 2 Hours

Servings: 8

Ingredients:

- 5 lb. Aussie Boneless Leg of lamb

Smoked Paprika Rub

- 1 tbsp raw sugar; 1 tbsp salt; 1 tbsp black pepper
- 1 tbsp smoked paprika; 1 tbsp garlic powder; 1 tbsp rosemary
- 1 tbsp onion powder; 1 tbsp cumin; 1/2 tbsp cayenne pepper

Roasted Carrots

- One bunch of rainbow carrots
- Olive oil; Salt and pepper

Directions:

1. Preheat your Traeger to 350F and trim any excess fat from the meat.
2. Combine the paprika rub ingredients and generously rub all over the meat.
3. Place the lamb on the preheated Traeger over indirect heat and smoke for 2 hours. Meanwhile, toss the carrots in oil, salt, and pepper.
4. Add the carrots to the grill after 1 ½ hour or until the internal temperature has reached 90F.
5. Cook until the internal meat temperature reaches 135F.
6. Remove the lamb from the Traeger and cover it with foil for 30 minutes. Once the carrots are cooked, serve with the meat and enjoy it.

Nutrition: Calories 257   Total fat 8g   Total carbs 6g   Protein 37g

Sugars 3g   Fiber 1g   Sodium 431mg   Potassium 666mg

81. Simple Traeger Grilled Lamb Chops

Preparation Time: 10 Minutes

Cooking Time: 20 Minutes

Servings: 6

Ingredients:

- 1/4 cup white vinegar, distilled
- 2 tbsp olive oil
- 2 tbsp salt
- 1/2 tbsp black pepper
- 1 tbsp minced garlic
- One onion, thinly sliced
- 2 lb. lamb chops

Directions:

1. In a resealable bag, mix vinegar, oil, salt, black pepper, garlic, and sliced onions until all salt has dissolved.

2. Add the lamb and toss until evenly coated. Place in a fridge to marinate for 2 hours.

3. Preheat your Traeger.

4. Remove the lamb from the resealable bag and leave any onion that is stuck on the meat. Use an aluminum foil to cover any exposed bone ends.

5. Grill until the desired doneness is achieved. Serve and enjoy when hot.

Nutrition:

Calories 519   Total fat 44.8g   Total carbs 2.3g

Protein 25g   Sugars 0.8g   Fiber 0.4g

Sodium 861mg   Potassium 358.6mg

82. Traeger Grilled Lamb with Sugar Glaze

Preparation Time: 15 Minutes

Cooking Time: 20 Minutes

Servings: 4

Ingredients:

- 1/4 cup sugar
- 2 tbsp ground ginger
- 2 tbsp dried tarragon
- 1/2 tbsp salt
- 1 tbsp black pepper, ground
- 1 tbsp ground cinnamon
- 1 tbsp garlic powder
- Four lamb chops

Directions:

1. In a mixing bowl, mix sugar, ground ginger, tarragon, salt, pepper, cinnamon, and garlic.

2. Rub the lamb chops with the mixture and refrigerate for an hour.

3. Meanwhile, preheat your Traeger.

4. Brush the grill grates with oil and place the marinated lamb chops on it—Cook for 5 minutes on each side.

5. Serve and enjoy.

Nutrition:

Calories 241   Total fat 13.1g   Total carbs 15.8g

Protein 14.6g   Sugars 13.6g   Fiber 0.7g

Sodium 339.2mg   Potassium 256.7mg

83. Traeger Grilled Leg of Lamb Steak

Preparation Time: 10 Minutes

Cooking Time: 10 Minutes

Servings: 4

Ingredients:

- 4 reaches lamb steaks, bone-in
- 1/4 cup olive oil
- Four garlic cloves, minced
- 1 tbsp rosemary, freshly chopped
- Salt and pepper to taste

Directions:

1. Arrange the steak in a dish in a single layer. Cover the meat with oil, garlic, fresh rosemary, salt, and pepper.
2. Flip the meat to coat on all sides and let it marinate for 30 minutes.
3. Preheat your Traeger and lightly oil the grates. Cook the meat on the grill until well browned on both sides, and the internal temperature reaches 140F. Serve and enjoy.

Nutrition:

- Calories 327.3
- Total fat 21.9g
- Total carbs 1.7g
- Protein 29.6g
- Sugars 0.1g
- Fiber 0.2g
- Sodium 112.1mg
- Potassium 409.8mg

84. Traeger Garlic Rack Lamb

Preparation Time: 45 Minutes

Cooking Time: 3 Hours

Servings: 4

Ingredients:

- Lamb Rack; Basil – 1 teaspoon

- Oregano – 1 teaspoon; Peppermill – 10 cranks

- Marsala wine – 3 oz.; Cram Sherry – 3 oz.

- Olive oil; Madeira wine – 3 oz

- Balsamic vinegar – 3 oz.; Rosemary – 1 teaspoon

Directions:

1. Add all of the ingredients into a zip bag the mix well to form an emulsion.

2. Place the rack lamb into the bag the release all of the air as you rub the marinade all over the lamb.

3. Let it stay in the bag for about 45 minutes

4. Get the wood pellet grill preheated to 250F, then cook the lamb for 3 hours as you turn on both sides.

5. Ensure that the internal temperature is at 165F before removing from the grill.

6. Allow to cool for a few minutes, then serve and enjoy.

Nutrition:

- Calories: 291 Cal

- Protein: 26 g

- Fat: 21 g

85. Traeger Braised Lamb Shank

Preparation Time: 20 Minutes

Cooking Time: 4 Hours

Servings: 6

Ingredients:

- Lamb shanks – 4
- Olive oil as required
- Beef broth – 1 cup
- Red wine – 1 cup
- Fresh thyme and sprigs – 4

Directions:

1. Season lamb shanks with prime rib rub, then allow resting.
2. Get the wood pellet grill temperature set to high, then cook the lamb shanks for about 30 minutes.
3. Place the shanks directly on the grill grate, then cook for another 20 minutes until browned on the outside.
4. Transfer the cooked lamb shanks into a Dutch oven, then pour beef broth, the herbs, and wine. Cover it with a fitting lid, then place it back on the grill grate and allow it to cook at a reduced temperature of 325F.
5. Brace the lamb shanks for about 3 hours or until the internal temperature gets to 180F.
6. Remove the lid once ready, then serve on a platter together with the accumulated juices and enjoy.

Nutrition:

Calories: 312 Cal   Protein: 27 g   Fat: 24 g

86. Wood Pellet Smoked Leg of Lamb

Preparation Time: 15 minutes

Cooking Time: 3 hours

Servings: 6

Ingredients:

- 1 leg lamb, boneless
- 4 garlic cloves, minced
- 1 tbsp black pepper, freshly ground
- 2 tbsp oregano; 2 tbsp salt
- 1 tbsp thyme; 2 tbsp olive oil

Intolerances:

- Gluten-Free
- Egg-Free
- Lactose-Free

Directions:

1. Trim any excess fat from the lamb and tie the lamb using twine to form a nice roast.

2. In a mixing bowl, mix garlic, spices, and oil. Rub all over the lamb, wrap with a plastic bag then refrigerate for an hour to marinate.

3. Place the lamb on a smoker set at 250 F. smoke the lamb for 4 hours or until the internal temperature reaches 145 F.

4. Remove from the smoker and let rest to cool. Serve and enjoy.

Nutrition:

Calories: 350   Fat: 16g

Carbs: 3g   Protein: 49g

87. Simple Grilled Lamb Chops

Preparation Time: 10 minutes

Cooking Time: 6 minutes

Servings: 6

Ingredients:

- 1/4 cup distilled white vinegar
- 2 tbsp salt; 1/2 tbsp black pepper
- 1 tbsp garlic, minced; 1 onion, thinly sliced
- 2 tbsp olive oil; 2 lb. lamb chops

Intolerances:

- Gluten-Free
- Egg-Free
- Lactose-Free

Directions:

1. In a resealable bag, mix vinegar, salt, black pepper, garlic, sliced onion, and oil until all salt has dissolved.

2. Add the lamb chops and toss until well coated. Place in the fridge to marinate for 2 hours. Preheat the wood pellet grill to high heat.

3. Remove the lamb from the fridge and discard the marinade. Wrap any exposed bones with foil.

4. Grill the lamb for 3 minutes per side. You can also broil in a broiler for more crispness. Serve and enjoy.

Nutrition:

Calories: 519   Fat: 45g

Carbs: 2g   Protein: 25g

88. Spicy Chinese Cumin Lamb Skewers

Preparation Time: 20 minutes

Cooking Time: 6 minutes

Servings: 10

Ingredients:

- 1 lb. lamb shoulder, cut into 1/2-inch pieces
- 10 skewers
- 2 tbsp ground cumin
- 2 tbsp red pepper flakes
- 1 tbsp salt

Intolerances:

- Gluten-Free
- Egg-Free
- Lactose-Free

Directions:

1. Thread the lamb pieces onto skewers.
2. Preheat the wood pellet grill to medium heat and lightly oil the grill grate.
3. Place the skewers on the grill grate and cook while turning occasionally. Sprinkle cumin, pepper flakes, and salt every time you turn the skewer.
4. Cook for 6 minutes or until nicely browned. Serve and enjoy.

Nutrition:

Calories: 77   Fat: 5g

Carbs: 2g   Protein: 6g

89. Garlic and Rosemary Grilled Lamb Chops

Preparation Time: 10 minutes

Cooking Time: 20 minutes

Servings: 4

Ingredients:

- 2 lb. lamb loin, thick cut; 4 garlic cloves, minced
- 1 tbsp rosemary leaves, fresh chopped
- 1 tbsp kosher salt; 1/2 tbsp black pepper
- 1 lemon zest; 1/4 cup olive oil

Intolerances:

- Gluten-Free
- Egg-Free
- Lactose-Free

Directions:

1. In a small mixing bowl, mix garlic, lemon zest, oil, salt, and black pepper then pour the mixture over the lamb.
2. Flip the lamb chops to make sure they are evenly coated. Place the chops in the fridge to marinate for an hour.
3. Preheat the wood pellet grill to high heat then sear the lamb for 3 minutes on each side.
4. Reduce the heat and cook the chops for 6 minutes or until the internal temperature reaches 150 F.
5. Remove the lamb from the grill and wrap it in a foil. Let it rest for 5 minutes before serving. Enjoy.

Nutrition:

Calories: 171   Fat: 8g   Carbs: 1g   Protein: 23g

90. Grilled Leg of Lambs Steaks

Preparation Time: 10 minutes

Cooking Time: 10 minutes

Servings: 4

Ingredients:

- 4 lamb steaks, bone-in
- 1/4 cup olive oil
- 4 garlic cloves, minced
- 1 tbsp rosemary, freshly chopped
- Salt and black pepper

Intolerances:

- Gluten-Free
- Egg-Free
- Lactose-Free

Directions:

1. Place the lamb in a shallow dish in a single layer. Top with oil, garlic cloves, rosemary, salt, and black pepper then flip the steaks to cover on both sides.
2. Let sit for 30 minutes to marinate.
3. Preheat the wood pellet grill to high and brush the grill grate with oil.
4. Place the lamb steaks on the grill grate and cook until browned and the internal is slightly pink. The internal temperature should be 140 F.
5. Let rest for 5 minutes before serving. Enjoy.

Nutrition:

Calories: 325   Fat: 22g

Carbs: 2g   Protein: 30g

91. Wood Pellet Grilled Lamb Loin Chops

Preparation Time: 10 minutes

Cooking Time: 10 minutes

Servings: 6

Ingredients:

- 2 tbsp herbs de Provence
- 1-1/2 tbsp olive oil
- 2 garlic cloves, minced
- 2 tbsp lemon juice
- 5 oz lamb loin chops
- Salt and black pepper to taste

Intolerances:

- Gluten-Free
- Egg-Free
- Lactose-Free

Directions:

1. In a small mixing bowl, mix herbs de Provence, oil, garlic, and juice. Rub the mixture on the lamb chops then refrigerate for an hour.

2. Preheat the wood pellet grill to medium-high then lightly oil the grill grate.

3. Season the lamb chops with salt and black pepper.

4. Place the lamb chops on the grill and cook for 4 minutes on each side.

5. Remove the chops from the grill and place them in an aluminum covered plate. Let rest for 5 minutes before serving. Enjoy.

Nutrition:

Calories: 570   Fat: 44g   Carbs: 1g   Protein: 42g

CHAPTER 7:
Seafood Recipes

92. Barbeque Shrimp

Preparation Time: 20 minutes
Cooking Time: 8 minutes
Servings: 6
Ingredients:

- 2-pound raw shrimp (peeled and deveined)
- ¼ cup extra virgin olive oil
- ½ tsp paprika
- ½ tsp red pepper flakes
- 2 garlic cloves (minced)
- 1 tsp cumin
- 1 lemon (juiced)
- 1 tsp kosher salt
- 1 tbsp chili paste
- Bamboo or wooden skewers (soaked for 30 minutes, at least)

Directions:

1. Combine the pepper flakes, cumin, lemon, salt, chili, paprika, garlic and olive oil. Add the shrimp and toss to combine.

2. Transfer the shrimp and marinade into a zip-lock bag and refrigerate for 4 hours.

3. Let shrimp rest in room temperature after pulling it out from marinade

4. Start your grill on smoke, leaving the lid opened for 5 minutes, or until fire starts. Use hickory wood pellet.

5. Keep lid unopened and preheat the grill to "high" for 15 minutes.

6. Thread shrimps onto skewers and arrange the skewers on the grill grate.

7. Smoke shrimps for 8 minutes, 4 minutes per side.

8. Serve and enjoy.

Nutrition:

- Calories: 267 Cal
- Fat: 11.6 g
- Carbohydrates: 4.9 g
- Protein: 34.9 g
- Fiber: 0.4 g

93. Traeger Grilled Tuna steaks

Preparation Time: 5 minutes

Cooking Time: 4 minutes

Servings: 4

Ingredients:

- 4 (6 ounce each) tuna steaks (1 inch thick)
- 1 lemon (juiced); 1 clove garlic (minced)
- 1 tsp chili; 2 tbsp extra virgin olive oil
- 1 cup white wine; 3 tbsp brown sugar
- 1 tsp rosemary

Directions:

1. Combine lemon, chili, white wine, sugar, rosemary, olive oil and garlic. Add the tuna steaks and toss to combine.

2. Transfer the tuna and marinade to a zip-lock bag. Refrigerate for 3 hours.

3. Remove the tuna steaks from the marinade and let them rest for about 1 hour

4. Start your grill on smoke, leaving the lid opened for 5 minutes, or until fire starts.

5. Do not open lid to preheat until 15 minutes to the setting "HIGH"

6. Grease the grill grate with oil and place the tuna on the grill grate. Grill tuna steaks for 4 minutes, 2 minutes per side.

7. Remove the tuna from the grill and let them rest for a few minutes.

Nutrition:

Calories: 137 Cal   Fat: 17.8 g   Fiber: 0.6 g

Carbohydrates: 10.2 g   Protein: 51.2 g

94. Oyster in Shells

Preparation Time: 25 minutes

Cooking Time: 8 minutes

Servings: 4

Ingredients:

- 12 medium oysters; 1 tsp oregano; 2 tbsp freshly chopped parsley
- 1 lemon (juiced); 1 tsp freshly ground black pepper
- 6 tbsp unsalted butter (melted); 1 tsp salt or more to taste
- 2 garlic cloves (minced); 2 ½ tbsp grated parmesan cheese

Directions:

1. Remove dirt
2. Open the shell completely. Discard the top shell.
3. Gently run the knife under the oyster to loosen the oyster foot from the bottom shell. Repeat step 2 and 3 for the remaining oysters.
4. Combine melted butter, lemon, pepper, salt, garlic and oregano in a mixing bowl. Pour ½ to 1 tsp of the butter mixture on each oyster.
5. Start your wood pellet grill on smoke, leaving the lid opened for 5 minutes, or until fire starts.
6. Keep lid unopened to preheat in the set "HIGH" with lid closed for 15 minutes. Gently arrange the oysters onto the grill grate.
7. Grill oyster for 6 to 8 minutes or until the oyster juice is bubbling and the oyster is plump.
8. Remove oysters from heat. Serve and top with grated parmesan and chopped parsley.

Nutrition:

Calories: 200 Cal   Fat: 19.2 g   Fiber: 0.8 g

Carbohydrates: 3.9 g   Protein: 4.6 g

95. Grilled King Crab Legs

Preparation Time: 10 minutes

Cooking Time: 25 minutes

Servings: 4

Ingredients:

- 4 pounds king crab legs (split)
- 4 tbsp lemon juice
- 2 tbsp garlic powder
- 1 cup butter (melted)
- 2 tsp brown sugar
- 2 tsp paprika
- Black pepper (depends to your liking)

Directions:

1. In a mixing bowl, combine the lemon juice, butter, sugar, garlic, paprika and pepper.
2. Arrange the split crab on a baking sheet, split side up.
3. Drizzle ¾ of the butter mixture over the crab legs.
4. Configure your pellet grill for indirect cooking and preheat it to 225°F, using mesquite wood pellets.
5. Arrange the crab legs onto the grill grate, shell side down.
6. Cover the grill and cook 25 minutes.
7. Remove the crab legs from the grill.
8. Serve and top with the remaining butter mixture.

Nutrition:

Calories: 480 Cal   Fat: 53.2 g   Fiber: 1.2 g

Carbohydrates: 6.1 g   Protein: 88.6 g

96. Cajun Smoked Catfish

Preparation Time: 15 minutes

Cooking Time: 2 hours

Servings: 4

Ingredients:

- 4 catfish fillets (5 ounces each); ½ cup Cajun seasoning
- 1 tsp ground black pepper; 1 tbsp smoked paprika
- 1/4 tsp cayenne pepper; 1 tsp hot sauce
- 1 tsp granulated garlic; 1 tsp onion powder
- 1 tsp thyme; 1 tsp salt or more to taste
- 2 tbsp chopped fresh parsley

Directions:

1. Pour water into the bottom of a square or rectangular dish. Add 4 tbsp salt. Arrange the catfish fillets into the dish. Cover the dish and refrigerate for 3 to 4 hours.

2. Combine the paprika, cayenne, hot sauce, onion, salt, thyme, garlic, pepper and Cajun seasoning in a mixing bowl.

3. Remove the fish from the dish and let it sit for a few minutes, or until it is at room temperature. Pat the fish fillets dry with a paper towel.

4. Rub the seasoning mixture over each fillet generously. Start your grill on smoke, leaving the lid opened for 5 minutes, or until fire starts.

5. Keep lid unopened and preheat to 200°F, using mesquite hardwood pellets. Arrange the fish fillets onto the grill grate and close the grill. Cook for about 2 hours, or until the fish is flaky.

6. Remove the fillets from the grill and let the fillets rest for a few minutes to cool. Serve and garnish with chopped fresh parsley.

Nutrition: Calories: 204 Fat: 11.1g Carbohydrates: 2.7g Protein: 22.9g

97. Smoked Scallops

Preparation Time: 10 minutes

Cooking Time: 15 minutes

Servings: 6

Ingredients:

- 2 pounds sea scallops
- 4 tbsp salted butter
- 2 tbsp lemon juice
- ½ tsp ground black pepper
- 1 garlic clove (minced)
- 1 kosher tsp salt
- 1 tsp freshly chopped tarragon

Directions:

1. Let the scallops dry using paper towels and drizzle all sides with salt and pepper to season

2. Place you're a cast iron pan in your grill and preheat the grill to 400°F with lid closed for 15 minutes.

3. Combine the butter and garlic in hot cast iron pan. Add the scallops and stir. Close grill lid and cook for 8 minutes.

4. Flip the scallops and cook for an additional 7 minutes.

5. Remove the scallop from heat and let it rest for a few minutes.

6. Stir in the chopped tarragon. Serve and top with lemon juice.

Nutrition:

Calories: 204 Cal   Fat: 8.9 g   Fiber: 0.1 g

Carbohydrates: 4 g   Protein: 25.6 g

98. Grilled Tilapia

Preparation Time: 10 minutes

Cooking Time: 20 minutes

Servings: 6

Ingredients:

- 2 tsp dried parsley; ½ tsp garlic powder
- 1 tsp cayenne pepper; ½ tsp ground black pepper
- ½ tsp thyme; ½ tsp dried basil
- ½ tsp oregano; 3 tbsp olive oil
- ½ tsp lemon pepper; 1 tsp kosher salt
- 1 lemon (juiced); 6 tilapia fillets
- 1 ½ tsp creole seafood seasoning

Directions:

1. In a mixing bowl, combine spices
2. Brush the fillets with oil and lemon juice.
3. Liberally, season all sides of the tilapia fillets with the seasoning mix.
4. Preheat your grill to 325°F. Place a non-stick BBQ grilling try on the grill and arrange the tilapia fillets onto it.
5. Grill for 15 to 20 minutes. Remove fillets and cool down

Nutrition:

- Calories: 176 Cal
- Fat: 9.6 g
- Carbohydrates: 1.5 g
- Protein: 22.3 g
- Fiber: 0.5 g

99. Traeger Salmon with Togarashi

Preparation Time: 5 Minutes

Cooking Time: 20 Minutes

Servings: 3

Ingredients:

- One salmon fillet
- 1/4 cup olive oil
- 1/2 tbsp kosher salt
- 1 tbsp Togarashi seasoning

Directions:

1. Preheat your Traeger to 4000F.
2. Place the salmon on a sheet lined with non-stick foil with the skin side down.
3. Rub the oil into the meat, then sprinkle salt and Togarashi.
4. Place the salmon on the grill and cook for 20 minutes or until the internal temperature reaches 145F with the lid closed.
5. Remove from the Traeger and serve when hot.

Nutrition:

- Calories 119
- Total fat 10g
- Saturated fat 2g
- Sodium 720mg

100. Trager Rockfish

Preparation Time: 10 Minutes

Cooking Time: 20 Minutes

Servings: 6

Ingredients:

- Six rockfish fillets
- One lemon, sliced
- 3/4 tbsp salt
- 2 tbsp fresh dill, chopped
- 1/2 tbsp garlic powder
- 1/2 tbsp onion powder
- 6 tbsp butter

Directions:

1. Preheat your Traeger to 400F.
2. Season the fish with salt, dill, garlic, and onion powder on both sides, then place it in a baking dish.
3. Place a pat of butter and a lemon slice on each fillet. Place the baking dish in the Traeger and close the lid.
4. Cook for 20 minutes or until the fish is no longer translucent and is flaky.
5. Remove from Traeger and let rest before serving.

Nutrition:

Calories 270   Total fat 17g

Saturated fat 9g   Total carbs 2g

Net carbs 2g   Protein 28g   Sodium 381mg

101. Traeger Grilled Lingcod

Preparation Time: 10 Minutes

Cooking Time: 15 Minutes

Servings: 6

Ingredients:

- 2 lb. lingcod fillets
- 1/2 tbsp salt
- 1/2 tbsp white pepper
- 1/4 tbsp cayenne pepper
- Lemon wedges

Directions:

1. Preheat your Traeger to 375F.
2. Place the lingcod on a parchment paper or a grill mat
3. Season the fish with salt, pepper, and top with lemon wedges.
4. Cook the fish for 15 minutes or until the internal temperature reaches 145F.

Nutrition:

- Calories 245
- Total fat 2g
- Total carbs 2g
- Protein 52g
- Sugars 1g
- Fiber 1g
- Sodium 442mg

102. Crab Stuffed Lingcod

Preparation Time: 20 Minutes

Cooking Time: 30 Minutes

Servings: 6

Ingredients:

Lemon cream sauce

- Four garlic cloves; One shallot; One leek
- 2 tbsp olive oil; 1 tbsp salt; 1/4 tbsp black pepper
- 3 tbsp butter; 1/4 cup white wine; 1 cup whipping cream
- 2 tbsp lemon juice; 1 tbsp lemon zest

Crab mix

- 1 lb. crab meat; 1/3 cup mayo
- 1/3 cup sour cream; 1/3 cup lemon cream sauce
- 1/4 green onion, chopped; 1/4 tbsp black pepper
- 1/2 tbsp old bay seasoning

Fish

- 2 lb. lingcod; 1 tbsp olive oil
- 1 tbsp salt; 1 tbsp paprika
- 1 tbsp green onion, chopped
- 1 tbsp Italian parsley

Directions:

Lemon cream sauce

1. Chop garlic, shallot, and leeks, then add to a saucepan with oil, salt, pepper, and butter.
2. Sauté over medium heat until the shallot is translucent.

3. Deglaze with white wine, then add whipping cream. Bring the sauce to boil, reduce heat, and simmer for 3 minutes.

4. Remove from heat and add lemon juice and lemon zest. Transfer the sauce to a blender and blend until smooth.

5. Set aside 1/3 cup for the crab mix

Crab mix

1. Add all the fixings to a mixing bowl and mix thoroughly until well combined.

2. Set aside

Fish

1. Fire up your Traeger to high heat, then slice the fish into 6-ounce portions.

2. Lay the fish on its side on a cutting board and slice it 3/4 way through the middle leaving a 1/2 inch on each end to have a nice pouch.

3. Rub the oil into the fish, then place them on a baking sheet. Sprinkle with salt.

4. Stuff crab mix into each fish, then sprinkle paprika and place it on the grill.

5. Cook for 15 minutes or more if the fillets are more than 2 inches thick.

6. Remove the fish and transfer to serving platters. Pour the remaining lemon cream sauce on each fish and garnish with onions and parsley.

Nutrition:

Calories 476   Total fat 33g

Saturated fat 14g   Total carbs 6g

Net carbs 5g   Protein 38g

Sugars 3g   Fiber 1g

Sodium 1032mg

103. Traeger Smoked Shrimp

Preparation Time: 10 Minutes

Cooking Time: 10 Minutes

Servings: 6

Ingredients:

- 1 lb. tail-on shrimp, uncooked
- 1/2 tbsp onion powder
- 1/2 tbsp garlic powder
- 1/2 tbsp salt
- 4 tbsp teriyaki sauce
- 2 tbsp green onion, minced
- 4 tbsp sriracha mayo

Directions:

1. Peel the shrimp shells leaving the tail on, then wash well and rise.
2. Drain well and pat dry with a paper towel.
3. Preheat your Traeger to 450F.
4. Season the shrimp with onion powder, garlic powder, and salt. Place the shrimp in the Traeger and cook for 6 minutes on each side.
5. Remove the shrimp from the Traeger and toss with teriyaki sauce, then garnish with onions and mayo.

Nutrition:

- Calories 87
- Total carbs 2g
- Net carbs 2g
- Protein 16g
- Sodium 1241mg

104. Grilled Shrimp Kabobs

Preparation Time: 5 Minutes

Cooking Time: 10 Minutes

Servings: 4

Ingredients:

- 1 lb. colossal shrimp, peeled and deveined
- 2 tbsp. oil
- 1/2 tbsp. garlic salt
- 1/2 tbsp. salt
- 1/8 tbsp. pepper
- Six skewers

Directions:

1. Preheat your Traeger to 375F.
2. Pat the shrimp dry with a paper towel.
3. In a mixing bowl, mix oil, garlic salt, salt, and pepper
4. Toss the shrimp in the mixture until well coated.
5. Skewer the shrimps and cook in the Traeger with the lid closed for 4 minutes.
6. Open the lid, flip the skewers, cook for another 4 minutes, or wait until the shrimp is pink and the flesh is opaque.
7. Serve.

Nutrition:

- Calories 325
- Protein 20g
- Sodium 120mg

105. Sweet Bacon-Wrapped Shrimp

Preparation Time: 20 Minutes

Cooking Time: 10 Minutes

Servings: 12

Ingredients:

- 1 lb. raw shrimp
- 1/2 tbsp salt
- 1/4 tbsp garlic powder
- 1 lb. bacon, cut into halves

Directions:

1. Preheat your Traeger to 350F.
2. Remove the shells and tails from the shrimp, then pat them dry with the paper towels.
3. Sprinkle salt and garlic on the shrimp, then wrap with bacon and secure with a toothpick.
4. Place the shrimps on a baking rack greased with cooking spray.
5. Cook for 10 minutes, flip and cook for another 10 minutes, or until the bacon is crisp enough.
6. Remove from the Traeger and serve.

Nutrition:

Calories 204   Total fat 14g

Saturated fat 5g   Total carbs 1g

Net carbs 1g   Protein 18g   Sodium 939mg

106. Traeger Spot Prawn Skewers

Preparation Time: 10 Minutes

Cooking Time: 10 Minutes

Servings: 6

Ingredients:

- 2 lb. spot prawns
- 2 tbsp oil
- Salt and pepper to taste

Directions:

1. Preheat your Traeger to 400F.
2. Skewer your prawns with soaked skewers, then generously sprinkle with oil, salt, and pepper.
3. Place the skewers on the grill, then cook with the lid closed for 5 minutes on each side.
4. Remove the skewers and serve when hot.

Nutrition:

- Calories 221
- Total fat 7g
- Saturated fat 1g
- Total carbs 2g
- Net carbs 2g
- Protein 34g
- Sodium 1481mg

107. Traeger Bacon-wrapped Scallops

Preparation Time: 15 Minutes

Cooking Time: 20 Minutes

Servings: 8

Ingredients:

- 1 lb. sea scallops
- 1/2 lb. bacon
- Sea salt

Directions:

1. Preheat your Traeger to 375F.

2. Pat dries the scallops with a towel, then wrap them with a piece of bacon and secure with a toothpick.

3. Lay the scallops on the grill with the bacon side down. Close the lid and cook for 5 minutes on each side.

4. Keep the scallops on the bacon side so that you will not get grill marks on the scallops.

5. Serve and enjoy.

Nutrition:

- Calories 261
- Total fat 14g
- Saturated fat 5g
- Total carbs 5g
- Net carbs 5g
- Protein 28g
- Sodium 1238mg

108. Traeger Lobster Tail

Preparation Time: 10 Minutes

Cooking Time: 15 Minutes

Servings: 2

Ingredients:

- 10 oz lobster tail
- 1/4 tbsp old bay seasoning
- 1/4 tbsp Himalayan salt
- 2 tbsp butter, melted
- 1 tbsp fresh parsley, chopped

Directions:

1. Preheat your Traeger to 450F.
2. Slice the tail down the middle, then season it with bay seasoning and salt.
3. Place the tails directly on the grill with the meat side down. Grill for 15 minutes or until the internal temperature reaches 140F.
4. Remove from the Traeger and drizzle with butter.
5. Serve when hot garnished with parsley.

Nutrition:

- Calories 305
- Total fat 14g
- Saturated fat 8g
- Total carbs 5g
- Net carbs 5g
- Protein 38g
- Sodium 684mg

109. Roasted Honey Salmon

Preparation Time: 5 Minutes

Cooking Time: 1 Hour

Servings: 4

Ingredients:

- Two cloves' garlic, grated
- Two tablespoon ginger, minced
- One teaspoon honey
- One teaspoon sesame oil
- Two tablespoon lemon juice
- One teaspoon chili paste
- Four salmon fillets
- Two tablespoon soy sauce

Directions:

1. Set your wood pellet grill to smoke while the lid is open.
2. Do this for 5 minutes.
3. Preheat your wood pellet grill to 400 degrees F.
4. Combine all the ingredients except salmon in a sealable plastic bag.
5. Shake to mix the ingredients. Add the salmon.
6. Marinate inside the refrigerator for 30 minutes.
7. Add the salmon to a roasting pan and place it on top of the grill.
8. Close the lid and cook for 3 minutes.
9. Flip the salmon and cook for another 3 minutes.

Nutrition:

Calories 119   Total fat 10g

Saturated fat 2g   Sodium 720mg

110. Blackened Salmon

Preparation Time: 10 Minutes

Cooking Time: 20 Minutes

Servings: 4

Ingredients:

- 2 lb. salmon, fillet, scaled and deboned
- Two tablespoons olive oil
- Four tablespoons sweet dry rub
- One tablespoon cayenne pepper
- Two cloves' garlic, minced

Directions:

1. Turn on your wood pellet grill.
2. Set it to 350 degrees F.
3. Brush the salmon with the olive oil.
4. Sprinkle it with the dry rub, cayenne pepper, and garlic.
5. Grill for 5 minutes per side.

Nutrition:

- Calories 119
- Total fat 10g
- Saturated fat 2g
- Sodium 720mg

111. Grilled Cajun Shrimp

Preparation Time: 5 Minutes

Cooking Time: 25 Minutes

Servings: 8

Ingredients:

Dip

- 1/2 cup mayonnaise; One teaspoon lemon juice
- 1 cup sour cream; One clove garlic, grated
- One tablespoon Cajun seasoning; One tablespoon hickory bacon rub
- One tablespoon hot sauce; Chopped scallions

Shrimp

- 1/2 lb. shrimp, peeled and deveined; Two tablespoons olive oil
- 1/2 tablespoon hickory bacon seasoning; 1 tablespoon Cajun seasoning

Directions:

1. Turn on your wood pellet grill. Set it to 350 degrees F.
2. Mix the dip ingredients in a bowl. Transfer to a small pan.
3. Cover with foil. Place on top of the grill. Cook for 10 minutes.
4. Coat the shrimp with the olive oil and sprinkle with the seasonings.
5. Grill for 5 minutes per side.
6. Pour the dip on top or serve with the shrimp.

Nutrition:

Calories 87   Total carbs 2g

Net carbs 2g   Protein 16g

Sodium 1241mg

112. Salmon Cakes

Preparation Time: 5 Minutes
Cooking Time: 25 Minutes
Servings: 4
Ingredients:

- 1 cup cooked salmon, flaked
- 1/2 red bell pepper, chopped
- Two eggs, beaten; 1/4 cup mayonnaise
- 1/2 tablespoon dry sweet rub
- 1 1/2 cups breadcrumbs; Olive oil
- One tablespoon mustard

Directions:

1. Combine all the fixings except the olive oil in a bowl.
2. Form patties from this mixture. Let sit for 15 minutes.
3. Turn on your wood pellet grill. Set it to 350 degrees F.
4. Add a baking pan to the grill. Drizzle a little olive oil on top of the pan.
5. Add the salmon cakes to the pan. Grill each side for 3 to 4 minutes.

Nutrition:

- Calories 119
- Total fat 10g
- Saturated fat 2g
- Sodium 720mg

113. Pineapple Maple Glaze Fish

Preparation Time: 10 minutes

Cooking Time: 15 Minutes

Servings: 6 Servings

Ingredients:

- 3 pounds of fresh salmon; 1/4 cup maple syrup
- 1/2 cup pineapple juice
- Brine Ingredients
- 3 cups of water; Sea salt, to taste
- 2 cups of pineapple juice; ½ cup of brown sugar
- 5 tablespoons of Worcestershire sauce
- 1 tablespoon of garlic salt

Directions:

1. Combine all the brine ingredients in a large cooking pan.
2. Place the fish into the brine and let it sit for 2 hours for marinating.
3. After 2 hours, take out the fish and pat dry with a paper towel and set aside.
4. Preheat the smoker grill to 250 degrees Fahrenheit, until the smoke started to appear.
5. Put salmon on the grill and cook for 15 minutes.
6. Meanwhile, mix pineapple and maple syrup in a bowl and baste fish every 5 minutes.
7. Once the salmon is done, serve and enjoy.

Nutrition:

Calories 123   Total Fat 4.9g6%   Saturated Fat 1.5g8%   Cholesterol 60mg20%

Sodium 29mg1%   Total Carbohydrate 0g0 %   Dietary Fiber 0g0%   Sugar 0g

114. Smoked Catfish Recipe

Preparation Time: 10 minutes

Cooking Time: 5 Minutes

Servings: 3 Servings

Ingredients:

Ingredients for The Rub

- 2 tablespoons paprika; 1/4 teaspoon salt
- 1 tablespoon garlic powder; 1 tablespoon onion powder
- 1/2 tablespoon dried thyme; 1/2 tablespoon cayenne

Other ingredients

- 2 pounds fresh catfish fillets
- 4 tablespoons butter, soften

Directions:

1. Take a mixing bowl, and combine all the rub ingredients in it, including the paprika, salt, garlic powder, onion powder, and thyme and cayenne paper.
2. Rub the fillet with the butter, and then sprinkle a generous amount of rub on top
3. Coat fish well with the rub.
4. Preheat the smoker grill at 200 degrees Fahrenheit for 15 minutes.
5. Cook fish on the grill for 10 minutes, 5minutes per side.
6. Once done, serve and enjoy.

Nutrition:

Calories 146   Total Fat 4.2g   Saturated Fat 2.5g

Cholesterol 61mg   Sodium 28mg

115. Classic Smoked Trout

Preparation Time: 10 minutes

Cooking Time: 1 Hour

Servings: 3 Servings

Ingredients:

Ingredients for The Brine

- 4 cups of water; 1 cup of sea salt
- 1-2 cups dark-brown sugar

Ingredients for The Trout's

- 3 pounds of trout, backbone and pin bones removed
- 4 tablespoons of olive oil

Directions:

1. Preheat the electrical smoker grill, by setting the temperature to 250 degrees F, for 15 minutes by closing the lid.
2. Take a cooking pot, and combine all the brine ingredients, including water, sugar, and salt.
3. Submerged the fish in the brine mixture for a few hours.
4. Afterward, take out the fish, and pat dry with the paper towel.
5. Drizzle olive oil over the fish, and then place it over the grill grate for cooking.
6. Smoke the fish, until the internal temperature reaches 140 degrees Fahrenheit for 1 hour. Then serve.

Nutrition:

Calories 254   Total Fat 4.8g   Saturated Fat 1.5g

Cholesterol 81mg   Sodium 18mg

116. Cajun Smoked Shrimp

Preparation Time: 10 minutes

Cooking Time: 10 Minutes

Servings: 2 Servings

Ingredients:

- 2 tablespoons of virgin olive oil
- 1/2 lemon, juiced; Salt, to taste
- 3 cloves garlic, finely minced
- 2 tablespoons of Cajun spice
- 1.5 pounds of shrimp, raw, peeled, deveined

Directions:

1. Take a zip lock bag and combine olive oil, lemon juice, garlic cloves, Cajun spice, salt, and shrimp.
2. Toss the ingredients well for fine coating.
3. Preheat the smoker grill for 10 minutes until the smoke starts to establish.
4. Put the fish on the grill grate and close lid.
5. Turn the temperature to high and allow the fish to cook the shrimp for 10 minutes, 5 minutes per side. Once done, serve.

Nutrition:

- Calories 446
- Total Fat 4.8g
- Saturated Fat 6.5g
- Cholesterol 53mg
- Sodium 48mg

117. Candied Smoked Salmon with Orange Ginger Rub

Preparation Time: 10 minutes

Cooking Time: 2 Hours 10 Minutes

Servings: 10 servings

Ingredients:

The Marinade

- Brown sugar – ¼ cup
- Salt – ½ teaspoon

The Rub

- Minced garlic – 2 tablespoons
- Grated fresh ginger – 1 teaspoon
- Grated orange zest – ½ teaspoon
- Chili powder – ½ teaspoon
- Cayenne pepper – ½ teaspoon

The Glaze

- Red wine – 2 tablespoons
- Dark rum – 2 tablespoons
- Brown sugar – 1 ½ cups
- Honey – 1 cup

Directions:

1. Mix salt with brown sugar then apply over the salmon fillet. Let it rest for approximately an hour or until the sugar is melted.

2. In the meantime, combine minced garlic with grated fresh ginger, orange zest, chili powder, and cayenne pepper. Mix well.

3. Rub the salmon fillet with the spice mixture then set aside.

4. Plug the wood pellet smoker then fill the hopper with the wood pellet. Turn the switch on.

5. Set the wood pellet smoker for indirect heat then adjust the temperature to 225°F (107°C).

6. Place the seasoned salmon in wood pellet smoker and smoke for 2 hours.

7. Mix red wine with dark rum, brown sugar, and honey then stir until dissolved.

8. During the smoking process, baste the honey mixture over the salmon fillet for several times.

9. Once the smoked salmon flakes, remove it from the wood pellet smoker and transfer it to a serving dish. Serve and enjoy.

Nutrition:

- Calories: 433
- Fats: 39g
- Carbs: 4g
- Fiber: 0g

CHAPTER 8:
Vegetarian Recipes

118. Traeger Grilled Zucchini

Preparation Time: 30 Minutes

Cooking Time: 10 Minutes

Servings: 4

Ingredients:

- Four zucchinis, sliced into strips; One tablespoon sherry vinegar
- Two tablespoons olive oil; Salt and pepper to taste
- Two fresh thyme, chopped

Directions:

1. Place the zucchini strips in a bowl.
2. Mix the remaining fixings and pour them into the zucchini.
3. Coat evenly.
4. Set the Traeger wood pellet grill to 350 degrees F.
5. Preheat for 15 minutes while the lid is closed.
6. Place the zucchini on the grill.
7. Cook for 3 minutes per side.

Nutrition:

Calories 118   Total fat 7.6g   Total carbs 10.8g   Protein 5.4g

Sugars 3.7g   Fiber 2.5g   Sodium 3500mg   Potassium 536mg

119. Smoked Potato Salad

Preparation Time: 1 Hour and 15 Minutes

Cooking Time: 40 Minutes

Servings: 4

Ingredients:

- 2 lb. potatoes
- Two tablespoons olive oil
- 2 cups mayonnaise
- One tablespoon white wine vinegar
- One tablespoon dry mustard
- 1/2 onion, chopped
- Two celery stalks, chopped
- Salt and pepper to taste

Directions:

1. Coat the potatoes with oil.
2. Smoke the potatoes in the Traeger wood pellet grill at 180 degrees F for 20 minutes.
3. Increase temperature to 450 degrees F and cook for 20 more minutes.
4. Transfer to a bowl and let cool.
5. Peel potatoes. Slice into cubes. Refrigerate for 30 minutes.
6. Stir in the rest of the ingredients.

Nutrition:

Calories 118   Total fat 7.6g

Total carbs 10.8g   Protein 5.4g

Sugars 3.7g   Fiber 2.5g,

Sodium 3500mg   Potassium 536mg

120. Baked Parmesan Mushrooms

Preparation Time: 15 Minutes

Cooking Time: 15 Minutes

Servings: 8

Ingredients:

- Eight mushroom caps
- 1/2 cup Parmesan cheese, grated
- 1/2 teaspoon garlic salt
- 1/4 cup mayonnaise
- Pinch paprika
- Hot sauce

Directions:

1. Place mushroom caps in a baking pan.
2. Mix the remaining ingredients in a bowl.
3. Scoop the mixture onto the mushroom.
4. Place the baking pan on the grill.
5. Cook in the Traeger wood pellet grill at 350 degrees F for 15 minutes while the lid is closed.

Nutrition:

Calories 118   Total fat 7.6g

Total carbs 10.8g   Protein 5.4g

Sugars 3.7g   Fiber 2.5g,

Sodium 3500mg   Potassium 536mg

121. Roasted Spicy Tomatoes

Preparation Time: 30 Minutes

Cooking Time: 1 Hour and 30 Minutes

Servings: 4

Ingredients:

- 2 lb. large tomatoes, sliced in half
- Olive oil
- Two tablespoons' garlic, chopped
- Three tablespoons parsley, chopped
- Salt and pepper to taste
- Hot pepper sauce

Directions:

1. Set the temperature to 400 degrees F.
2. Preheat it for 15 minutes while the lid is closed.
3. Add tomatoes to a baking pan.
4. Drizzle with oil and sprinkle with garlic, parsley, salt, and pepper.
5. Roast for 1 hour and 30 minutes.
6. Drizzle with hot pepper sauce and serve.

Nutrition:

Calories 118   Total fat 7.6g

Total carbs 10.8g   Protein 5.4g

Sugars 3.7g   Fiber 2.5g,

Sodium 3500mg   Potassium 536mg

122. Grilled Corn with Honey and Butter

Preparation Time: 30 Minutes

Cooking Time: 10 Minutes

Servings: 4

Ingredients:

- Six pieces of corn
- Two tablespoons olive oil
- 1/2 cup butter
- 1/2 cup honey
- One tablespoon smoked salt
- Pepper to taste

Directions:

1. Preheat the wood pellet grill too high for 15 minutes while the lid is closed.
2. Brush the corn with oil and butter.
3. Grill the corn for 10 minutes, turning from time to time.
4. Mix honey and butter.
5. Brush corn with this mixture and sprinkle with smoked salt and pepper.

Nutrition:

Calories 118   Total fat 7.6g

Total carbs 10.8g   Protein 5.4g

Sugars 3.7g   Fiber 2.5g,

Sodium 3500mg   Potassium 536mg

123. Grilled Sweet Potato Planks

Preparation Time: 30 Minutes

Cooking Time: 30 Minutes

Servings: 8

Ingredients:

- Five sweet potatoes, sliced into planks
- One tablespoon olive oil
- One teaspoon onion powder
- Salt and pepper to taste

Directions:

1. Set the Traeger wood pellet grill to high.
2. Preheat it for 15 minutes while the lid is closed.
3. Coat the sweet potatoes with oil.
4. Sprinkle with onion powder, salt, and pepper.
5. Grill the sweet potatoes for 15 minutes.

Nutrition:

- Calories 118
- Total fat 7.6g
- Total carbs 10.8g
- Protein 5.4g
- Sugars 3.7g
- Fiber 2.5g,
- Sodium 3500mg
- Potassium 536mg

124. Roasted Veggies and Hummus

Preparation Time: 30 Minutes

Cooking Time: 20 Minutes

Servings: 4

Ingredients:

- One white onion, sliced into wedges
- 2 cups butternut squash
- 2 cups cauliflower, sliced into florets
- 1 cup mushroom buttons
- Olive oil
- Salt and pepper to taste
- Hummus

Directions:

1. Set the Traeger wood pellet grill to high.
2. Preheat it for 10 minutes while the lid is closed.
3. Add the veggies to a baking pan.
4. Roast for 20 minutes.
5. Serve roasted veggies with hummus.

Nutrition:

Calories 118   Total fat 7.6g

Total carbs 10.8g   Protein 5.4g

Sugars 3.7g   Fiber 2.5g,

Sodium 3500mg   Potassium 536mg

125. Traeger Smoked Mushrooms

Preparation Time: 15 Minutes

Cooking Time: 45 Minutes

Servings: 2

Ingredients:

- 4 cups whole baby portobello, cleaned
- 1 tbsp canola oil
- 1 tbsp onion powder
- 1 tbsp garlic, granulated
- 1 tbsp salt
- 1 tbsp pepper

Directions:

1. Place all the ingredients in a bowl, mix, and combine.
2. Set your Traeger to 180F.
3. Place the mushrooms on the grill directly and smoke for about 30 minutes.
4. Increase heat to high and cook the mushroom for another 15 minutes.
5. Serve warm and enjoy!

Nutrition:

Calories 118   Total fat 7.6g

Total carbs 10.8g   Protein 5.4g

Sugars 3.7g   Fiber 2.5g,

Sodium 3500mg   Potassium 536mg

126. Grilled Zucchini Squash Spears

Preparation Time: 5 Minutes

Cooking Time: 10 Minutes

Servings: 4

Ingredients:

- Four zucchinis, medium
- 2 tbsp olive oil
- 1 tbsp sherry vinegar
- Two thyme leaves pulled
- Salt to taste
- Pepper to taste

Directions:

1. Clean zucchini, cut ends off, half each lengthwise, and cut each half into thirds.
2. Combine all the other ingredients in a zip lock bag, medium, then add spears.
3. Toss well and mix to coat the zucchini.
4. Preheat Traeger to 350F with the lid closed for 15 minutes.
5. Remove spears from the zip lock bag and place them directly on your grill grate with the cut side down.
6. Cook for about 3-4 minutes until zucchini is tender and grill marks show.
7. Remove them from the grill and enjoy.

Nutrition:

Calories 93   Total fat 7.4g   Total carbs 7.1g   Protein 2.4g

Sugars 3.4g   Fiber 2.5g   Sodium 3500mg   Potassium 536mg

127. Grilled Asparagus & Honey-Glazed Carrots

Preparation Time: 15 Minutes

Cooking Time: 35 Minutes

Servings: 4

Ingredients:

- One bunch asparagus, woody ends removed
- 2 tbsp olive oil
- 1 lb. peeled carrots
- 2 tbsp honey
- Sea salt to taste
- Lemon zest to taste

Directions:

1. Rinse the vegetables under cold water.
2. Splash the asparagus with oil and generously with a splash of salt.
3. Drizzle carrots generously with honey and splash lightly with salt.
4. Preheat your Traeger to 350F with the lid closed for about 15 minutes.
5. Place the carrots first on the grill and cook for about 10-15 minutes.
6. Now place asparagus on the grill and cook both for about 15-20 minutes or until done to your liking.
7. Top with lemon zest and enjoy.

Nutrition:

Calories 184   Total fat 7.3g

Total carbs 28.6g   Protein 6g

Sugars 18.5g   Fiber 7.6g,

Sodium 142mg   Potassium 826mg

128. Traeger Grilled Vegetables

Preparation Time: 5 Minutes

Cooking Time: 15 Minutes

Servings: 12

Ingredients:

- One veggie tray
- 1/4 cup vegetable oil
- 1-2 tbsp Traeger veggie seasoning

Directions:

1. Preheat your Traeger to 375F.
2. Meanwhile, toss the veggies in oil placed on a sheet pan, large, then splash with the seasoning.
3. Place on the Traeger and grill for about 10-15 minutes.
4. Remove, serve, and enjoy.

Nutrition:

- Calories 44
- Total fat 5g
- Total carbs 10.8g
- Protein 0g
- Sugars 0g
- Fiber 0g,
- Sodium 36mg
- Potassium 116mg

129. Smoked Acorn Squash

Preparation Time: 10 Minutes

Cooking Time: 2 Hours

Servings: 6

Ingredients:

- Three acorn squash, seeded and halved
- 3 tbsp olive oil; 1/4 cup butter, unsalted
- 1 tbsp cinnamon, ground; 1 tbsp chili powder
- 1 tbsp nutmeg, ground; 1/4 cup brown sugar

Directions:

1. Brush the cut sides of your squash with olive oil, then cover with foil poking holes for smoke and steam to get through.

2. Preheat your Traeger to 225F.

3. Place the squash halves on the grill with the cut side down and smoke for about 1½- 2 hours. Remove from the Traeger.

4. Let it sit while you prepare spiced butter. Melt butter in a saucepan, then adds spices and sugar, stirring to combine.

5. Remove the foil from the squash halves.

6. Place 1 tbsp of the butter mixture onto each half. Serve and enjoy!

Nutrition:

Calories 149   Total fat 10g

Total carbs 14g   Protein 2g

Sugars 2g   Fiber 2g

Sodium 19mg   Potassium 101mg

130. Roasted Green Beans with Bacon

Preparation Time: 15 minutes

Cooking Time: 20 minutes

Servings: 6

Ingredients:

- 1-pound green beans
- 4 strips bacon, cut into small pieces
- 4 tablespoons extra virgin olive oil
- 2 cloves garlic, minced
- 1 teaspoon salt

Directions:

1. Fire the Traeger Grill to 400F. Use desired wood pellets when cooking. Keep lid unopened and let it preheat for at most 15 minutes

2. Toss all ingredients on a sheet tray and spread out evenly.

3. Place the tray on the grill grate and roast for 20 minutes.

Nutrition:

- Calories: 65 Cal
- Fat: 5.3 g
- Carbohydrates: 3 g
- Protein: 1.3 g
- Fiber: 0 g

131. Smoked Watermelon

Preparation Time: 15 minutes

Cooking Time: 45-90 minutes

Servings: 5

Ingredients:

- 1 small seedless watermelon
- Balsamic vinegar
- Wooden skewers

Directions:

1. Slice ends of small seedless watermelons
2. Slice the watermelon in 1-inch cubes. Put the cubes in a container and drizzle vinegar on the cubes of watermelon.
3. Preheat the smoker to 225°F. Add wood chips and water to the smoker before starting preheating.
4. Place the cubes on the skewers.
5. Place the skewers on the smoker rack for 50 minutes. Cook
6. Remove the skewers. Serve!

Nutrition:

- Calories: 20 Cal
- Fat: 0 g
- Carbohydrates: 4 g
- Protein: 1 g
- Fiber: 0.2 g

132. Grilled Corn with Honey Butter

Preparation Time: 15 minutes

Cooking Time: 10 minutes

Servings: 6

Ingredients:

- 6 pieces corn, husked
- 2 tablespoons olive oil
- Salt and pepper to taste
- ½ cup butter, room temperature
- ½ cup honey

Directions:

1. Fire the Traeger Grill to 350F. Use desired wood pellets when cooking. Keep lid unopened to preheat until 15 minutes
2. Coat corn with oil and add salt and pepper
3. Place the corn on the grill grate and cook for 10 minutes. Make sure to flip the corn halfway through the cooking time for even cooking.
4. Meanwhile, mix the butter and honey on a small bowl. Set aside.
5. Remove corn from grill and coat with honey butter sauce

Nutrition:

- Calories: 387 Cal
- Fat: 21.6 g
- Carbohydrates: 51.2 g
- Protein: 5 g
- Fiber: 0 g

133. Smoked Mushrooms

Preparation Time: 20 minutes

Cooking Time: 2 hours

Servings: 6

Ingredients:

- 6-12 large Portobello mushrooms
- Sea salt
- black pepper
- Extra virgin olive oil
- Herbs de Provence

Directions:

1. Preheat the smoker to 200°F while adding water and wood chips to the smoker bowl and tray, respectively.

2. Wash and dry mushrooms

3. Rub the mushrooms with olive oil, salt and pepper seasoning with herbs in a bowl.

4. Place the mushrooms with the cap side down on the smoker rack. Smoke the mushrooms for 2 hours while adding water and wood chips to the smoker after every 60 minutes.

5. Remove the mushrooms and serve

Nutrition:

- Calories: 106 Cal
- Fat: 6 g
- Carbohydrates: 5 g
- Protein: 8 g
- Fiber: 0.9 g

134. Smoked Cherry Tomatoes

Preparation Time: 20 minutes

Cooking Time: 1 ½ hours

Servings: 8-10

Ingredients:

- 2 pints of tomatoes

Directions:

1. Preheat the electric smoker to 225°F while adding wood chips and water to the smoker.

2. Clean the tomatoes with clean water and dry them off properly.

3. Place the tomatoes on the pan and place the pan in the smoker.

4. Smoke for 90 minutes while adding water and wood chips to the smoker.

Nutrition:

- Calories: 16 Cal

- Fat: 0 g

- Carbohydrates: 3 g

- Protein: 1 g

- Fiber: 1 g

135. Smoked and Smashed New Potatoes

Preparation Time: 5 minutes

Cooking Time: 8 hours

Servings: 4

Ingredients:

- 1-1/2 pounds small new red potatoes or fingerlings
- Extra virgin olive oil
- Sea salt and black pepper
- 2 tbsp softened butter

Directions:

1. Let the potatoes dry. Once dried, put in a pan and coat with salt, pepper, and extra virgin olive oil.
2. Place the potatoes on the topmost rack of the smoker.
3. Smoke for 60 minutes.
4. Once done, take them out and smash each one
5. Mix with butter and season

Nutrition:

- Calories: 258 Cal
- Fat: 2.0 g
- Carbohydrates: 15.5 g
- Protein: 4.1 g
- Fiber: 1.5 g

136. Smoked Brussels Sprouts

Preparation Time: 15 minutes

Cooking Time: 45 minutes

Servings: 6

Ingredients:

- 1-1/2 pounds Brussels sprouts
- 2 cloves of garlic minced
- 2 tbsp extra virgin olive oil
- Sea salt and cracked black pepper

Directions:

1. Rinse sprouts
2. Remove the outer leaves and brown bottoms off the sprouts.
3. Place sprouts in a large bowl then coat with olive oil.
4. Add a coat of garlic, salt, and pepper and transfer them to the pan.
5. Add to the top rack of the smoker with water and woodchips.
6. Smoke for 45 minutes or until reaches 250 F temperature.
7. Serve

Nutrition:

- Calories: 84 Cal
- Fat: 4.9 g
- Carbohydrates: 7.2 g
- Protein: 2.6 g
- Fiber: 2.9 g

137. Apple Veggie Burger

Preparation Time: 10 minutes

Cooking Time: 35 minutes

Servings: 6

Ingredients:

- 3 tbsp ground flax or ground chia; 1/3 cup of warm water
- 1/2 cups rolled oats; 1 cup chickpeas, drained and rinsed
- 1 tsp cumin; 1/2 cup onion
- 1 tsp dried basil; 2 granny smith apples
- 1/3 cup parsley or cilantro, chopped
- 2 tbsp soy sauce; 2 tsp liquid smoke
- 2 cloves garlic, minced; 1 tsp chili powder
- 1/4 tsp black pepper

Directions:

1. Preheat the smoker to 225°F while adding wood chips and water to it.
2. In a separate bowl, add chickpeas and mash. Mix together the remaining ingredients along with the dipped flax seeds.
3. Form patties from this mixture.
4. Put the patties on the rack of the smoker and smoke them for 20 minutes on each side.
5. When brown, take them out, and serve.

Nutrition:

Calories: 241 Cal   Fat: 5 g   Fiber: 10.3 g

Carbohydrates: 40 g   Protein: 9 g

138. Smoked Tofu

Preparation Time: 10 minutes

Cooking Time: 41 hour and 30 minutes

Servings: 4

Ingredients:

- 400g plain tofu
- Sesame oil

Directions:

1. Preheat the smoker to 225°F while adding wood chips and water to it.
2. Till that time, take the tofu out of the packet and let it rest
3. Slice the tofu in one-inch-thick pieces and apply sesame oil
4. Place the tofu inside the smoker for 45 minutes while adding water and wood chips after one hour.
5. Once cooked, take them out and serve!

Nutrition:

- Calories: 201 Cal
- Fat: 13 g
- Carbohydrates: 1 g
- Protein: 20 g
- Fiber: 0 g

139. Easy Smoked Vegetables

Preparation Time: 15 minutes

Cooking Time: 1 ½ hour

Servings: 6

Ingredients:

- 1 cup of pecan wood chips; 1 medium yellow squash, 1/2-inch slices
- 1 ear fresh corn, silk strands removed, and husks, cut corn into 1-inch pieces
- 1 small red onion, thin wedges; 1 small green bell pepper, 1-inch strips
- 1 small red bell pepper, 1-inch strips
- 1 small yellow bell pepper, 1-inch strips; 1 cup mushrooms, halved
- 2 tbsp vegetable oil; vgetable seasonings

Directions:

1. Take a large bowl and toss all the vegetables together in it.
2. Sprinkle it with seasoning and coat all the vegetables well with it.
3. Place the wood chips and a bowl of water in the smoker.
4. Preheat the smoker at 100°F or ten minutes.
5. Put the vegetables in a pan and add to the middle rack of the electric smoker.
6. Smoke for thirty minutes until the vegetable becomes tender.
7. When done, serve, and enjoy.

Nutrition:

Calories: 97 Cal   Fat: 5 g   Fiber: 3 g

Carbohydrates: 11 g   Protein: 2 g

140. Zucchini with Red Potatoes

Preparation Time: 15 minutes

Cooking Time: 4 hours

Servings: 4

Ingredients:

- 2 zucchinis, sliced in 3/4-inch-thick disks
- 1 red pepper, cut into strips
- 2 yellow squash, sliced in 3/4-inch-thick disks
- 1 medium red onion, cut into wedges
- 6 small red potatoes, cut into chunks; Balsamic Vinaigrette:
- 1/3 cup extra virgin olive oil; 1/4 teaspoon salt
- 1/4 cup balsamic vinegar; 2 tsp Dijon mustard
- 1/8 teaspoon pepper

Directions:

1. For Vinaigrette: Take a medium-sized bowl and blend together olive oil, Dijon mustard, salt, pepper, and balsamic vinegar.

2. Place all the veggies into a large bowl and pour the vinaigrette mixture over it and evenly toss.

3. Put the vegetable in a pan and then smoke for 4 hours at a temperature of 225°F.

4. Serve and enjoy the food.

Nutrition:

Calories: 381 Cal   Fat: 17.6 g   Fiber: 6.5 g

Carbohydrates: 49 g   Protein: 6.7 g

141. Shiitake Smoked Mushrooms

Preparation Time: 15 minutes

Cooking Time: 45 minutes

Servings: 4-6

Ingredients:

- 4 Cup Shiitake Mushrooms
- 1 tbsp canola oil
- 1 tsp onion powder
- 1 tsp granulated garlic
- 1 tsp salt
- 1 tsp pepper

Directions:

1. Combine all the ingredients together
2. Apply the mix over the mushrooms generously.
3. Preheat the smoker at 180°F. Add wood chips and half a bowl of water in the side tray.
4. Place it in the smoker and smoke for 45 minutes.
5. Serve warm and enjoy.

Nutrition:

- Calories: 301 Cal
- Fat: 9 g
- Carbohydrates: 47.8 g
- Protein: 7.1 g
- Fiber: 4.8 g

142. Garlic and Herb Smoke Potato

Preparation Time: 5 minutes

Cooking Time: 2 hours

Servings: 6

Ingredients:

- 1.5 pounds bag of Gemstone Potatoes
- 1/4 cup Parmesan, fresh grated; For the Marinade
- 2 tbsp olive oil; 6 garlic cloves, freshly chopped
- 1/2 tsp dried oregano; 1/2 tsp dried basil
- 1/2 tsp dried dill; 1/2 tsp salt
- 1/2 tsp dried Italian seasoning; 1/4 tsp ground pepper

Directions:

1. Preheat the smoker to 225°F.
2. Wash the potatoes thoroughly and add them to a sealable plastic bag.
3. Add garlic cloves, basil, salt, Italian seasoning, dill, oregano, and olive oil to the zip lock bag. Shake.
4. Place in the fridge for 2 hours to marinate.
5. Next, take an Aluminum foil and put 2 tbsp of water along with the coated potatoes. Fold the foil so that the potatoes are sealed in
6. Place in the preheated smoker. Smoke for 2 hours
7. Remove the foil and pour the potatoes into a bowl.
8. Serve with grated Parmesan cheese.

Nutrition:

Calories: 146 Cal   Fat: 6 g   Fiber: 2.1 g

Carbohydrates: 19 g   Protein: 4 g

143. Smoked Baked Beans

Preparation Time: 15 minutes

Cooking Time: 3 hours

Servings: 12

Ingredients:

- 1 medium yellow onion diced
- 3 jalapenos; 2 tbsp molasses
- 56 oz pork and beans
- 3/4 cup barbeque sauce
- 1/2 cup dark brown sugar
- 1/4 cup apple cider vinegar
- 2 tbsp Dijon mustard

Directions:

1. Preheat the smoker to 250°F.
2. Pour the beans along with all the liquid in a pan. Add brown sugar, barbeque sauce, Dijon mustard, apple cider vinegar, and molasses.
3. Stir. Place the pan on one of the racks.
4. Smoke for 3 hours until thickened
5. Remove after 3 hours. Serve

Nutrition:

- Calories: 214 Cal
- Fat: 2 g
- Carbohydrates: 42 g
- Protein: 7 g
- Fiber: 7 g

144. Corn & Cheese Chile Rellenos

Preparation time: 30 minutes

Cooking time: 65 minutes

Servings: 8-12

Ingredients:

- Pellet: hardwood, maple; 2 lbs. Ripe tomatoes, chopped
- Four cloves' garlic, chopped; 1/2 cup sweet onion, chopped
- One jalapeno stemmed, seeded, and chopped
- Eight large green new Mexican or poblano chiles
- Three ears sweet corn, husked
- 1/2 tsp. Dry oregano, Mexican, crumbled
- 1 tsp. ground cumin; 1 tsp. Mild Chile powder
- 1/8 tsp. Ground cinnamon; Salt and freshly ground pepper
- 3 cups grated Monterey jack; 1/2 cup Mexican crema
- 1 cup queso fresco, crumbled; Fresh cilantro leaves

Directions:

1. Place the tomatoes, garlic, onions and jalapeno in a shallow baking dish and place it on the grill grate before starting. This vegetable will expose more wood smoke.

2. When prepared to cook, start the grill on Smoke with the lid open until the fire is established (4 to 5 minutes). S

3. Mix the cooled tomato mixture in a blender and liquefy. Put in a pot.

4. Stir in the cumin, oregano, some chile powder, cinnamon, and some salt and pepper to taste.

5. Carefully peel the New Mexican chiles' blistered outer skin: Leave the stem ends intact and try not to tear the flesh.

6. Cut the corn off the cobs and put it in a large mixing bowl.

7. Bake or cook the Rellenos for 25 to 30 minutes or until the filling is bubbling and the cheese has melted.

8. Sprinkle with queso fresco and garnish it with fresh cilantro leaves, if desired. Enjoy!

Nutrition:

- Calories: 206
- Carbs: 5g
- Fat: 14g
- Protein: 9g

145. Roasted Tomatoes with Hot Pepper Sauce

Preparation time: 20 minutes

Cooking time: 90 minutes

Servings: 4-6

Ingredients:

- Pellet: hardwood, alder; 2 lbs. roman fresh tomatoes
- 3 tbsps. parsley, chopped; 2 tbsps. garlic, chopped
- Black pepper, to taste; 1/2 cup olive oil
- Hot pepper, to taste; 1 lb. spaghetti or other pasta

Directions:

1. Prepare and ready to cook, set the temperature to 400degrees F and preheat, lid closed for 15 minutes
2. Rinse with water the tomatoes and cut them in half, length width and then place them in a baking dish cut side up.
3. Sprinkle with chopped parsley, garlic, then add salt and black pepper, and then pour 1/4 cup of olive oil over them.
4. Place on pre-heated and bake for 1 1/2 hours and then tomatoes will shrink, and the skins will be partly blackened.
5. Take the tomatoes from the baking dish and place them in a food processor, leaving the cooking oil and puree them.
6. Put the pasta into boiling salted water and cook until tender. Then drain and mix immediately with the pureed tomatoes.
7. Add the remaining 1/4 cup of raw olive oil and crumbled hot red pepper to taste. Toss and serve. Enjoy!

Nutrition:

Calories: 111   Carbs: 5g

Fat: 11g   Protein: 1g

146. Grilled Fingerling Potato Salad

Preparation time: 15 minutes

Cooking time: 15 minutes

Servings: 6-8

Ingredients:

- Pellet: hardwood, pecan; Ten scallions
- 1-1/2 lbs. Fingerling potatoes cut in half lengthwise
- 2/3 cup Evo (extra virgin olive oil), divided use
- 2 tbsps. rice vinegar; 2 tsp. lemon juice
- One small jalapeno, sliced; 2 tsp. kosher salt

Directions:

1. Prepare and ready to cook, turn temperature to High and preheat, lid closed for 15 minutes.

2. Brush the spring onions with the oil and place them on the grill. Cook for about 2-3 minutes until they are slightly charred. Remove and let cool. Once the spring onions have cooled, slice them and set aside.

3. Brush the Fingerlings with oil (reserving 1/3 cup for later use), then salt and pepper. Place cut side down on the grill cooked through, about 4-5 minutes.

4. In a bowl, mix the remaining 1/3 cup of olive oil, rice vinegar, salt, and lemon juice, then mix the green onions, potatoes and slices jalapeno.

5. Season with salt and pepper and serve. Enjoy!

Nutrition:

- Calories: 270
- Carbs: 18g
- Fat: 18g
- Protein: 3g

147. Smoked Jalapeño Poppers

Preparation time: 15 minutes

Cooking time: 60 minutes

Servings: 4-6

Ingredients:

- Pellet: hardwood, mesquite
- 12 medium jalapeños
- Six slices bacon, cut in half
- 8 oz. cream cheese, softened
- 1 cup cheese, grated
- 2 tbsps. pork & poultry rub

Directions:

1. Prepare and ready to cook, turn temperature up to 180 degrees F and preheat, lid closed for 15 minutes.

2. Cut jalapeños in half lengthwise. Remove the seeds and ribs.

3. Combine softened cream cheese with Pork & Poultry rub and grated cheese.

4. Divide the mixture over each jalapeño half. Wrap in bacon and secure with a toothpick.

5. Put the jalapeños on a rimmed baking sheet. Place on the grill and smoke for 30 minutes.

6. Increase the temperature of the grill to 375 encores and cook for another 30 minutes or until the bacon is cooked to the desired doneness. Serve hot, enjoy!

Nutrition:

Calories: 280   Carbs: 24g

Fat: 19g   Protein: 4g

148. Grilled Veggie Sandwich

Preparation time: 30 minutes

Cooking time: 30 minutes

Servings: 4-6

Ingredients:

- Pellet: hardwood, pecan; Smoked hummus
- 1-1/2 cups chickpeas; 1/3 cup tahini
- 1 tbsp. minced garlic; 2 tbsps. olive oil
- 1 tsp. kosher salt; 4 tbsps. lemon juice
- Grilled veggie sandwich; One small eggplant, sliced into strips
- One small zucchini, cut into strips
- One small yellow squash, sliced into strips
- Two large Portobello mushrooms; Olive oil
- Salt and pepper to taste; Two heirloom tomatoes, sliced
- One bunch of basil leaves pulled; Four ciabatta buns
- 1/2 cup ricotta; Juice of 1 lemon
- One garlic clove minced; Salt and pepper to taste

Directions:

1. Ready to cook, turn temperature to 180 degrees F and preheat, lid closed for 15 minutes.

2. In a prepared bowl of a food processor, combine the smoked chickpeas, tahini, garlic, olive oil, salt and lemon juice and blend until smooth but not completely smooth. Transfer to a bowl and reserve.

3. Increase grill temp to high (400-500 degrees F).

4. While the vegetables are cooking, mix the ricotta, the lemon juice, garlic, salt and some pepper.

5. Cut the ciabatta buns in half and then open them up—spread the hummus on one side and ricotta on the other. Stack the grilled veggies and top with tomatoes and basil. Enjoy!

Nutrition:

- Calories: 376
- Carbs: 57g
- Fat: 16g
- Protein: 10g

149. Smoked Healthy Cabbage

Preparation time: 10 minutes

Cooking time: 2 hours

Servings: 5

Ingredients:

- Pellet: maple pellets
- One head cabbage, cored
- 4 tbsp. butter
- 2 tbsp. rendered bacon fat
- One chicken bouillon cube
- 1 tsp. fresh ground black pepper
- One garlic clove, minced

Directions:

1. Pre-heat your smoker to 240 degrees Fahrenheit using your preferred wood
2. Fill the hole of your cored cabbage with butter, bouillon cube, bacon fat, pepper, and garlic
3. Wrap the cabbage in foil about two-thirds of the way up
4. Make sure to leave the top open
5. Transfer to your smoker rack and smoke for 2 hours
6. Unwrap and enjoy!

Nutrition:

- Calories: 231
- Fats: 10g
- Carbs: 26g
- Fiber: 1g

150. Garlic and Rosemary Potato Wedges

Preparation time: 15 minutes

Cooking time: 1 hour 30 minutes

Servings: 4

Ingredients:

- Pellet: maple pellets
- 4-6 large russet potatoes, cut into wedges
- ¼ cup olive oil; 2 tsp. salt
- Two garlic cloves, minced
- 2 tbsp. rosemary leaves, chopped
- 1 tsp. fresh ground black pepper
- 1 tsp. sugar; 1 tsp. onion powder

Directions:

1. Pre-heat your smoker to 250 degrees Fahrenheit using maple wood
2. Take a large bowl and add potatoes and olive oil. Toss well
3. Take another small bowl and stir garlic, salt, rosemary, pepper, sugar, onion powder
4. Sprinkle the mix on all sides of the potato wedge
5. Transfer the seasoned wedge to your smoker rack and smoke for one and a ½ hours. Serve and enjoy!

Nutrition:

- Calories: 291
- Fats: 10g
- Carbs: 46g
- Fiber: 2g

151. Smoked Tomato and Mozzarella Dip

Preparation time: 5 minutes

Cooking time: 1 hour

Servings: 4

Ingredients:

- Pellet: mesquite; 8 ounces Colby cheese, shredded
- 8 ounces smoked mozzarella cheese, shredded
- ½ cup parmesan cheese, grated; 1 cup sour cream
- 1 cup sun-dried tomatoes; 1 and ½ tsp. salt
- 1 tsp. fresh ground pepper; 1 tsp. dried basil
- 1 tsp. dried oregano; 1 tsp. red pepper flakes
- One garlic clove, minced; ½ teaspoon onion powder
- French toast, serving

Directions:

1. Pre-heat your smoker to 275 degrees Fahrenheit using your preferred wood
2. Take a large bowl and stir in the cheeses, tomatoes, pepper, salt, basil, oregano, red pepper flakes, garlic, and onion powder and mix well
3. Transfer the mix to a small metal pan and transfer to a smoker
4. Smoke for 1 hour
5. Serve with toasted French bread Enjoy!

Nutrition:

- Calories: 174
- Fats: 11g
- Carbs: 15g
- Fiber: 2g

152. Feisty Roasted Cauliflower

Preparation time: 15 minutes

Cooking time: 10 minutes

Servings: 4

Ingredients:

- Pellet: maple; One cauliflower head, cut into florets
- 1 tbsp. oil; 1 cup parmesan, grated
- Two garlic cloves, crushed; ½ teaspoon pepper
- ½ teaspoon salt; ¼ teaspoon paprika

Directions:

1. Pre-heat your Smoker to 180 degrees F
2. Transfer florets to smoker and smoke for 1 hour
3. Take a bowl and add all ingredients except cheese
4. Once smoking is done, remove florets
5. Increase temperature to 450 degrees F, brush florets with the brush, and transfer to grill
6. Smoke for 10 minutes more
7. Sprinkle cheese on top and let them sit (Lid closed) until cheese melts
8. Serve and enjoy!

Nutrition:

- Calories: 45
- Fats: 2g
- Carbs: 7g
- Fiber: 1g

153. Savory Applesauce on the Grill

Preparation Time: 0 minutes

Cooking Time: 45 minutes

Servings: 2

Ingredients:

- 1½ pounds whole apples
- Salt

Directions:

1. Start the coals or turn a gas grill for medium direct cooking. Just make sure the grates are clean.

2. Put the apples on the grill directly over the fire. Close the lid and cook until the fruit feels soft when gently squeezed with tongs, 10 to 20 minutes total, depending on their size. Move to a cutting board and then let sit until cool enough to touch.

3. Cut the flesh from around the core of each apple; discard the cores. Put the chunks in a blender or food processor and process until smooth, or put them in a bowl and purée with an immersion blender until as chunky or smooth as you like. Add some salt and then taste adjusts the seasoning. Serve or refrigerate in a container for up to 3 days.

Nutrition:

- Calories: 15
- Fats: 0 g
- Cholesterol: 0 mg
- Carbohydrates: 3 g
- Fiber: 0 g
- Sugars: 3 g
- Proteins: 0 g

154. Avocado with Lemon

Preparation Time: 5 minutes

Cooking Time: 20 minutes

Servings: 4

Ingredients:

- Two ripe avocados
- Good-quality olive oil for brushing
- One lemon halved
- Salt and pepper

Directions:

1. Start the coals or turn a gas grill for medium direct cooking. Just make sure the grates are clean.

2. Cut the avocados in half lengthwise. Carefully strike a chef's knife into the pit, then wiggle it a bit to lift and remove it. Insert a spoon underneath the flesh against the skin and run it all the way around to separate the entire half of the avocado. Repeat with the other avocado. Brush with oil, and then squeeze one of the lemon halves over them thoroughly on both sides so they don't discolor. Cut the other lemon half into four wedges.

3. Put the avocados on the grill directly over the fire, cut side down. Cover with lid and cook, turning once, until browned in places, 5 to 10 minutes total. Serve the halved avocados as is, or slice and fan them for a prettier presentation. Sprinkle with salt and pepper and garnish with the lemon wedges.

Nutrition:

Calories: 50.3   Fats: 4.6 g   Cholesterol: 0 mg   Fiber: 1.7 g

Carbohydrates: 2.8 g   Sugars: 0.2 g   Proteins: 0.6 g

155. Simplest Grilled Asparagus

Preparation Time: 0 minutes

Cooking Time: 25 minutes

Servings: 4

Ingredients:

- 1½–2 pounds asparagus
- 1–2 tablespoons good-quality olive oil or melted butter
- Salt

Directions:

1. Start the coals or turn the heat of a gas grill for direct hot cooking. Make sure the grates are clean.

2. Cut the tough bottoms from the asparagus. If they're thick, trim the ends with a vegetable peeler. Mix with the oil and then sprinkle with salt.

3. Put the asparagus on the grill directly over the fire, perpendicular to the grates, so they don't fall through. Cover with the lid and cook, turning once, until the thick part of the stalks can barely be pierced with a skewer or thin knife, 5 to 10 minutes total. Transfer to a platter and serve.

Nutrition:

- Calories: 225
- Fats: 20.6 g
- Cholesterol: 0 mg
- Carbohydrates: 9.1 g
- Fiber: 4.2 g
- Sugars: 0 g
- Proteins: 4.6 g

156. Beets and Greens with Lemon-Dill Vinaigrette

Preparation Time: 0 minutes

Cooking Time: 1 hour

Servings: 4

Ingredients:

- 1½ pounds small beets, with fresh-looking greens still attached if possible
- ½ cup plus 2 tbsp. good-quality olive oil
- Salt and pepper
- 3 tbsp. fresh lemon juice
- 2 tbsp. minced fresh dill

Directions:

1. Start the coals or turn a gas grill for medium to medium-low direct cooking. Make sure the grates are clean.

2. Cut the greens off the beets. Throw away any wilted or discolored leaves; rinse the remainder thoroughly to remove any grit and drain. Trim the root ends of the beets and scrub well under running water. Pat the leaves and beets dry. Toss the beets with two tablespoons of oil and a sprinkle of salt until evenly coated.

3. Put the beets on the grill directly over the fire. (No need to wash the bowl.) Close the lid and cook, turning them every 5 to 10 minutes, until a knife inserted in the center goes through with no resistance, 30 to 40 minutes total. Transfer to a plate and then let sit until cool enough to handle.

4. Toss the beet greens in the reserved bowl to coat in oil. Put them on the grill directly over the fire. Close the lid and cook, tossing once or twice, until they're bright green and browned in spots, 2 to 5 minutes total. Take a look; if they're on too long, they'll crisp up to the point where they'll shatter. Transfer to a plate.

5. Put the remaining ½ cup oil and the lemon juice in a serving bowl and whisk until thickened. Stir in the dill and some salt and pepper. Peel off the skin from the beets and cut into halves or quarters. Cut the stems from the leaves in 1-inch lengths; cut the leaves across into ribbons. Put the beets, leaves, and stems in the bowl and toss with the vinaigrette until coated. Serve warm or at room temperature. Or makeup to several hours ahead, covers, and refrigerates to serve chilled.

Nutrition:

- Calories: 73
- Fats: 3.8 g
- Cholesterol: 0 mg
- Carbohydrates: 9.6 g
- Fiber: 3.6 g
- Sugars: 2 g
- Proteins: 2.2 g

157. Baby Bok Choy with Lime-Miso Vinaigrette

Preparation Time: 10 minutes

Cooking Time: 25 minutes

Servings: 4

Ingredients:

- ¼ cup good-quality vegetable oil; Grated zest of 1 lime
- 2 tbsp. fresh lime juice; 2 tbsp. white or light miso
- 1 tbsp. rice vinegar; Salt and pepper
- 1½ pounds baby bok choy

Directions:

1. Start the coals or turn a gas grill for medium direct cooking. Make sure the grates are clean.

2. Whisk together the oil, lime zest and juice, miso and vinegar in a small bowl until combined and thickened. Taste and adjust the seasoning with salt and pepper.

3. Trim the bottoms from the bok choy and cut them into halves or quarters as needed. Pour half of the vinaigrette into a baking dish. Add the bok choy and twist in the vinaigrette until completely coated.

4. Put the bok choy on the grill directly over the fire. Close the lid and cook, turning once, until the leaves brown, and you can insert a knife through the core with no resistance, 5 to 10 minutes per side, depending on their size. Transfer to a platter; drizzle with the reserved vinaigrette and serve warm or at room temperature.

Nutrition:

Calories: 209.7   Fats: 9.4 g

Cholesterol: 7.4 mg   Carbohydrates: 25.9 g

Fiber: 4.5 g   Sugars: 3 g   Proteins: 10.1 g

158. Grilled Carrots

Preparation Time: 5 minutes

Cooking Time: 20 minutes

Servings: 6

Ingredients:

- 1 lb. carrots, large; 1/2 tbsp. salt
- 6 oz. butter; Fresh thyme
- 1/2 tbsps. black pepper

Directions:

1. Thoroughly wash the carrots and do not peel. Pat them dry and coat with olive oil. Add salt to your carrots.

2. Meanwhile, preheat a pellet grill to 350F.

3. Now place your carrots directly on the grill or on a raised rack.

4. Close and cook for about 20 minutes.

5. While carrots cook, cook butter in a saucepan, small, over medium heat until browned. Stir frequently to avoid burning. Remove from heat.

6. Remove carrots from the grill onto a plate, and then drizzle with browned butter.

7. Add pepper and splash with thyme. Serve and enjoy.

Nutrition:

Calories: 250   Total Fat: 25 g

Saturated Fat: 15 g   Total Carbs: 6 g

Net Carbs: 4g   Protein: 1 g

Sugars: 3 g   Fiber: 2 g

Sodium: 402 mg

159. Grilled Brussels Sprouts

Preparation Time: 15 minutes

Cooking Time: 20 minutes

Servings: 8

Ingredients:

- 1/2 lb. bacon, grease reserved
- 1 lb. Brussels Sprouts
- 1/2 tbsp. pepper
- 1/2 tbsp. salt

Directions:

1. Cook bacon until crispy on a stovetop, reserve its grease, and then chop into small pieces.
2. Meanwhile, wash the Brussels sprouts, trim off the dry end and remove dried leaves, if any. Half them and set aside.
3. Place 1/4 cup reserved grease in a pan, cast-iron, over medium-high heat.
4. Season the Brussels sprouts with pepper and salt.
5. Brown the sprouts on the pan with the cut side down for about 3-4 minutes.
6. In the meantime, preheat your pellet grill to 350-375F.
7. Place bacon pieces and browned sprouts into your grill-safe pan.
8. Cook for about 20 minutes. Serve immediately.

Nutrition:

Calories: 153   Total Fat: 10 g   Sugars: 1 g

Total Carbs: 5 g   Protein: 11 g

160. Wood Pellet Spicy Brisket

Preparation Time: 20 minutes

Cooking Time: 9 hours

Servings: 10

Ingredients:

- 2 tbsps. garlic powder; 2 tbsps. onion powder
- 2 tbsps. Paprika; 2 tbsps. chili powder
- 1/3 cup salt; 1/3 cup black pepper
- 12 lb. whole packer brisket, trimmed
- 1-1/2 cup beef broth

Directions:

1. Set your wood pellet temperature to 225 degrees F. Let preheat for 15 minutes with the lid closed.
2. Meanwhile, mix garlic, onion, paprika, chili, salt, and pepper in a mixing bowl.
3. The brisket generously on all sides.
4. Place the meat on the grill with the fat side down and let it cool until the internal temperature reaches 160degrees F.
5. Remove the meat from the grill and double wrap it with foil. Return it to the grill and cook until the internal temperature reaches 204degrees F.
6. Remove from grill, unwrap the brisket and let rest for 15 minutes.
7. Slice and serve.

Nutrition:

Calories: 270   Saturated Fat: 8 g

Net Carbs: 3 g   Protein: 20 g

161. Pellet Grill Funeral Potatoes

Preparation Time: 10 minutes

Cooking Time: 1 hour

Servings: 8

Ingredients:

- 32 oz., package frozen hash browns
- 1/2 cup cheddar cheese, grated
- One can cream of chicken soup
- 1 cup sour cream; 1 cup Mayonnaise
- 3 cups corn flakes, whole or crushed
- 1/4 cup melted butter

Directions:

1. Preheat your pellet grill to 350F.
2. Spray a 13 x 9 baking pan, aluminum, using a cooking spray, non-stick.
3. Mix hash browns, cheddar cheese, chicken soup cream, sour cream, and mayonnaise in a large bowl.
4. Spoon the mixture into a baking pan gently.
5. Mix corn flakes and melted butter, then sprinkle over the casserole.
6. Grill for about 1-1/2 hours until potatoes become tender. If the top browns too much, cover using a foil until potatoes are done.
7. Remove from the grill and serve hot.

Nutrition:

Calories: 403   Total Fat: 37 g   Protein: 4 g

Saturated Fat: 12 g   Total Carbs: 14 g

162. Smoky Caramelized Onions on the Pellet Grill

Preparation Time: 5 minutes

Cooking Time: 1 hour

Servings: 4

Ingredients:

- Five large sliced onions
- 1/2 cup fat of your choice
- Pinch of Sea salt

Directions:

1. Place all the ingredients into a pan. For a deep rich brown, caramelized onion, cook them off for about 1hour on a stovetop.

2. Keep the grill temperatures not higher than 250 - 275F.

3. Now transfer the pan into the grill.

4. Cook for about 1-1½ hours until brown. Check and stir with a spoon, wooden, after every 15 minutes. Make sure not to run out of pellets.

5. Now remove from the grill and season with more salt if necessary.

6. Serve immediately or place in a refrigerator for up to 1 week.

Nutrition:

- Calories: 286
- Saturated Fat: 10.3 g
- Total Carbs: 12.8 g
- Protein: 1.5 g

163. Hickory Smoked Green Beans

Preparation Time: 15 minutes

Cooking Time: 3 hours

Servings: 10

Ingredients:

- 6 cups fresh green beans, halved and ends cut off
- 2 cups chicken broth; 1 tbsp. pepper, ground
- 1/4 tbsp. salt; 2 tbsps. apple cider vinegar
- 1/4 cup diced onion; 6-8 bite-size bacon slices
- Optional: sliced almonds

Directions:

1. Add green beans to a colander, then rinse thoroughly. Set aside.
2. Place chicken broth, pepper, salt, and apple cider in a large pan. Add green beans.
3. Blanch over medium heat for about 3-4 minutes, and then remove from heat.
4. Transfer the mixture into an aluminum pan, disposable. Make sure all of them go into the pan, so do not drain them.
5. Place bacon slices over the beans and place the pan into the wood pellet smoker,
6. Smoke for about 3 hours uncovered.
7. Remove from the smoker and top with almond slices.
8. Serve immediately.

Nutrition:

Calories: 57   Total Fat: 3 g

Net Carbs: 4 g   Protein: 4 g

164. Easy Grilled Corn

Preparation Time: 5 minutes

Cooking Time: 40 minutes

Servings: 6

Ingredients:

- Six fresh corn ears, still in the husk
- Pepper, salt, and butter

Directions:

1. Preheat your wood pellet grill to 375-40F.
2. Cut off the large silk ball from the corn top and any hanging or loose husk pieces.
3. Place the corn on your grill grate directly, and do not peel off the husk.
4. Grill for about 30-40 minutes. Flip a few times to grill evenly all rounds.
5. Transfer the corn to a platter, serve.
6. Now top with pepper, salt, and butter.
7. Enjoy!

Nutrition:

- Calories: 77
- Total Fat: 1 g
- Saturated Fat: 1 g
- Total Carbs: 17 g
- Net Carbs: 15 g
- Protein: 3 g

165. Seasoned Potatoes on Smoker

Preparation Time: 10 minutes

Cooking Time: 45 minutes

Servings: 6

Ingredients:

- 1-1/2 lb. creamer potatoes
- 2 tbsps. olive oil
- 1 tbsp. garlic powder
- 1/4 tbsp. oregano
- 1/2 tbsp. thyme, dried
- 1/2 tbsp. parsley, dried

Directions:

1. Preheat your pellet grill to 350F.
2. Spray an 8x8 inch foil pan using non-stick spray.
3. Mix all ingredients in the pan and place it into the grill.
4. Cook for about 45 minutes until potatoes are done. Stir after every 15 minutes.
5. Serve and enjoy!

Nutrition:

- Calories: 130
- Total Fat: 4 g
- Saturated Fat: 2 g
- Total Carbs: 20 g
- Net Carbs: 18 g
- Protein: 2 g

166. Smoked Deviled Eggs

Preparation Time: 15 minutes

Cooking Time: 30 minutes

Servings: 5

Ingredients

- hard-boiled eggs, peeled
- 3 tbsp mayonnaise; 3 tbsp chives, diced
- 1 tbsp brown mustard; 1 tbsp apple cider vinegar
- Dash of hot sauce; Salt and pepper
- 2 tbsp cooked bacon, crumbled
- Paprika to taste

Directions:

1. Preheat the Traeger to 180°F for 15 minutes with the lid closed.
2. Place the eggs on the grill grate and smoke the eggs for 30 minutes. Remove the eggs from the grill and let cool.
3. Half the eggs and scoop the egg yolks into a zip lock bag.
4. Add all other ingredients in the zip lock bag except bacon and paprika. Mix until smooth.
5. Pipe the mixture into the egg whites then top with bacon and paprika.
6. Let rest then serve and enjoy.

Nutrition:

Calories 140   Total fat 12g   Saturated fat 3g

Total Carbs 1g   Net Carbs 1g   Protein 6g

Sugar 0g   Fiber 0g   Sodium: 210mg   Potassium 100mg

167. Traeger Grilled Stuffed Zucchini

Preparation Time: 5 minutes

Cooking Time: 11 minutes

Servings: 8

Ingredients

- 4 zucchinis; tbsp olive oil
- 2 tbsp red onion, chopped
- 1/4 tbsp garlic, minced
- 1/2 cup bread crumbs
- 1/2 cup mozzarella cheese, shredded
- 1 tbsp fresh mint; 1/2 tbsp salt
- 3 tbsp parmesan cheese

Directions:

1. Cut the zucchini lengthwise and scoop out the pulp then brush the shells with oil.

2. In a non-stick skillet sauté pulp, onion, and remaining oil. Add garlic and cook for a minute.

3. Add bread crumbs and cook until golden brown. Remove from heat and stir in mozzarella cheese, fresh mint, and salt.

4. Spoon the mixture into the shells and sprinkle parmesan cheese.

5. Place in a grill and grill for 10 minutes or until the zucchini are tender.

Nutrition:

Calories 186   Total fat 10g   Saturated fat 5g   Total Carbs 17g

Net Carbs 14g   Protein 9g   Sugar 4g   Fiber 3g   Sodium: 553mg

168. Traeger Bacon Wrapped Jalapeno Poppers

Preparation Time: 10 minutes

Cooking Time: 20 minutes

Servings: 6

Ingredients

- jalapenos, fresh
- 4 oz cream cheese
- 1/2 cup cheddar cheese, shredded
- 1 tbsp vegetable rub
- 12 slices cut bacon

Directions:

1. Preheat the Traeger smoker and grill to 375°F.
2. Slice the jalapenos lengthwise and scrape the seed and membrane. Rinse them with water and set aside.
3. In a mixing bowl, mix cream cheese, cheddar cheese, vegetable rub until well mixed.
4. Fill the jalapeno halves with the mixture then wrap with the bacon pieces.
5. Smoke for 20 minutes or until the bacon crispy.
6. Serve and enjoy.

Nutrition:

Calories 1830   Total fat 11g   Saturated fat 6g   Total Carbs 5g

Net Carbs 4g   Protein 6g   Sugar 4g   Fiber 1g

169. Green Beans with Bacon

Preparation Time: 10 minutes

Cooking Time: 20 minutes

Servings: 6

Ingredients:

- 4 strips of bacon, chopped
- 1 1/2-pound green beans, ends trimmed
- 1 teaspoon minced garlic ; 1 teaspoon salt
- 4 tablespoons olive oil

Directions:

1. Switch on the Traeger grill, fill the grill hopper with flavored Traeger's, power the grill on by using the control panel, select 'smoke' on the temperature dial, or set the temperature to 450 degrees F and let it preheat for a minimum of 15 minutes.

2. Meanwhile, take a sheet tray, place all the ingredients in it and toss until mixed.

3. When the grill has preheated, open the lid, place prepared sheet tray on the grill grate, shut the grill and smoke for 20 minutes until lightly browned and cooked.

4. When done, transfer green beans to a dish and then serve.

Nutrition:

- Calories: 93 Cal
- Fat: 4.6 g
- Carbs: 8.2 g
- Protein: 5.9 g
- Fiber: 2.9 g

CHAPTER 9:
Vegan Recipes

170. Smoke-Roasted Root Vegetables

Preparation Time: 15 minutes

Cooking Time: 1 hour

Servings: 4

Ingredients:

The Vegetables

- Large carrots – 2
- Medium-size potatoes – 2
- Medium-size sweet potatoes – 2

The Spice Mix

- Sea salt – 1 ½ teaspoon
- Ground black pepper – 1 teaspoon
- Olive oil – 1/4 cup, and more for drizzling

Other Ingredients:

- Chopped parsley – 2 tablespoons

Directions:

1. In the meantime, prepare vegetables.
2. For this, do not peel vegetables and sliced into 2-inch pieces.

3. Place these vegetables in a large bowl, add ingredients for spice mix and toss to coat.

4. Transfer these vegetables into an aluminum tray, about 8 by 12 inch.

5. When ready to smoke, place a prepared pouch of woodchips over charcoal and when start to smoke, place aluminum tray containing vegetables on the grate above the drip pan.

6. Set lid on smoker and monitor temperature through temperature gauge or temperature probes and maintain it.

7. Let smoke for 1 hour or until vegetables are very tender.

8. When done, drizzle oil over vegetables, then garnish with parsley and serve.

Nutrition:

Calories - 225 | Fat - 17.2g

Saturated fat - 2.5g | Carbohydrates - 16.8g

Protein - 2.8g | Sodium - 196mg

Cholesterol - 0mg | Calcium - 35mg

Potassium - 483mg | Iron - 1mg

171. Traeger Smoked Corn the Cob

Preparation Time: 15 minutes

Cooking Time: 1 hour

Servings: 6

Ingredients:

The Vegetable

- Ears of corn, with husk – 6
- Green onions, thinly sliced – 3

The Sauce

- Melted butter, unsalted – ¼ cup
- Brown sugar – 1 tablespoon
- Paprika – 1 teaspoon
- Onion powder – 1 teaspoon
- Garlic powder – ½ teaspoon
- Salt – ½ teaspoon

Directions:

1. Before setting smoker, prepare corn.
2. For this, remove back husk from corn by pulling it away and then remove silks.
3. Fill a large pot half full with water, add ears of corn and pour in more water if corns are covered with water completely.
4. Let corn soak for 4 hours, then drain them, pat dry completely using paper towels and gently pull back husk over corn.
5. Stir together ingredients for sauce in a bowl until well combined.
6. Brush this sauce generously over corns and sprinkle with green onions.

7. When ready to smoke, place a prepared pouch of woodchips over charcoal and when start to smoke, add ears of corn on the grate above the drip pan.

8. Set lid on smoker and monitor temperature through temperature gauge or temperature probes and maintain it.

9. Close down the lower air vent if the temperature is above 250 degrees or open up the lower air vent if the temperature drops below 255 degrees F and add few more hot coals.

10. Let smoke for 1 hour, corns halfway through, or until cooked through.

11. When done, remove corns from smokers, let rest for 10 minutes and serve.

Nutrition:

Calories- 125 | Fat- 17.2g

Saturated fat - 3.5g | Carbohydrates - 6.8g

Protein - 2.8g | Sodium - 196mg

Cholesterol - 0mg | Calcium - 35mg

Potassium - 283mg | Iron - 1mg

172. Smoked Artichokes

Preparation Time: 15 minutes

Cooking Time: 2 hours

Servings: 3

Ingredients:

The Vegetable

- Whole artichoke hearts, canned – 15

The Seasoning

- Cajun seasoning – 1 tablespoon
- Cayenne pepper – 1 tablespoon

Directions:

1. In the meantime, prepare artichoke hearts.
2. For this, cut each artichoke heart into halve.
3. Stir together ingredients for seasoning and sprinkle generously all over artichoke hearts.
4. When ready to smoke, place a prepared pouch of woodchips over charcoal and when start to smoke, brush the smoking grate with oil generously, place seasoned artichoke hearts on the grate above the drip pan.
5. Set lid on smoker and monitor temperature through temperature gauge or temperature probes and maintain it.
6. Close down the lower air vent if the temperature is above 250 degrees or open up the lower air vent if the temperature drops below 255 degrees F and add few more hot coals.
7. Check every hour if more water needs to add in the drip pan and add more hot coals using tongs along with another pouch of wood chips to keep the smoke going.

8. Let smoke for 2 hours or until artichoke hearts are cooked through and tender.

9. Serve with herb mayonnaise and pork steaks.

Nutrition:

Calories – 225 | Fat - 17.2g

Saturated fat - 2.5g | Carbohydrates - 16.8g

Protein - 2.8g | Sodium - 196mg

Cholesterol - 0mg | Calcium - 35mg

Potassium - 483mg | Iron - 1mg|

173. Smoked Tomatillo Salsa

Preparation Time: 15 minutes

Cooking Time: 1 Hour and 30 Minutes

Servings: 6

Ingredients:

The Vegetable

- Tomatillos – 6

The Seasoning

- Salt – 1 teaspoon
- Ground black pepper – ¾ teaspoon

The Salsa

- Chopped cilantro – ¼ cup
- Salt – 1 teaspoon
- Ground black pepper – 1 teaspoon
- Apple cider vinegar – 1/3 cup
- Water – 3 tablespoons

Directions:

1. In the meantime, prepare tomatillos.
2. For this, remove casing of tomatillos, then cut into quarters and then place in a sheet pan.
3. Sprinkle with salt and black pepper and toss to coat.
4. When ready to smoke, place a prepared pouch of woodchips over charcoal and when start to smoke, brush the smoking grate with oil generously, place sheet pan containing tomatillos on the grate above the drip pan.

5. Set lid on smoker and monitor temperature through temperature gauge or temperature probes and maintain it.

6. Close down the lower air vent if the temperature is above 250 degrees or open up the lower air vent if the temperature drops below 255 degrees F and add few more hot coals.

7. Check every hour if more water needs to add in the drip pan and add more hot coals using tongs along with another pouch of wood chips to keep the smoke going.

8. Let smoke for 1 hour and 30 minutes or until tender and roasted.

9. When done, remove sheet pan from the smoker and transfer tomatillos into a blender.

10. Add ingredients for salsa and pulse for 2 to 3 minutes at high speed or until smooth.

11. Serve salsa with meats.

Nutrition:

Calories – 223 | Fat - 7.2g

Saturated fat - 2.5g | Carbohydrates - 13g

Protein - 2.8g | Sodium - 196mg

Cholesterol - 0mg | Calcium - 35mg

Potassium - 483mg | Iron - 1mg

174. Traeger Smoked Jalapeño Pop

Preparation Time: 15 minutes

Cooking Time: 1 Hour and 45 Minutes

Servings: 6

Ingredients:

- Medium jalapeno peppers, halved lengthwise – 10
- Slices of bacon, thick cut – 4
- Grated cheddar cheese – 1 cup
- Cream cheese, softened – 4 ounces

Directions:

1. Place a prepared pouch of woodchips over charcoal and when start to smoke, place slices of bacon on the grate above the drip pan.

2. Close down the lower air vent if the temperature is above 250 degrees or open up the lower air vent if the temperature drops below 255 degrees F and add few more hot coals. Let smoke for 1 hour or until crispy.

3. In the meantime, cut each jalapeno pepper in half and remove its seeds and ribs. Arrange these pepper halves on a sheet tray in a single layer and set aside until required.

4. When bacon is done, chop it finely and transfer to a bowl. Add cheeses and stir until well mixed. Stuff this mixture into jalapeno peppers, about 1 tablespoon per pepper and then place a sheet pan on the smoker.

5. Let smoke for 30 to 45 minutes or until cheese melt completely and peppers are slightly roasted. Serve straightaway.

Nutrition: Calories – 225 | Fat - 17.2g | Saturated fat - 2.5g | Carbohydrates - 16.8g | Protein - 2.8g | Sodium - 196mg | Cholesterol - 0mg | Calcium - 35mg | Potassium - 483mg | Iron- 1mg

175. Wood Pellet Smoked Mushrooms

Preparation Time: 15 minutes,

Cooking Time: 45 minutes.

Servings: 5

Ingredients:

- 4 cup Portobello, whole and cleaned
- 1 tbsp. canola oil
- 1 tbsp. onion powder
- 1 tbsp. granulated garlic
- 1 tbsp. salt; 1 tbsp. pepper

Directions:

1. Put all the ingredients and mix well.
2. Set the wood pellet temperature to 180°F then place the mushrooms directly on the grill.
3. Smoke the mushrooms for 30 minutes.
4. Increase the temperature to high and cook the mushrooms for a further 15 minutes. Serve and enjoy.

Nutrition:

Calories: 1680 | Fat: 30g

Carbs: 10g | Protein: 4g

Sodium: 514mg | Potassium: 0mg

176. Wood Pellet Grilled Zucchini Squash Spears

Preparation Time: 5 minutes,

Cooking Time: 10 minutes.

Servings: 5

Ingredients:

- 4 zucchinis, cleaned and ends cut
- 2 tbsp. olive oil
- 1 tbsp. sherry vinegar
- 2 thyme leaves pulled
- Salt and pepper to taste

Directions:

1. Cut the zucchini into halves then cut each half thirds.
2. Add the rest of the ingredients in a zip lock bag with the zucchini pieces. Toss to mix well.
3. Preheat the wood pellet temperature to 350°F with the lid closed for 15 minutes.
4. Remove the zucchini from the bag and place them on the grill grate with the cut side down.
5. Cook for 4 minutes until the zucchini are tender
6. Remove from grill and serve with thyme leaves. Enjoy.

Nutrition:

Calories: 74 | Fat: 5.4g

Carbs: 6.1g | Protein: 2.6g

Sugar: 3.9g | Fiber: 2.3g

Sodium: 302mg | Potassium: 599mg:

177. Wood Pellet Cold Smoked Cheese

Preparation Time: 5 minutes

Cooking Time: 2 minutes

Servings: 10

Ingredients:

- Ice
- 1 aluminum pan, full-size and disposable
- 1 aluminum pan, half-size, and disposable
- Toothpicks
- A block of cheese

Directions:

1. Preheat the wood pellet to 165°F with the lid closed for 15 minutes.
2. Place the small pan in the large pan. Fill the surrounding of the small pan with ice.
3. Place the cheese in the small pan on top of toothpicks then place the pan on the grill and close the lid.
4. Smoke cheese for 1 hour, flip the cheese, and smoke for 1 more hour with the lid closed.
5. Remove the cheese from the grill and wrap it in parchment paper. Store in the fridge for 2 3 days for the smoke flavor to mellow.
6. Remove from the fridge and serve. Enjoy.

Nutrition:

Calories: 1910 | Total Fat: 7g | Saturated Fat: 6g

Total Carbs: 2g | Net Carbs: 2g | Protein: 6g

Sugar: 1g | Fiber: 0g | Sodium: 340mg | Potassium: 0mg

178. Wood Pellet Grilled Asparagus and Honey Glazed Carrots

Preparation Time: 15 minutes

Cooking Time: 35 minutes

Servings: 5

Ingredients:

- 1 bunch asparagus, trimmed ends
- 1 lb. carrots, peeled
- 2 tbsp. olive oil
- Sea salt to taste
- 2 tbsp. honey
- Lemon zest

Directions:

1. Sprinkle the asparagus with oil and sea salt. Drizzle the carrots with honey and salt.

2. Preheat the wood pellet to 165°F with the lid closed for 15 minutes.

3. Place the carrots in the wood pellet and cook for 15 minutes. Add asparagus and cook for 20 more minutes or until cooked through.

4. Top the carrots and asparagus with lemon zest. Enjoy.

Nutrition:

Calories: 1680 | Total Fat: 30g

Saturated Fat: 2g | Total Carbs: 10g

Net Carbs: 10g | Protein: 4g | Sodium: 514mg

179. Wood Pellet Grilled Vegetables

Preparation Time: 5 minutes

Cooking Time: 15 minutes

Servings: 8

Ingredients:

- 1 veggie tray
- 1/4 cup vegetable oil
- 2 tbsp. veggie seasoning

Directions:

1. Preheat the wood pellet grill to 375°F
2. Toss the vegetables in oil then place on a sheet pan.
3. Sprinkle with veggie seasoning then place on the hot grill.
4. Grill for 15 minutes or until the veggies are cooked
5. Let rest then serve. Enjoy.

Nutrition:

Calories: 44 | Total Fat: 5g

Saturated Fat: 0g | Total Carbs: 1g

Net Carbs: 1g | Sodium: 36mg | Potassium: 10mg

180. Wood Pellet Smoked Asparagus

Preparation Time: 5 minutes

Cooking Time: 1 hour

Servings: 4

Ingredients:

- 1 bunch fresh asparagus ends cut
- 2 tbsp. olive oil
- Salt and pepper to taste

Directions:

1. Fire up your wood pellet smoker to 230°F
2. Place the asparagus in a mixing bowl and drizzle with olive oil. Season with salt and pepper.
3. Place the asparagus in a tinfoil sheet and fold the sides such that you create a basket.
4. Smoke the asparagus for 1 hour or until soft turning after half an hour.
5. Remove from the grill and serve. Enjoy.

Nutrition:

Calories: 43 | Total Fat: 2g

Total Carbs: 4g | Net Carbs: 2g

Protein: 3g | Sugar: 2g

Fiber: 2g | Sodium: 148mg

181 Wood Pellet Smoked Acorn Squash

Preparation Time: 10 minutes

Cooking Time: 2 hours

Servings: 6

Ingredients:

- 3 tbsp. olive oil; 1 tbsp. chili powder
- 3 acorn squash, halved and seeded
- 1/4 cup unsalted butter; 1/4 cup brown Sugar:
- 1 tbsp. cinnamon, ground
- 1 tbsp. nutmeg, ground

Directions:

1. Brush olive oil on the acorn squash cut sides then covers the halves with foil. Poke holes on the foil to allow steam and smoke through.

2. Fire up the wood pellet to 225°F and smoke the squash for 1 ½-2 hours.

3. Remove the squash from the smoker and allow it to sit.

4. Meanwhile, melt butter, Sugar: and spices in a saucepan. Stir well to combine.

5. Remove the foil from the squash and spoon the butter mixture in each squash half. Enjoy.

Nutrition:

Calories: 149 | Total Fat: 10g

Saturated Fat: 5g | Total Carbs: 14g

Net Carbs: 12g | Protein: 2g

Sugar: 0g | Fiber: 2g

Sodium: 19mg | Potassium: 0mg

182. Wood Pellet Smoked Vegetables

Preparation Time: 5 minutes

Cooking Time: 15 minutes

Servings: 6

Ingredients:

- 1 ear corn, fresh, husks and silk strands removed
- 1yellow squash, sliced; 1 red onion, cut into wedges
- 1 green pepper, cut into strips; 1 red pepper, cut into strips
- 1 yellow pepper, cut into strips; 1 cup mushrooms, halved
- 2 tbsp. oil; 2 tbsp. chicken seasoning

Directions:

1. Soak the pecan wood pellets in water for an hour. Remove the pellets from water and fill the smoker box with the wet pellets.

2. Place the smoker box under the grill and close the lid. Heat the grill on high heat for 10 minutes or until smoke starts coming out from the wood chips.

3. Meanwhile, toss the veggies in oil and seasonings then transfer them into a grill basket.

4. Grill for 10 minutes while turning occasionally. Serve and enjoy.

Nutrition:

Calories: 97 | Total Fat: 5g

Saturated Fat: 2g | Total Carbs: 11g

Net Carbs: 8g | Protein: 2g

Sugar: 1g | Fiber: 3g

Sodium: 251mg | Potassium: 171mg

183. Wood Pellet Grill Spicy Sweet Potatoes

Preparation Time: 10 minutes

Cooking Time: 35 minutes

Servings: 6

Ingredients:

- 2 lb. sweet potatoes, cut into chunks
- 1 red onion, chopped; 2 tbsp. oil
- 2 tbsp. orange juice; 1 tbsp. salt
- 1 tbsp. roasted cinnamon
- 1/4 tbsp. Chipotle chili pepper

Directions:

1. Preheat the wood pellet grill to 425°F with the lid closed.
2. Toss the sweet potatoes with onion, oil, and juice.
3. In a mixing bowl, mix cinnamon, salt, and pepper then sprinkle the mixture over the sweet potatoes.
4. Spread the potatoes on a lined baking dish in a single layer.
5. Place the baking dish in the grill and grill for 30 minutes or until the sweet potatoes are tender. Serve and enjoy.

Nutrition:

Calories: 145 | Total Fat: 5g

Saturated Fat: 0g | Total Carbs: 23g

Net Carbs: 19g | Protein: 2g

Sugar: 3g | Fiber: 4g

Sodium: 428mg | Potassium: 230mg

184 Wood Pellet Grilled Mexican Street Corn

Preparation Time: 5 minutes

Cooking Time: 25 minutes

Servings: 6

Ingredients:

- 6 ears of corn on the cob; 1 tbsp. olive oil
- Kosher salt and pepper to taste
- 1/4 cup mayo; 1/4 cup sour cream
- 1 tbsp. garlic paste; 1/2 tbsp. chili powder
- Pinch of ground red pepper
- 1/2 cup coria cheese, crumbled
- 1/4 cup cilantro, chopped; 6 lime wedges

Directions:

1. Brush the corn with oil. Sprinkle with salt.
2. Place the corn on a wood pellet grill set at 350°F. Cook for 25 minutes as you turn it occasionally.
3. Meanwhile mix mayo, cream, garlic, chili, and red pepper until well combined.
4. Let it rest for some minutes then brush with the mayo mixture.
5. Sprinkle cottage cheese, more chili powder, and cilantro. Serve with lime wedges. Enjoy.

Nutrition:

Calories: 144 | Total Fat: 5g | Saturated Fat: 2g

Total Carbs: 10g | Net Carbs: 10g | Protein: 0g Sugar: 0g

Fiber: 0g | Sodium: 136mg | Potassium: 173mg

185. Smoked Potatoes

Preparation Time: 30 minutes

Cooking Time: 2 hours

Servings: 4

Ingredients:

- 1.5 lb. potatoes (gemstone)
- Fresh parsley (chopped)
- 1/4 cup Parmesan (grated)

Marinade ingredients:

- 6 cloves garlic (minced); 2 tablespoons olive oil
- 1/2 teaspoon dried dill; 1/2 teaspoon basil (dried)
- 1/2 teaspoon oregano (dried)
- 1/2 teaspoon Italian seasoning (dried)
- 1/4 teaspoon fresh pepper (ground)
- 1/2 teaspoon kosher salt

Directions:

1. Initial step is rinsing the potatoes with water. When done, place the potatoes in a large zip lock bag.

2. In a mixing bowl, add and combine the minced garlic cloves, dill, Italian seasoning, basil and ground pepper. Add this mixture in the zip lock bag together with the potatoes.

3. Coat the potatoes by shaking the zip lock bag and refrigerate for 2 hours. Once ready to cook, preheat your smoker to 225F.

4. Use aluminum foil to make a foil packet and place in the potatoes.

5. Pour in two tablespoons of water in the foil and fold it in half on its edges.

6. Put the foil packet on the smoker rack and smoke for 2 hours.

7. Remove from the smoker and top with the grated parmesan and parsley.

Nutrition:

Calories – 210 | Saturated fat - 2.1g

Fiber -4.3g | Sugars - 2.1g | Fat - 8.9g

Protein - 5.5g | Sodium - 368mg

Cholesterol - 5mg | Carbohydrates - 28.9g

186. Smoked Cabbage

Preparation Time: 15 minutes

Cooking Time: 1 hour

Servings: 4

Ingredients:

- 1 cabbage
- 1/4 cup olive oil
- Kosher salt
- Garlic powder
- Black pepper

Sauce ingredients:

- 1/4 cup cilantro
- 2 cloves garlic (minced)
- 2 green onions (divided in green parts & white parts)
- Lime juice (2 limes)
- 1 jalapeno (chopped)
- 1 green pear (chopped)
- 2 tablespoons olive oil
- 2 tablespoons buttermilk
- 1 tablespoon mayonnaise
- 1 teaspoon black pepper
- 1 teaspoon sea salt

Directions:

1. Preheat your smoker to 250F

2. Peel off the outer cabbage leaves and use a knife to cut 4 quarters.

3. Coat the 4 quarters with olive oil, seasoning with pepper and salt.

4. Place the cabbage quarters on the tray and smoke with the wedge side up for 20 minutes. Flip the cabbage quarters to one wedge side and smoke for 20 minutes and do the same for the other remaining side, smoking for an additional 20 minutes.

5. Remove the cabbage once well-cooked.

6. Put all sauce ingredients in a blender and process. You can adjust its consistency by adding the liquid ingredients to get your preference.

7. Enjoy!

Nutrition:

Calories – 303 | Protein - 3g

Fat - 23g | Sat fat - 3g

Carbohydrates - 22g | Sugar - 12g

Fiber - 7g | Sodium - 1236mg

Potassium - 457mg | Calcium - 110mg

Vitamin C - 91.1mg | Vitamin A - 390IU

187. Smoked Vegetables with Vinaigrette

Preparation Time: 15 minutes

Cooking Time: 4 hours

Servings: 4

Ingredients:

Zucchini (thickly Sliced)

- Red potatoes (small in size & chopped)
- Red onions (chopped); Red pepper (chopped)
- Yellow medium squash (thickly sliced)

Vinaigrette ingredients:

- 1/3 cup olive oil; 1/4 cup vinegar (balsamic)
- 2 teaspoons Dijon mustard
- Pepper; Salt

Directions:

1. Add and combine balsamic vinegar, olive oil, Mustard, pepper and salt in a bowl.
2. In a casserole dish, add all the vegetables and combine. Coat the vegetables with the balsamic vinaigrette by tossing.
3. Preheat your smoker to 225F.
4. Put the dish with the vegetables in the smoker and smoke for 4 hours.

Nutrition:

Calories – 225 | Fat - 17.2g | Saturated fat - 2.5g | Iron - 1mg

Carbohydrates - 16.8g | Protein - 2.8g | Sodium - 196mg

Cholesterol - 0mg | Calcium - 35mg | Potassium - 483mg

CHAPTER 10:
Poultry Recipes

188. Traeger Grilled Buffalo Chicken

Preparation Time: 5 Minutes

Cooking Time: 10 Minutes

Servings: 6

Ingredients

- 5 chicken breasts, boneless and skinless
- 2 tbsp homemade BBQ rub
- 1 cup homemade Cholula Buffalo sauce

Directions:

1. Preheat the Traeger to 400F.
2. Slice the chicken breast lengthwise into strips. Season the slices with BBQ rub.
3. Place the chicken slices on the grill and paint both sides with buffalo sauce.
4. Cook for 4 minutes with the lid closed. Flip the breasts, paint again with sauce, and cook until the internal temperature reaches 165F.
5. Remove the chicken from the Traeger and serve when warm.

Nutrition: Calories 176 | Total fat 4g | Saturated fat 1g | Total carbs 1g Net carbs 1g | Protein 32g | Sugars 1g | Fiber 0g | Sodium 631mg

189. Traeger Sheet Pan Chicken Fajitas

Preparation Time: 10 Minutes

Cooking Time: 10 Minutes

Servings: 10

Ingredients

- 2 lb. chicken breast; 1 onion, sliced
- 1 red bell pepper, seeded and sliced
- 1 orange-red bell pepper, seeded and sliced
- 1 tbsp salt; 1/2 tbsp onion powder
- 1/2 tbsp granulated garlic; 2 tbsp oil
- 2 tbsp Spice ologist Chile Margarita Seasoning

Directions:

1. Preheat the Traeger to 450 F and line a baking sheet with parchment paper.
2. In a mixing bowl, combine seasonings and oil then toss with the peppers and chicken.
3. Place the baking sheet in the Traeger and let heat for 10 minutes with the lid closed.
4. Open the lid and place the veggies and the chicken in a single layer. Close the lid and cook for 10 minutes or until the chicken is no longer pink.
5. Serve with warm tortillas and top with your favorite toppings.

Nutrition:

Calories 211 | Total fat 6g | Saturated fat 1g | Total carbs 5g

Net carbs 4g | Protein 29g | Sugars 4g | Fiber 1g | Sodium 360mg

190. Traeger Asian Miso Chicken wings

Preparation Time: 15 Minutes

Cooking Time: 25 Minutes

Servings: 6

Ingredients

- 2 lb. chicken wings; 3/4 cup soy
- 1/2 cup pineapple juice
- 1 tbsp sriracha; 1/8 cup miso
- 1/8 cup gochujang; 1/2 cup water
- 1/2 cup oil; Togarashi

Directions:

1. Preheat the Traeger to 375 F
2. Combine all the ingredients except togarashi in a zip lock bag. Toss until the chicken wings are well coated. Refrigerate for 12 hours
3. Pace the wings on the grill grates and close the lid. Cook for 25 minutes or until the internal temperature reaches 165 F
4. Remove the wings from the Traeger and sprinkle Togarashi.
5. Serve when hot and enjoy.

Nutrition:

Calories 703 | Total fat 56g | Saturated fat 14g | Total carbs 24g

Net carbs 23g | Protein 27g | Sugars 6g | Fiber 1g | Sodium 1156mg

191. Yan's Grilled Quarters

Preparation Time: 20 minutes (additional 2-4 hours marinade)

Cooking Time: 1 to 1.5 hours

Servings: 4

Ingredients:

- 4 fresh or thawed frozen chicken quarters
- 4-6 glasses of extra virgin olive oil
- 4 tablespoons of Yang's original dry lab

Directions:

1. Configure a wood pellet smoker grill for indirect cooking and use the pellets to preheat to 325 ° F.

2. Place chicken on grill and cook at 325 ° F for 1 hour.

3. After one hour, raise the pit temperature to 400 ° F to finish the chicken and crisp the skin.

4. When the inside temperature of the thickest part of the thighs and feet reaches 180 ° F and the juice becomes clear, pull the crispy chicken out of the grill.

5. Let the crispy grilled chicken rest under a loose foil tent for 15 minutes before eating.

Nutrition:

Calories 956 | Total fat 47g | Saturated fat 13g | Total carbs 1g |
Net carbs 1g | Protein 124g | Sugars 0g | Fiber 0g | Sodium 1750mg

192. Cajun Patch Cock Chicken

Preparation Time: 30 minutes (additional 3 hours marinade)

Cooking Time: 2.5 hours

Servings: 4

Ingredients:

- 4-5 pounds of fresh or thawed frozen chicken
- 4-6 glasses of extra virgin olive oil
- Cajun Spice Lab 4 tablespoons or Lucile Bloody Mary Mix Cajun Hot Dry Herb Mix Seasoning

Directions:

1. Use hickory, pecan pellets, or blend to configure a wood pellet smoker grill for indirect cooking and preheat to 225 ° F.

2. If the unit has a temperature meat probe input, such as a MAK Grills 2 Star, insert the probe into the thickest part of the breast.

3. Make chicken for 1.5 hours.

4. After one and a half hours at 225 ° F, raise the pit temperature to 375 ° F and roast until the inside temperature of the thickest part of the chest reaches 170 ° F and the thighs are at least 180 ° F.

5. Place the chicken under a loose foil tent for 15 minutes before carving.

Nutrition:

Calories 956 | Total fat 47g | Saturated fat 13g | Total carbs 1g

Net carbs 1g | Protein 124g | Sugars 0g | Fiber 0g | Sodium 1750mg

193. Roasted Tuscan Thighs

Preparation Time: 20 minutes (plus 1-2 hours marinade)

Cooking Time: 40-60 minutes

Servings: 4

Ingredients:

- 8 chicken thighs, with bone, with skin
- 3 extra virgin olive oils with roasted garlic flavor
- 3 cups of Tuscan or Tuscan seasoning per thigh

Directions:

1. Set the wood pellet smoker grill for indirect cooking and use the pellets to preheat to 375 degrees Fahrenheit.

2. Depending on the grill of the wood pellet smoker, roast for 40-60 minutes until the internal temperature of the thick part of the chicken thigh reaches 180 ° F. Place the roasted Tuscan thighs under a loose foil tent for 15 minutes before serving.

Nutrition:

Calories 956 | Total fat 47g | Saturated fat 13g | Total carbs 1g |

Net carbs 1g | Protein 124g | Sugars 0g | Fiber 0g | Sodium 1750mg

194. Smoked Bone In-Turkey Breast

Preparation Time: 20 minutes

Cooking Time: 3-4 hours

Servings: 6-8

Ingredients:

- 1 (8-10 pounds) boned turkey breast
- 6 tablespoons extra virgin olive oil
- 5 Yang original dry lab or poultry seasonings

Directions:

1. Configure a wood pellet smoker grill for indirect cooking and preheat to 225 ° F using hickory or pecan pellets.

2. Smoke the boned turkey breast directly in a V rack or grill at 225 ° F for 2 hours.

3. After 2 hours of hickory smoke, raise the pit temperature to 325 ° F. Roast until the thickest part of the turkey breast reaches an internal temperature of 170 ° F and the juice is clear.

4. Place the hickory smoked turkey breast under a loose foil tent for 20 minutes, then scrape the grain.

Nutrition:

Calories 956 | Total fat 47g | Saturated fat 13g | Total carbs 1g

Net carbs 1g | Protein 124g | Sugars 0g | Fiber 0g | Sodium 1750mg

195. Teriyaki Smoked Drumstick

Preparation Time: 15 minutes (more marinade overnight)

Cooking Time: 1.5 hours to 2 hours

Servings: 4

Ingredients:

- 3 cup teriyaki marinade and cooking sauce like Yoshida's original gourmet
- Poultry seasoning 3 tsp
- 1 tsp garlic powder
- 10 chicken drumsticks

Directions:

1. Configure a wood pellet smoking grill for indirect cooking.

2. Place the skin on the drumstick and, while the grill is preheating, hang the drumstick on a poultry leg and wing rack to drain the cooking sheet on the counter. If you do not have a poultry leg and feather rack, you can dry the drumstick by tapping it with a paper towel.

3. Preheat wood pellet smoker grill to 180 ° F using hickory or maple pellets.

4. Make marinated chicken leg for 1 hour.

5. After 1 hour, raise the hole temperature to 350 ° F and cook the drumstick for another 30-45 minutes until the thickest part of the stick reaches an internal temperature of 180 ° F.

6. Place the chicken drumstick under the loose foil tent for 15 minutes before serving.

Nutrition:

Calories 956 | Total fat 47g | Saturated fat 13g | Total carbs 1g

Net carbs 1g | Protein 124g | Sugars 0g | Fiber 0g | Sodium 1750mg

196. Hickory Smoke Patchcock Turkey

Preparation Time: 20 minutes

Cooking Time: 3-4 hours

Servings: 8-10

Ingredients:

- 1 (14 lb.) fresh or thawed frozen young turkey
- ¼ Extra virgin olive oil with cup roasted garlic flavor
- poultry seasonings or original dry lab in January

Directions:

1. Configure a wood pellet smoking grill for indirect cooking and preheat to 225 ° F using hickory pellets.
2. Place the turkey skin down on a non-stick grill mat made of Teflon-coated fiberglass.
3. Suck the turkey at 225 ° F for 2 hours.
4. After 2 hours, raise the pit temperature to 350 ° F.
5. Roast turkey until the thickest part of the chest reaches an internal temperature of 170 ° F and the juice is clear.
6. Place the Hickory smoked roast turkey under a loose foil tent for 20 minutes before engraving.

Nutrition:

Calories 956 | Total fat 47g | Saturated fat 13g | Total carbs 1g |
Net carbs 1g | Protein 124g | Sugars 0g | Fiber 0g | Sodium 1750mg

197. Lemon Cornish Chicken Stuffed with Crab

Preparation Time: 30 minutes (additional 2-3 hours marinade)

Cooking Time: 1 hour 30 minutes

Servings: 2-4

Ingredients:

- 2 Cornish chickens (about 1¾ pound each)
- Half lemon, half
- 4 tbsp western rub or poultry rub
- 2 cups stuffed with crab meat

Directions:

1. Set wood pellet smoker grill for indirect cooking and preheat to 375 ° F with pellets.

2. Place the stuffed animal on the rack in the baking dish. If you do not have a rack that is small enough to fit, you can also place the chicken directly on the baking dish.

3. Roast the chicken at 375 ° F until the inside temperature of the thickest part of the chicken breast reaches 170 ° F, the thigh reaches 180 ° F, and the juice is clear.

4. Test the crab meat stuffing to see if the temperature has reached 165 ° F.

5. Place the roasted chicken under a loose foil tent for 15 minutes before serving.

Nutrition:

Calories 956 | Total fat 47g | Saturated fat 13g | Total carbs 1g

Net carbs 1g | Protein 124g | Sugars 0g | Fiber 0g | Sodium 1750mg

198. Bacon Cordon Blue

Preparation Time: 30 minutes

Cooking Time: 2 to 2.5 hours

Servings: 6

Ingredients:

- 24 bacon slices
- 3 large boneless, skinless chicken breasts, butterfly
- 3 extra virgin olive oils with roasted garlic flavor
- 3 Yang original dry lab or poultry seasonings
- 12 slice black forest ham; 12-slice provolone cheese

Directions:

1. Using apple or cherry pellets, configure a wood pellet smoker grill for indirect cooking and preheat (180 ° F to 200 ° F) for smoking.
2. Inhale bacon cordon blue for 1 hour.
3. After smoking for 1 hour, raise the pit temperature to 350 ° F.
4. Bacon cordon blue occurs when the internal temperature reaches 165 ° F and the bacon becomes crispy.
5. Rest for 15 minutes under a loose foil tent before serving.

Nutrition:

Calories 956 | Total fat 47g | Saturated fat 13g | Total carbs 1g

Net carbs 1g | Protein 124g | Sugars 0g | Fiber 0g | Sodium 1750mg

199. Roast Duck à I Orange

Preparation Time: 30 minutes

Cooking Time: 2 to 2.5 hours

Servings: 3-4

Ingredients:

- 1 (5-6 lb.) Frozen Long Island, Beijing or Canadian ducks
- 3 tbsp west or 3 tbsp; 1 large orange, cut into wedges
- Three celery stems chopped into large chunks
- Half a small red onion, a quarter; Orange sauce:
- 2 orange cups; 2 tablespoons soy sauce
- 2 tablespoons orange marmalade
- 2 tablespoons honey; 3g tsp grated raw

Directions:

1. Set the wood pellet smoker grill for indirect cooking and use the pellets to preheat to 350 ° F.
2. Roast the ducks at 350 ° F for 2 hours.
3. After 2 hours, brush the duck freely with orange sauce.
4. Roast the orange glass duck for another 30 minutes, making sure that the inside temperature of the thickest part of the leg reaches 165 ° F.
5. Place duck under loose foil tent for 20 minutes before serving.
6. Discard the orange wedge, celery and onion. Serve with a quarter of duck with poultry scissors.

Nutrition:

Calories 956 | Total fat 47g | Saturated fat 13g | Total carbs 1g

Net carbs 1g | Protein 124g | Sugars 0g | Fiber 0g | Sodium 1750mg

200. Herb Roasted Turkey

Preparation Time: 30 minutes (additional 2-3 hours marinade)

Cooking Time: 1 hour 30 minutes

Servings: 2-4

Ingredients:

- 8 Tbsp. Butter, Room Temperature; 3 Tbsp. Butter
- 2 Tbsp. Mixed Herbs Such as Parsley, Sage, Rosemary, And Marjoram, Chopped
- 1/4 Tsp. Black Pepper, Freshly Ground
- 1 (12-14 Lbs.) Turkey, Thawed If pre-frozen

Directions:

1. In a small mixing bowl, combine the 8 tablespoons of softened butter, mixed herbs, and black pepper and beat until fluffy with a wooden spoon.

2. Remove any giblets from the turkey cavity and save them for gravy making, if desired. Wash the turkey, inside and out, under cold running water. Dry with paper towels.

3. Using your fingers or the handle of a wooden spoon, gently push some of the herbed butter underneath the turkey skin onto the breast halves, being careful not to tear the skin.

4. Rub the outside of the turkey with the melted butter and sprinkle with the Traeger Pork and Poultry Rub. Pour the chicken broth in the bottom of the roasting pan.

5. When ready to cook, set temperature to 325 F and preheat, lid closed for 15 minutes.

Nutrition:

Calories 956 | Total fat 47g | Saturated fat 13g | Total carbs 1g

Net carbs 1g | Protein 124g | Sugars 0g | Fiber 0g | Sodium 1750mg

201. Smoked Bourbon & Orange Brined Turkey

Preparation Time: 30 minutes

Cooking Time: 1 hour 30 minutes

Servings: 2-4

Ingredients:

- Traeger Orange Brine (From Kit)
- Traeger Turkey Rub (From Kit)
- 1.25-2.5 Gallons Cold Water
- 1 Cup Bourbon; 1 Tbsp. Butter, Melted

Directions:

1. Mix Traeger Orange Brine seasoning (from Orange Brine & Turkey Rub Kit) with one quart of water. Boil for 5 minutes. Remove from heat, add 1 gallon of cold water and bourbon.

2. Place turkey breast side down in a large container. Pour cooled brine mix over bird. Add cold water until bird is submerged. Refrigerate for 24 hours.

3. Remove turkey and disregard brine. Blot turkey dry with paper towels. Combine butter and Grand Marnier and coat outside of turkey.

4. Season outside of turkey with Traeger Turkey Rub (from Orange Brine & Turkey Rub Kit).

5. When ready to cook, set temperature to 225 F and preheat, lid closed for 15 minutes.

Nutrition:

Calories 956 | Total fat 47g | Saturated fat 13g | Total carbs 1g

Net carbs 1g | Protein 124g | Sugars 0g | Fiber 0g | Sodium 1750mg

202. Traeger Leftover Turkey Soup

Preparation Time: 30 minutes

Cooking Time: 1 hour 30 minutes

Servings: 2-4

Ingredients:

- 1 Turkey Carcass
- 16 Cups Cold Water
- 2 Large Celery Ribs, Sliced
- 2 Large Carrots, Scraped and Sliced
- 2 Red Onions, Quartered

Directions:

1. Strip a turkey carcass of all meat; set aside in a container.
2. Break up the bones of the turkey carcass and place them in a large pot. Add any turkey skin or other assorted "bits" that are not edible meat.
3. Once the stock has come to a boil, add all remaining Ingredients and turn heat down until the bubbles barely break the surface. Let simmer for 3 to 4 hours, stirring occasionally.
4. When the stock is ready, strain it through a fine-meshed sieve into a large bowl; if your sieve is not fine, line it first with cheesecloth.
5. Refrigerate stock, covered, for several hours or preferably overnight. You can either make soup the then day, or freeze the stock.

Nutrition:

Calories 956 | Total fat 47g | Saturated fat 13g | Total carbs 1g

Net carbs 1g | Protein 124g | Sugars 0g | Fiber 0g | Sodium 1750mg

203. Smoked Turkey by Rob Cooks

Preparation Time: 30 minutes

Cooking Time: 1 hour 30 minutes

Servings: 2-4

Ingredients:

- Smoked Turkey by Rob's cooks
- 1 (12-14 Lb.) Turkey, Fresh or Thawed
- 3/4 Lb. (3 Sticks) Unsalted Butter
- 1 (5 Gal) Bucket or Stock Pot
- Foil Pan, Large Enough for Turkey

Directions:

1. This method requires an overnight brining so collect everything the day before your meal.

2. The afternoon before, prepare your brine by adding the kosher salt and sugar to a medium saucepan. Cover with water and bring to a boil. Stir to dissolve the salt and sugar.

3. Prepare your turkey by removing the neck, gizzards and truss, if pre-trussed. Trim off excess skin and fat near the cavity and neck. Place the turkey in bucket with the brine.

4. When ready to cook, set temperature to 180 F and preheat, lid closed for 15 minutes.

5. Remove your turkey from the brine. Remember there's a cavity full of water so make sure to do this over the sink, otherwise you'll have brine all over the place.

Nutrition:

Calories 956 | Total fat 47g | Saturated fat 13g | Total carbs 1g

Net carbs 1g | Protein 124g | Sugars 0g | Fiber 0g | Sodium 1750mg

204. Smoked Turkey Legs

Preparation Time: 30 minutes

Cooking Time: 1 hour 30 minutes

Servings: 2-4

Ingredients:

- 1 Gal Warm Water
- 1/2-Gal Cold Water; 4 Cups Ice
- 1 Cup Traeger BBQ Rub
- 1/2 Cup Curing Salt

Directions:

1. In a large stockpot, combine one gallon of warm water, the rub, curing salt, brown sugar, allspice (if using), peppercorns, bay leaves and liquid smoke.

2. Bring to a boil over high heat to dissolve the salt granules. Cool to room temperature.

3. Add cold water and ice; chill in the refrigerator. Add the turkey legs, making sure they're completely submerged in the brine.

4. After 24 hours, drain the turkey legs and discard the brine. Rinse the brine off the legs with cold water, then dry thoroughly with paper towels. Brush off any clinging solid spices.

5. When ready to cook, set temperature to 250 F and preheat, lid closed for 15 minutes.

Nutrition:

Calories 956 | Total fat 47g | Saturated fat 13g | Total carbs 1g

Net carbs 1g | Protein 124g | Sugars 0g | Fiber 0g | Sodium 1750mg

205. Traditional Thanksgiving Turkey

Preparation Time: 30 minutes

Cooking Time: 1 hour 30 minutes

Servings: 2-4

Ingredients:

- 1 (18-20lb) Turkey
- 1/2 Lb. Butter, Softened
- 8 Sprigs Thyme
- 6 Cloves Garlic, Minced
- 1 Sprig Rosemary, Rough Chop

Directions:

1. In a small bowl, combine butter with the minced garlic, thyme leaves, chopped rosemary, black pepper and kosher salt.

2. Prepare the turkey by separating the skin from the breast creating a pocket to stuff the butter-herb mixture in.

3. Cover the entire breast with 1/4" thickness of butter mixture.

4. Season the whole turkey with kosher salt and black pepper. As an option, you can also stuff the turkey cavity with Traditional Stuffing.

5. When ready to cook, set the temperature to 300 F and preheat, lid closed for 15 minutes.

Nutrition:

Calories 956 | Total fat 47g | Saturated fat 13g | Total carbs 1g

Net carbs 1g | Protein 124g | Sugars 0g | Fiber 0g | Sodium 1750mg

206. Turkey Jalapeno Meatballs

Preparation Time: 30 minutes

Cooking Time: 1 hour 30 minutes

Servings: 2-4

Ingredients:

- Turkey Jalapeño Meatballs
- 1 1/4 Lbs. Ground Turkey
- 1 Jalapeño Pepper, Deseeded and Finely Diced
- 1/2 Tsp Garlic Salt
- 1 Tsp Onion Powder

Directions:

1. In a separate small bowl, combine the milk and bread crumbs.
2. In a large bowl, mix together turkey, garlic salt, onion powder, salt, pepper, Worcestershire sauce, cayenne pepper, egg and jalapeños.
3. Add the bread crumb milk mixture to the bowl and combine. Cover with plastic and refrigerate for up to 1 hour.
4. When ready to cook, set the temperature to 350°F and preheat, lid closed for 15 minutes
5. Roll the turkey mixture into balls, about one tablespoon each and place the meatballs in a single layer on a parchment lined baking sheet.

Nutrition:

Calories 956 | Total fat 47g | Saturated fat 13g | Total carbs 1g

Net carbs 1g | Protein 124g | Sugars 0g | Fiber 0g | Sodium 2750mg

207. Wild Turkey Southwest Egg Rolls

Preparation Time: 30 minutes

Cooking Time: 1 hour 30 minutes

Servings: 2-4

Ingredients:

- 2 Cups Leftover Wild Turkey Meat
- 1/2 Cup Corn; 1/2 Cup Black Beans
- 3 Tbsp Taco Seasoning
- 1/2 Cup White Onion, Chopped

Directions:

1. Add olive oil to a large skillet and heat on the stove over medium heat. Add onions and peppers and sauté 2-3 minutes until soft. Add garlic, cook 30 seconds, then Rote and black beans.

2. Pour taco seasoning over meat and add 1/3 cup of water and mix to coat well. Add to veggie mixture and stir to mix well. If it seems dry, add 2 tbsp water. Cook until heated all the way through.

3. Remove from the heat and transfer the mixture to the fridge. The mixture should be completely cooled prior to stuffing the egg rolls or the wrappers will break.

4. Place spoonful of the mixture in each wrapper and wrap tightly. Repeat with remaining wrappers. When ready to cook, set temperature to High and preheat, lid closed for 15 minutes.

5. Brush each egg roll with oil or butter and place directly on the Traeger grill grate. Cook until the exterior is crispy, about 20 min per side.

Nutrition:

Calories 456 | Total fat 37g | Saturated fat 13g | Total carbs 1g

Net carbs 1g | Protein 124g | Sugars 0g | Fiber 0g | Sodium 1750mg

208. Smoked Wild Turkey Breast

Preparation Time: 30 minutes

Cooking Time: 1 hour 30 minutes

Servings: 2-4

Ingredients:

- Brine; 1 Cup Brown Sugar
- 2 Lbs. Turkey Breast and Deboned Thigh, Tied with Skin On
- 1/4 Cup Salt; 2 Tbsp Cracked Pepper
- 4 Cups Cold Water; BBQ Rub
- 2 Tbsp Garlic Powder; 2 Tbsp Onions, Dried
- 2 Tbsp Black Pepper; 2 Tbsp Brown Sugar
- 1 Tbsp Cayenne Pepper; 2 Tbsp Chili Powder
- 1/4 Cup Paprika; 1 Tbsp Salt
- 2 Tbsp Sugar; 2 Tbsp Cumin, Ground

Directions:

1. For the Brine: In a large glass bowl combine brown sugar, salt, pepper and water. Add turkey and weigh down to completely submerge if necessary. Transfer to the refrigerator and brine.

2. Remove turkey from the brine and discard the brine.

3. When ready to cook, set the temperature 180 F and preheat lid closed for 15 minutes.

4. Combine Ingredients for the BBQ Rub. Season turkey with rub and place directly on the grill grate skin side up.

5. Smoke for 5-8 hours or until the internal temperature reaches 160 F degrees when an instant read thermometer is inserted into the center.

6. Remove from the smoker and let rest for 10 minutes. Turkey will continue to cook once taken off grill to reach a final temperature of 165 F in the breast.

7. Slice and serve with your favorite sides. Enjoy!

Nutrition:

Calories 856 | Total fat 47g | Saturated fat 13g | Total carbs 2g

Net carbs 1g | Protein 124g | Sugars 0g | Fiber 0g | Sodium 1750mg

209. Grilled Wild Turkey Orange Cashew Salad

Preparation Time: 30 minutes

Cooking Time: 1 hour 30 minutes

Servings: 2-4

Ingredients:

- 2 Wild Turkey Breast Halves, Without Skin
- 1/4 Cup Teriyaki Sauce; Turkey Breast
- 1 (12 Oz) Can Blood Orange Kill Cliff or Similar Citrus Soda
- 2 Tbsp Traeger Chicken Rub; 1 Tsp Fresh Ginger
- Cashew Salad; 4 Cups Romaine Lettuce, Chopped
- 1/2 Head Red or White Cabbage, Chopped
- 1/2 Cup Shredded Carrots; 1/2 Cup Edamame, Shelled
- 1 Smoked Yellow Bell Pepper, Sliced into Circles
- 1 Smoked Red Bell Pepper, Sliced into Circles
- 3 Chive Tips, Chopped; 1/2 Cup Smoked Cashews
- Blood Orange Vinaigrette; 1 Tsp Orange Zest
- Juice From 1/2 Large Orange; 1 Tsp Finely Grated Fresh Ginger
- 2 Tbsp Seasoned Rice Vinegar; 1 Tsp Honey
- Sea Salt, To Taste; 1/4 Cup Light Vegetable Oil

Directions:

1. For the Marinade: Combine teriyaki sauce, Kill Cliff soda and fresh ginger. Pour marinade over turkey breasts in a Ziplock bag or dish and seal.

2. When ready to cook, set temperature to 375 F and preheat, lid closed for 15 minutes.

3. Remove turkey from the refrigerator, drain the marinade and pat turkey dry with paper towels.

4. Place turkey into a shallow oven proof dish and season with Traeger Chicken Rub.

5. Place dish in the Traeger and cook for 30-45 minutes or until the breast reaches an internal temperature of 160 F.

6. Remove the breast from the grill and wrap in Traeger Butcher Paper. Let turkey rest for 10 minutes. While turkey is resting, prepare salad.

7. Assemble salad Ingredients in a bowl and toss to mix. Combine all Ingredients in list for vinaigrette.

8. After resting for 10 minutes, slice turkey and serve with cashew salad and blood orange vinaigrette. Enjoy!

Nutrition:

Calories 956 | Total fat 47g | Saturated fat 13g | Total carbs 1g

Net carbs 1g | Protein 124g | Sugars 0g | Fiber 0g | Sodium 1750mg

210. Baked Cornbread Turkey Tamale Pie

Preparation Time: 30 minutes

Cooking Time: 1 hour 30 minutes

Servings: 2-4

Ingredients:

- Filling; 2 Cups Shredded Turkey; 2 Cobs of Corn
- 1 (15 Oz) Can Black Beans, Rinsed and Drained
- 1 Yellow Bell Pepper; 1 Orange Bell Pepper
- 2 Jalapeños; 2 Tbsp Cilantro
- 1 Bunch Green Onions; 1/2 Tsp Cumin
- 1/2 Tsp Paprika; 1 (7 Oz) Can Chipotle Sauce
- 1 (15 Oz) Can Enchilada Sauce
- 1/2 Cup Shredded Cheddar Cheese
- Cornbread Topping; 1 Cup All-Purpose Flour
- 1 Cup Yellow or White Cornmeal; 1 Tbsp Sugar
- 2 Tsp Baking Powder; 1/2 Tsp Salt; 3 Tbsp Butter
- 1 Cup Buttermilk; 1 Large Egg, Lightly Beaten

Directions:

1. For the filling: Mix to combine filling Ingredients Place in the bottom of a butter greased 10-inch pan.

2. For the cornbread topping: In a mixing bowl, combine the flour, cornmeal, sugar, baking powder, and salt. Melt the butter in a small saucepan.

3. Add the milk-egg mixture to the dry Ingredients and stir to combine. Do not over mix.

4. To assemble Tamale Pie: Fill the bottom of a butter greased 10-inch pan with the shredded turkey filling. Top with the cornbread topping and smooth to the edges of pan.

5. When ready to cook, set the temperature to 375 F and preheat, lid closed for 15 minutes.

6. Place directly on the grill grate and cook for 45-50 minutes or until the cornbread is lightly browned and cooked through. Enjoy!

Nutrition:

Calories 956 | Total fat 47g | Saturated fat 13g | Total carbs 1g

Net carbs 1g | Protein 124g | Sugars 0g | Fiber 0g | Sodium 1750mg

211. Traeger BBQ simple Turkey Sandwiches

Preparation Time: 30 minutes

Cooking Time: 45 minutes

Servings: 10

Ingredients:

- 6 Turkey Thighs, Skin-On; Pork & Poultry Rub
- 1 1/2 Cups Chicken or Turkey Broth
- 1 Cup barbeque Sauce, Or More as Needed
- 6 Buns or Kaiser Rolls, Split and Buttered

Directions:

1. Season turkey thighs on both sides with the Pork & Poultry rub.
2. When ready to cook, turn temperature to 180 degrees F and preheat, lid closed for 15 minutes.
3. Arrange the turkey thighs exactly on the grill grate and smoke for 30 minutes.
4. Transfer the thighs to sturdy disposable aluminum foil or baking tray. Pour the broth around the thighs and then cover the pan with foil or a lid.
5. Increase temperature to 325 degrees F and preheat, lid closed. Roast the thighs until it reaches an internal temperature of 180 degrees F.
6. Remove pan from the grill, but leave the grill on. Let the turkey thighs cool slightly up to they can be handled comfortably.
7. Let the drops drip off and keep. Remove skin and discard.
8. Pull out the shredded turkey meat with your fingers and return it to the roasting pan.
9. Add a cup or more of your favorite BBQ Sauce along with some of the drippings.

10. Recover the pan with foil and reheat the BBQ turkey on the grill for 20 to 30 minutes.

11. Serve with toasted buns if desired. Enjoy!

Nutrition:

Energy (calories): 25 kcal | Protein: 0.7 g

Fat: 1.53 g | Carbohydrates: 2.59 g

212. Roasted Spatchcock Turkey

Preparation Time: 30 minutes

Cooking Time: 3-4 hours

Servings: 4

Ingredients:

- 1 (18-20 Lb.) Whole Turkey
- 4 tbsps. Turkey Rub
- 1 tbsp. Jacobsen Sea Salt
- 4 Cloves Garlic, Minced
- 3 tbsps. Parsley, Chopped
- 1 tbsp. Rosemary, Chopped
- 2 tbsps. Thyme Leaves, Chopped
- 2 Scallions, Chopped
- 3 tbsps. Olive Oil

Directions:

1. When ready to cook, turn temperature to High and preheat, lid closed for 15 minutes.

2. On a cutting board, mix the garlic, parsley, thyme, rosemary and green onions. Chop the mixture until it turns into a paste. Set aside.

3. Spatchcock the turkey: With a large knife or shears, cut the bird open along the backbone on both sides, through the ribs, and remove the backbone.

4. Once the bird is open, split the breastbone to spread the bird flat, allowing it to roast evenly.

5. With the bird's breast facing up, season the outside with half of the Turkey Rub, then follow 2/3 of the herb mixture by rubbing it into the bird. Drizzle with olive oil.

6. Roll over the bird and then season generously with the remaining Turkey Rub.

7. Place the turkey exactly on the grill grate and cook for 30 minutes.

8. Turn to low temperature on the grill to 300 degrees F and continue to cook for 3-4 hours or until the internal temperature reaches 160 degrees F in the breast.

9. The finished inside temperature should reach 165 degrees F, but it will continue to rise after the bird is totally removed it from the grill.

10. Prepare the bird and let it rest 20-25 minutes before carving. Enjoy!

213. Spatchcocked Maple Brined Turkey

Preparation Time: 40 minutes

Cooking Time: 2-3 hours

Servings: 6

Ingredients:

- 1 (12-14 Lbs.) Turkey, Thawed If Frozen
- Qtrs. Hot Water ; 1 1/2 Cups Kosher Salt
- 3/4 cup of Bourbon; 1 cup of Pure Maple Syrup
- 1/2 Cup of Brown Sugar; 1 Onion
- 3-4 Strips Orange Peel
- 3 Bay Leaves, Broken into Pieces
- 2 tbsps. Black Peppercorns; 1 tbsp. Whole Cloves
- 3 Qtrs. Ice; 1 cup Butter, Melted
- Pork & Poultry Rub, As Needed
- Sprigs of Fresh Sage and Thyme, To Garnish
- Orange Wedges, Lady Apples, Or Kumquats, To Serve

Directions:

<u>Note</u>: Do not use kosher turkey or basting turkey for this recipe as they have already been fortified with saline.

For the Brine:

1. In a large stockpot or container, combine the hot water, kosher salt, bourbon, 3/4 cup of the maple syrup, brown sugar, onion, bay leaves, orange peel, peppercorns, and cloves and stir until well mixed. Add the ice.

2. Rinse or drain the turkey, inside and out, under cold running water. Remove giblets and discard or save for another use. Some turkeys come with a gravy packet as well; remove it before roasting the bird.

3. Add the turkey to the brine and refrigerate 8 to 12 hours, or overnight—weight with an ice pack to keep the bird immerse

4. Rinse and pat dry it with paper towels; discard the brine.

5. Spatchcock the turkey: Using a knife or shears, cut the bird open along the spine on both sides, then through the ribs and removes the backbone.

6. Once the bird is open, split the breastbone to spread the bird flat, allowing it to roast evenly.

7. Mix together the melted butter and the remaining 1/4 cup of maple syrup and divide in half. Brush half of the blend on the bird and then sprinkle with Pork and Poultry Rub or the salt and black pepper.

8. Set aside the other half of the blend mixture until ready to use.

9. Prepare and ready to cook, set the temperature to 350 degrees F and preheat, lid closed for 15 minutes.

10. Roast or cook the turkey until the internal temperature in the thickest part of the breast reaches 165 degrees F, about 2-3 hours.

11. Brush with the remaining butter-maple syrup glaze while having the last 30 minutes of cooking the meat.

12. Let the turkey remain rest for 15 to 20 minutes and then garnish, if desired, with fresh herbs and or kumquats. Enjoy!

Nutrition:

Energy (calories): 748 kcal | Protein: 18.11 g

Fat: 50.92 g | Carbohydrates: 55.01 g

CHAPTER 11:
Appetizer

214. Grilled Corn

Preparation Time: 15 minutes

Cooking Time: 25 minutes

Servings: 6

Ingredients:

- Six fresh ears of corn
- Salt; Black pepper; Olive oil
- Vegetable seasoning
- Butter for serving

Directions:

1. Preheat the grill to high with a closed lid.
2. Peel the husks. Remove the corn's silk. Rub with black pepper, salt, vegetable seasoning, and oil.
3. Close the husks and grill for 25 minutes. Turn them occasionally.
4. Serve topped with butter and enjoy.

Nutrition:

Calories: 70 | Protein: 3g

Carbs: 18g | Fat: 2g

215. Thyme - Rosemary Mash Potatoes

Preparation Time: 20 minutes

Cooking Time: 1 hour

Servings: 6

Ingredients:

- 4 ½ lbs. Potatoes, russet
- Salt, 1 pint of Heavy cream
- 3 Thyme sprigs + 2 tablespoons for garnish
- 2 Rosemary sprigs; Sage leaves
- Black peppercorns; Black pepper to taste
- Two stick Butter softened; 2 Garlic cloves, chopped

Directions:

1. Preheat the grill to 350F with a closed lid.

2. Peel the russet potatoes.

3. Cut into small pieces and place them in a baking dish. Fill it with water (1 ½ cups). Place on the grill and cook with a closed lid for about 1 hour.

4. In the meantime, in a saucepan, combine the garlic, peppercorns, herbs, and cream. Place on the grate and cook covered for about 15 minutes. Once done, strain to remove the garlic and herbs. Keep warm.

5. Take out the water of the potatoes and place them in a stockpot. Rice them with a fork and pour 2/3 of the mixture. Add one stick of softened butter and salt. Serve right away.

Nutrition:

Calories: 180 | Protein: 4g

Carbs: 28g | Fat: 10g

216. Grilled Broccoli

Preparation Time: 15 minutes

Cooking Time: 10 minutes

Servings: 4 to 6

Ingredients:

- Four bunches of Broccoli
- Four tablespoons Olive oil
- Black pepper and salt to taste
- ½ Lemon, the juice
- ½ Lemon cut into wedges

Directions:

1. Preheat the grill to High with a closed lid.
2. In a bowl, add the broccoli and drizzle with oil. Coat well—season with salt.
3. Grill for 5 minutes and then flip. Cook for 3 minutes more.
4. I have once done transfer on a plate. Squeeze lemon on top and serve with lemon wedges. Enjoy!

Nutrition:

Calories: 35g | Protein: 2.5g

Carbs: 5g | Fat: 1g

217. Smoked Coleslaw

Preparation Time: 15 minutes

Cooking Time: 25 minutes

Servings: 8

Ingredients:

- One shredded Purple Cabbage
- One shredded Green Cabbage
- 2 Scallions, sliced; 1 cup Carrots, shredded

Dressing

- One tablespoon of Celery Seed
- 1/8 cup of White vinegar; 1 ½ cups Mayo
- Black pepper and salt to taste

Directions:

1. Preheat the grill to 180F with a closed lid.
2. On a tray, spread the carrots and cabbage. Place the tray on the grate and smoke for about 25 minutes. Transfer to the fridge to cool.
3. In the meantime, make the dressing. In a bowl, combine the ingredients. Mix well.
4. Transfer the veggies to a bowl. Drizzle with the sauce and toss
5. Serve sprinkled with scallions.

Nutrition:

Calories: 35g | Protein: 1g

Carbs: 5g | Fat: 5g

218. The Best Potato Roast

Preparation Time: 15 minutes

Cooking Time: 35 minutes

Servings: 6

Ingredients:

- 4 Potatoes, large (scrubbed)
- 1 ½ cups gravy (beef or chicken)
- Rib seasoning to taste
- 1 ½ cups Cheddar cheese
- Black pepper and salt to taste
- Two tablespoons sliced Scallions

Directions:

1. Preheat the grill to high with a closed lid.
2. Slice each potato into wedges or fries. Transfer into a bowl and drizzle with oil—season with Rib seasoning.
3. Spread the wedges/fries on a baking sheet (rimmed)—roast for about 20 minutes. Turn the wedges/fries and cook for 15 minutes more.
4. In the meantime, in a saucepan, warm the chicken/beef gravy. Cut the cheese into small cubes.
5. It was once done cooking, place the potatoes on a plate or into a bowl. Distribute the cut cheese and pour hot gravy on top.
6. Serve garnished with scallion—season with pepper. Enjoy!

Nutrition:

Calories: 220 | Protein: 3g

Carbs: 38g | Fat: 15g

219. Smoked Corn on the Cob

Preparation Time: 5 Minutes

Cooking Time: 60 Minutes

Servings: 4

Ingredients

- 4 corn ears, husk removed
- 4 tbsp olive oil
- Pepper and salt to taste

Directions:

1. Preheat your smoker to 225F.
2. Meanwhile, brush your corn with olive oil. Season with pepper and salt.
3. Place the corn on a smoker and smoke for about 1 hour 15 minutes.
4. Remove from the smoker and serve.
5. Enjoy!

Nutrition:

Calories 180 | Total fat 7g | Saturated fat 4g | Total Carbs 31g | Net Carbs 27g
Protein 5g | Sugars 5g | Fiber 4g | Sodium 23mg | Potassium 416mg

220. Traeger Smoked Vegetables

Preparation Time: 5 Minutes

Cooking Time: 20 Minutes

Servings: 4

Ingredients

- 1 head of broccoli; 4 carrots

- 16 oz snow peas; 1 tbsp olive oil

- 1 cup mushrooms, chopped

- 1-1/2 tbsp pepper; 1 tbsp garlic powder

Directions:

1. Cut broccoli and carrots into bite-size pieces. Add snow peas and combine.

2. Toss the veggies with oil and seasoning.

3. Now cover a pan, sheet, with parchment paper. Place veggies on top.

4. Meanwhile, set your wood pellet smoker to 180F.

5. Place the pan into the smoker. Smoke for about 5 minutes.

6. Adjust smoker temperature to 40F and continue cooking for another 10-15 minutes until slightly brown broccoli tips.

7. Remove, Serve, and enjoy.

Nutrition:

Calories 111 | Total fat 4g | Saturated fat 1g | Total Carbs 15g | Net Carbs 9g Protein 5g | Sugars 7g | Fiber 6g | Sodium 0mg | Potassium 109mg

221. Traeger Smashed Potato Casserole 1

Preparation Time: 30-45 minutes

Cooking Time: 45-60 minutes

Servings: 8

Recommended pellet: Optional

Ingredients:

- 8-10 bacon slices; 1 sliced red onion
- ¼ cup (½ stick) salt butter or bacon grease
- 1 sliced small pepper; 1 sliced small red pepper
- 1 sliced small pepper; 3 cups mashed potatoes
- ¾ cup sour cream; 1.5 teaspoon Texas BBQ Love
- 3 cups of sharp cheddar cheese
- 4 cups hashed brown potato

Directions:

1. Cook the bacon in a large skillet over medium heat until both sides are crispy for about 5 minutes. Set the bacon aside.

2. Transfer the rendered bacon grease to a glass container.

3. In the same large frying pan, heat the butter or bacon grease over medium heat and fry the red onions and peppers until they become al dente. Set aside.

4. Spray a 9 x 11-inch casserole dish with a non-stick cooking spray and spread the mashed potatoes to the bottom of the dish.

5. Layer sour cream on mashed potatoes and season with Texas BBQ Love.

6. Layer the stir-fried vegetables on the potatoes and pour butter or bacon grease into a pan.

7. Sprinkle 1.5 cups of sharp cheddar cheese followed by frozen hash brown potatoes.

8. Spoon the remaining butter or bacon grease from the stir-fried vegetables over the hash browns and place the crushed bacon.

9. Place the remaining 1.5 cups of sharp cheddar cheese and cover the casserole dish with a lid or aluminum foil.

10. Using the selected pellets, set up a wood pellet smoking grill for indirect cooking and preheat to 350 ° F.

11. Bake the crushed potato casserole for 45-60 minutes until the cheese foams.

12. Rest for 10 minutes before eating.

Nutrition:

Calories 77 | Total fat 1g | Saturated fat 1g | Total carbs 17g | Net carbs 15g Protein 3g | Sugars 6g | Fiber 2g | Sodium 14mg | Potassium 243mg

222. Mushrooms Stuffed with Crab Meat

Preparation Time: 20 minutes

Cooking Time: 30-45 minutes

Servings: 4-6

Recommended pellet: Optional

Ingredients:

- 6 medium-sized portobello mushrooms
- Extra virgin olive oil 1/3 Grated parmesan cheese cup

Club Beat Staffing:

- 8 oz fresh crab meat or canned or imitation crab meat
- 2 tablespoons extra virgin olive oil
- 1/3 Chopped celery; Chopped red peppers
- ½ cup chopped green onion
- ½ cup Italian breadcrumbs; ½Cup mayonnaise
- 8 oz cream cheese at room temperature
- 1/2 teaspoon of garlic; 1 tablespoon dried parsley
- Grated parmesan cheese cup
- 1 1 teaspoon of Old Bay seasoning
- ¼ teaspoon of kosher salt; ¼ teaspoon black pepper

Directions:

1. Clean the mushroom cap with a damp paper towel. Cut off the stem and save it.
2. Remove the brown gills from the bottom of the mushroom cap with a spoon and discard.
3. Prepare crab meat stuffing. If you are using canned crab meat, drain, rinse, and remove shellfish.

4. Heat the olive oil in a frying pan over medium high heat. Add celery, peppers and green onions and fry for 5 minutes. Set aside for cooling.

5. Gently pour the chilled sauteed vegetables and the remaining ingredients into a large bowl.

6. Cover and refrigerate crab meat stuffing until ready to use.

7. Put the crab mixture in each mushroom cap and make a mound in the center.

8. Sprinkle extra virgin olive oil and sprinkle parmesan cheese on each stuffed mushroom cap. Put the mushrooms in a 10 x 15-inch baking dish.

9. Use the pellets to set the wood pellet smoker grill to indirect heating and preheat to 375 ° F.

10. Bake for 30-45 minutes until the filling becomes hot (165 degrees Fahrenheit as measured by an instant-read digital thermometer) and the mushrooms begin to release juice.

Nutrition:

Calories 77 | Total fat 1g | Saturated fat 1g | Total carbs 17g | Net carbs 15g Protein 3g | Sugars 6g | Fiber 2g | Sodium 14mg | Potassium 243mg

223. Bacon Wrapped with Asparagus

Preparation Time: 15 minutes

Cooking Time: 25-30 minutes

Servings: 4-6

Recommended pellet: Optional

- 1-pound fresh thick asparagus (15-20 spears)
- Extra virgin olive oil; 5 sliced bacon
- 1 teaspoon of Western Love or salted pepper

Directions:

1. Cut off the wooden ends of the asparagus and make them all the same length.

2. Divide the asparagus into a bundle of three spears and split with olive oil. Wrap each bundle with a piece of bacon, then dust with seasonings or salt pepper for seasoning.

3. Set the wood pellet smoker grill for indirect cooking and place a Teflon coated fiberglass mat on the grate (to prevent asparagus from sticking to the grate grate). Preheat to 400 degrees Fahrenheit using all types of pellets. The grill can be preheated during asparagus Preparation Guide.

4. Bake the asparagus wrapped in bacon for 25-30 minutes until the asparagus is soft and the bacon is cooked and crispy.

Nutrition:

Calories 77 | Total fat 1g | Saturated fat 1g | Total carbs 17g | Net carbs 15g
Protein 3g | Sugars 6g | Fiber 2g | Sodium 14mg | Potassium 243mg

224. Bacon Cheddar Slider

Preparation Time: 30 minutes

Cooking Time: 15 minutes

Servings: 6-10 (1-2 sliders each as an appetizer)

Recommended pellet: Optional

Ingredients:

- 1-pound ground beef (80% lean)
- 1/2 teaspoon of garlic salt; 1/2 teaspoon salt
- 1/2 teaspoon of garlic; 1/2 teaspoon onion
- 1/2 teaspoon black pepper; 6 bacon slices, cut in half
- ½Cup mayonnaise; Sliced red onion; Ketchup
- 2 teaspoons of creamy wasabi (optional)
- 6 (1 oz) sliced sharp cheddar cheese, cut in half (optional)
- ½Cup sliced kosher dill pickles
- 12 mini breads sliced horizontally

Directions:

1. Place ground beef, garlic salt, seasoned salt, garlic powder, onion powder and black hupe pepper in a medium bowl.

2. Divide the meat mixture into 12 equal parts, shape into small thin round patties (about 2 ounces each) and save.

3. Cook the bacon on medium heat over medium heat for 5-8 minutes until crunchy. Set aside.

4. To make the sauce, mix the mayonnaise and horseradish in a small bowl, if used.

5. Set up a wood pellet smoker grill for direct cooking to use griddle accessories. Contact the manufacturer to see if there is a griddle accessory that works with the wooden pellet smoker grill.

6. Spray a cooking spray on the griddle cooking surface for best non-stick results.

7. Preheat wood pellet smoker grill to 350 ° F using selected pellets. Griddle surface should be approximately 400 ° F.

8. Grill the putty for 3-4 minutes each until the internal temperature reaches 160 ° F.

9. If necessary, place a sharp cheddar cheese slice on each patty while the patty is on the griddle or after the patty is removed from the griddle. Place a small amount of mayonnaise mixture, a slice of red onion, and a hamburger pate in the lower half of each roll. Pickled slices, bacon, and ketchup.

Nutrition:

Calories 77 | Total fat 1g | Saturated fat 1g | Total carbs 17g | Net carbs 15g Protein 3g | Sugars 6g | Fiber 2g | Sodium 14mg | Potassium 243mg

225. Garlic Parmesan Wedge

Preparation Time: 15 minutes

Cooking Time: 30-35 minutes

Servings: 3

Recommended pellet: Optional

- 3 large russet potatoes
- ¼ cup of extra virgin olive oil
- 1 tsp salt
- ¾ teaspoon black hu pepper
- 2 tsp garlic powder
- ¾ cup grated parmesan cheese
- 3 tablespoons of fresh coriander or flat leaf parsley (optional)
- ½ cup blue cheese or ranch dressing per serving, for soaking (optional)

Directions:

1. Gently rub the potatoes with cold water using a vegetable brush to dry the potatoes.

2. Cut the potatoes in half vertically and cut them in half.

3. Wipe off any water released when cutting potatoes with a paper towel. Moisture prevents wedges from becoming crunchy.

4. Put the potato wedge, olive oil, salt, pepper, and garlic powder in a large bowl and shake lightly by hand to distribute the oil and spices evenly.

5. Place the wedges on a single layer of non-stick grill tray / pan / basket (about 15 x 12 inches).

6. Set the wood pellet r grill for indirect cooking and use all types of wood pellets to preheat to 425 degrees Fahrenheit.

7. Put the grill tray in the preheated smoker grill, roast the potato wedge for 15 minutes, and turn. Roast the potato wedge for an additional 15-20 minutes until the potatoes are soft inside and crispy golden on the outside.

8. Sprinkle potato wedge with parmesan cheese and add coriander or parsley as needed. If necessary, add blue cheese or ranch dressing for the dip.

Nutrition:

Calories 87 | Total fat 1g | Saturated fat 2g | Total carbs 27g | Net carbs 15g Protein 3g | Sugars 6g | Fiber 2g | Sodium 14mg | Potassium 143mg

226. Roasted Vegetables

Preparation Time: 20 Minutes

Cooking Time: 20 to 40 Minutes

Servings: 4

Ingredients:

- 1 cup cauliflower floret
- 1 cup small mushroom, half
- One medium zucchini, sliced in half
- One medium yellow squash, sliced in half
- One medium-sized red pepper, chopped to 1.5-2 inches One small red onion, chopped to 1½-2 inch
- ounces small baby carrot
- Six mid-stem asparagus spears, cut into 1-inch pieces
- 1 cup cherry or grape tomato
- ¼ Extra virgin olive oil with cup roasted garlic flavor
- 2 tbsp. of balsamic vinegar
- Three garlic, chopped; 1 tsp. dry time
- 1 tsp. dried oregano
- One teaspoon of garlic salt
- ½ teaspoon black pepper

Directions:

1. Put cauliflower florets, mushrooms, zucchini, yellow pumpkin, red peppers, red onions, carrots, asparagus, and tomatoes in a large bowl.
2. Add olive oil, balsamic vinegar, garlic, thyme, oregano, garlic salt, and black hu to add to the vegetables.

3. Gently throw the vegetables by hand until completely covered with olive oil, herbs, and spices.

4. Spread the seasoned vegetables evenly on a non-stick grill tray/bread/basket (about 15 x 12 inches).

5. Set the wood pellet smoker and grill for indirect cooking and preheat to 425 degrees Fahrenheit using all wood pellets.

6. Transfer the grill tray to a preheated smoker and grill and roast the vegetables for 20-40 minutes or until the vegetables are perfectly cooked. Please put it out immediately.

Nutrition:

Calories: 114 | Carbs: 17g

Fat: 4g | Protein: 3g

227. Grilled Mushroom Skewers

Preparation Time: 5 Minutes

Cooking Time: 60 Minutes

Servings: 6

Ingredients:

- 16 - oz 1 lb. Baby Portobello Mushrooms

For the marinade:

- ¼ - cup olive oil ; ¼ - cup lemon juice
- Small handful of parsley; 1 - tsp sugar
- 1 - tsp salt; ¼ - tsp pepper
- ¼ - tsp cayenne pepper
- 1 to 2 - garlic cloves
- 1 - Tbsp balsamic vinegar

What you will need:

- 10 - inch bamboo/wood skewers

Directions:

1. Add the beans to the plate of a lipped container, in an even layer. Shower the softened spread uniformly out ludicrous, and utilizing a couple of tongs tenderly hurl the beans with the margarine until all around covered.

2. Season the beans uniformly, and generously, with salt and pepper.

3. Preheat the smoker to 275 degrees. Include the beans, and smoke 3-4 hours, hurling them like clockwork or until delicate wilted, and marginally seared in spots.

4. Spot 10 medium sticks into a heating dish and spread with water. It's critical to douse the sticks for in any event 15 minutes (more is better) or they will consume too rapidly on the flame broil.

5. Spot the majority of the marinade fixings in a nourishment processor and heartbeat a few times until marinade is almost smooth.

6. Flush your mushrooms and pat dry. Cut each mushroom down the middle, so each piece has half of the mushroom stem.

7. Spot the mushroom parts into an enormous gallon-size Ziploc sack, or a medium bowl and pour in the marinade. Shake the pack until the majority of the mushrooms are equally covered in marinade. Refrigerate and marinate for 30mins to 45mins.

8. Preheat your barbecue about 300F

9. Stick the mushrooms cozily onto the bamboo/wooden sticks that have been dousing (no compelling reason to dry the sticks). Piercing the mushrooms was a bit of irritating from the outset until I got the hang of things.

10. I've discovered that it's least demanding to stick them by bending them onto the stick. In the event that you simply drive the stick through, it might make the mushroom break.

11. Spot the pierced mushrooms on the hot barbecue for around 3mins for every side, causing sure the mushrooms don't consume to the flame broil. The mushrooms are done when they are delicate; as mushrooms ought to be Remove from the barbecue. Spread with foil to keep them warm until prepared to serve

Nutrition:

Calories: 230 | Carbs: 10g

Fat: 20g | Protein: 5g

228. Caprese Tomato Salad

Preparation Time: 5 Minutes

Cooking Time: 60 Minutes

Servings: 4

Ingredients:

- 3 - cups halved multicolored cherry tomatoes
- 1/8 - teaspoon kosher salt
- ½ - cup fresh basil leaves
- 1 - tablespoon extra-virgin olive oil
- 1 - tablespoon balsamic vinegar
- ½ - teaspoon black pepper
- ¼ - teaspoon kosher salt
- 1 - ounce diced fresh mozzarella cheese (about 1/3 cup)

Directions:

1. Join tomatoes and 1/8 tsp. legitimate salt in an enormous bowl. Let represent 5mins. Include basil leaves, olive oil, balsamic vinegar, pepper, 1/4 tsp. fit salt, and mozzarella; toss.

Nutrition:

Calories 80 | Fat 5.8g

Protein 2g | Carb 5g | Sugars 4g

229. Watermelon-Cucumber Salad

Preparation Time: 12 Minutes

Cooking Time: 0 Minutes

Servings: 4

Ingredients:

- 1 - tablespoon olive oil
- 2 - teaspoons fresh lemon juice
- ¼ - teaspoon salt
- 2 - cups cubed seedless watermelon
- 1 - cup thinly sliced English cucumber
- ¼ - cup thinly vertically sliced red onion
- 1 - tablespoon thinly sliced fresh basil

Directions:

1. Consolidate oil, squeeze, and salt in a huge bowl, mixing great. Include watermelon, cucumber, and onion; toss well to coat. Sprinkle plate of mixed greens equally with basil.

Nutrition:

Calories 60 | Fat 3.5g

Protein 0.8g | Carb 7.6g

230. Fresh Creamed Corn

Preparation Time: 5 Minutes

Cooking Time: 30 Minutes

Servings: 4

Ingredients:

- 2 - teaspoons unsalted butter
- 2 - cups fresh corn kernels
- 2 - tablespoons minced shallots
- ¾ - cup 1% low-fat milk
- 2 - teaspoons all-purpose flour
- ¼ - teaspoon salt

Directions:

1. Melt butter in a huge nonstick skillet over medium-excessive warmness.

2. Add corn and minced shallots to pan; prepare dinner 1 minute, stirring constantly.

3. Add milk, flour, and salt to pan; bring to a boil.

4. Reduce warmness to low; cover and cook dinner 4 minutes.

Nutrition:

Calories 107 | Fat 3.4g

Protein 4g | Carb 18g

231. Spinach Salad with Avocado and Orange

Preparation Time: 5 Minutes

Cooking Time: 20 Minutes

Servings: 4

Ingredients:

- 1 ½ - tablespoons fresh lime juice
- 4 - teaspoons extra-virgin olive oil
- 1 - tablespoon chopped fresh cilantro
- 1/8 - teaspoon kosher salt
- ½ - cup diced peeled ripe avocado
- ½ - cup fresh orange segments
- 1 - (5-ounce) package baby spinach
- 1/8 - teaspoon freshly ground black pepper

Directions:

1. Combine first 4 substances in a bowl, stirring with a whisk.
2. Combine avocado, orange segments, and spinach in a bowl. Add oil combination; toss. Sprinkle salad with black pepper.

Nutrition:

Calories 103 |Fat 7.3g | Sodium 118mg

232. Raspberry and Blue Cheese Salad

Preparation Time: 5 Minutes

Cooking Time: 20 Minutes

Servings: 4

Ingredients:

- 1 ½ - tablespoons olive oil
- 1 ½ - teaspoons red wine vinegar
- ¼ - teaspoon Dijon mustard
- 1/8 - teaspoon salt
- 1/8 - teaspoon pepper
- 5 - cups mixed baby greens
- ½ - cup raspberries
- ¼ - cup chopped toasted pecans
- 1 - ounce blue cheese

Directions:

1. Join olive oil, vinegar, Dijon mustard, salt, and pepper.
2. Include blended infant greens; too.
3. Top with raspberries, walnuts, and blue cheddar.

Nutrition:

Calories 133 | Fat 12.2g | Sodium 193mg

233. Crunchy Zucchini Chips

Preparation Time: 15 Minutes

Cooking Time: 25 Minutes

Servings: 4

Ingredients:

- 1/3 - cup whole-wheat panko
- 3 - tablespoons uncooked amaranth
- ½ - teaspoon garlic powder
- ¼ - teaspoon kosher salt
- ¼ - teaspoon freshly ground black pepper
- 1 - ounce Parmesan cheese, finely grated
- 12 - ounces zucchini, cut into
- ¼ - inch-thick slices
- 1 - tablespoon olive oil Cooking spray

Directions:

1. Preheat stove to 425°. Join the initial 6 ingre-dients in a shallow dish. Join zucchini and oil in an enormous bowl; toss well to coat. Dig zucchini in panko blend, squeezing tenderly to follow. Spot covered cuts on an ovenproof wire rack covered with cooking shower; place the rack on a preparing sheet or jam move dish.

2. Heat at 425° for 26 minutes or until cooked and fresh. Serve chips right away.

Nutrition:

Calories 132 | |Protein 6g

Fat 6.5g | Carb 14g | Sugars 2g

234. Grilled Green Onions and Orzo and Sweet Peas

Preparation Time: 5 Minutes

Cooking Time: 15 Minutes

Servings: 4

Ingredients:

- ¾ - cup whole-wheat orzo
- 1 - cup frozen peas
- 1 - bunch green onions, trimmed
- 1 - teaspoon olive oil
- ½ - teaspoon grated lemon rind
- 1 - tablespoon lemon juice
- 1 - teaspoon olive oil
- ¼ - teaspoon salt
- 1 - ounce shaved Montego cheese

Directions:

1. Plan orzo as indicated by way of headings, discarding salt and fat. Include peas throughout most recent 2mins of cooking; channel.

2. Warm a fish fry skillet over high warmness. Toss inexperienced onions with 1 teaspoon olive oil. Cook 2 minutes on each facet. Cleave onions; upload to orzo. Include lemon skin, lemon juice, 1 teaspoon olive oil, and salt; toss. Sprinkle with shaved Manchego cheddar.

Nutrition:

Calories 197 | Fat 5.6g | Sodium 204mg

235. Tequila Slaw with Lime and Cilantro

Preparation Time: 5 Minutes

Cooking Time: 5 Minutes

Servings: 6

Ingredients:

- ¼ - cup canola mayonnaise (such as Hellmann's)
- 3 - tablespoons fresh lime juice
- 1 - tablespoon silver tequila
- 2 - teaspoons sugar
- ¼ - teaspoon kosher salt
- 1/3 - cup thinly sliced green onions
- ¼- cup chopped fresh cilantro
- 1 - (14-ounce) package coleslaw

Directions:

1. Add the first 5 ingredients in a big bowl. Add remaining ingredients; toss.

Nutrition:

Calories 64 | Fat 3g

Protein 0.8g | Carb 6.4g

236. Cranberry-Almond Broccoli Salad

Preparation Time: 10 Minutes

Cooking Time: 60 Minutes

Servings: 8

Ingredients:

- ¼ - cup finely chopped red onion
- 1/3 - cup canola mayonnaise
- 3 - tablespoons 2% reduced-fat Greek yogurt
- 1 - tablespoon cider vinegar
- 1 - tablespoon honey
- ¼ - teaspoon salt
- ¼ - teaspoon freshly ground black pepper
- 4 - cups coarsely chopped broccoli florets
- 1/3 - cup slivered almonds, toasted
- 1/3 - cup reduced-sugar dried cranberries
- 4 - center-cut bacon slices, cooked and crumbled

Directions:

1. Absorb red onion cold water for 5 minutes; channel.
2. Consolidate mayonnaise and then 5 fixings (through pepper), blending admirably with a whisk. Mix in red onion, broccoli, and remaining fixings. Spread and chill 1 hour before serving.

Nutrition:

Calories 104 | Fat 5.9g

Carb 11g | Sugars 5g

237. Onion Bacon Ring

Preparation Time: 10 Minutes

Cooking Time: 1 Hour and 30 Minutes

Servings: 6 to 8

Ingredients:

- 2 large Onions, cut into ½ inch slices
- 1 Package of Bacon
- 1 tsp. of Honey
- 1 tbsp. Mustard, yellow
- 1 tbsp. Garlic chili sauce

Direction:

1. Wrap Bacon around onion rings. Wrap until you out of bacon. Place on skewers.
2. Preheat the grill to 400F with closed lid.
3. In the meantime, on a bowl combine the mustard and garlic chili sauce. Add honey and stir well.
4. Grill the onion bacon rings for 1 h and 30 minutes. Flip once.
5. Serve with the sauce and enjoy!

Nutrition:

Calories: 90 | Protein: 2g

Carbs: 9g | Fat: 7g

238. Grilled Watermelon juice

Preparation Time: 10 Minutes

Cooking Time: 15 Minutes

Servings: 4

Ingredients:

- 2 Limes
- 2 tbsp. oil
- ½ Watermelon, sliced into wedges
- ¼ Tsp. Pepper flakes
- 2 tbsp. Salt

Directions:

1. Preheat the grill to high with closed lid.
2. Brush the watermelon with oil. Grill for 15 minutes. Flip once.
3. In a blender mix the salt and pepper flakes until combined.
4. Transfer the watermelon on a plate.
5. Serve and enjoy!

Nutrition:

Calories: 40 | Protein: 1g

Carbs: 10g | Fat: 0

239. Smoked Popcorn with Parmesan Herb

Preparation Time: 10 Minutes

Cooking Time: 10 Minutes

Servings: 2 to 4

Ingredients:

- ¼ cup of Popcorn Kernels
- 1 tsp. of salt
- 1 tsp. of Garlic powder
- ½ cup grated Parmesan
- 2 tsp. of Italian seasoning
- 2 tbsp. oil
- 4 tbsp. of Butter

Directions:

1. Preheat the grill to 250F with closed lid.
2. In a saucepan add the butter and oil. Melt and add the salt, garlic powder, and Italian seasoning.
3. Add the kernels in a paper bag. Fold it two times to close.
4. Place in the microwave. Turn on high heat and set 2 minutes.
5. Open and transfer into a bowl.
6. Pour the butter. Toss. Transfer on a baking tray and grill for about 10 minutes.
7. Serve and enjoy!

Nutrition:

Calories: 60 | Protein: 1g

Carbs: 5g | Fat: 3g

240. Smoked Mushrooms 1

Preparation Time: 5 Minutes

Cooking Time: 45 Minutes

Servings: 4 to 6

Ingredients:

- 4 cups Mushrooms (whole) baby Portobello, cleaned
- 1 tsp. of Onion powder
- 1 tbsp. of Canola Oil
- 1 tsp. garlic, granulated
- 1 tsp. of Pepper
- 1 tsp. of Salt

Directions:

1. Add the ingredients in a bowl.
2. Preheat the grill to smoke with closed lid.
3. Smoke the mushrooms for about 30 minutes.
4. Serve and enjoy!

Nutrition:

Calories: 55 | Protein: 2.5g

Carbs: 3g | Fat: 3.5g

CHAPTER 12:
Dessert Recipe

241. Pellet Grill Chocolate Chip Cookies

Preparation Time: 20 Minutes

Cooking Time: 45 Minutes

Servings: 12

Ingredients:

- 1cup salted butter softened
- 1cup of sugar
- 1cup light brown sugar
- 2tsp vanilla extract
- 2large eggs
- 3cups all-purpose flour
- 1tsp baking soda
- 1/2 tsp baking powder
- 1tsp natural sea salt
- 2cups semi-sweet chocolate chips or chunks

Directions:

1. Preheat pellet grill to 375°F.

2. Line a large baking sheet with parchment paper and set aside.

3. In a medium bowl, mix flour, baking soda, salt, and baking powder. Once combined, set aside.

4. In stand mixer bowl, combine butter, white sugar, and brown sugar until combined. Beat in eggs and vanilla. Beat until fluffy.

5. Mix in dry ingredients, continue to stir until combined.

6. Add chocolate chips and mix thoroughly.

7. Roll 3 tbsp of dough at a time into balls and place them on your cookie sheet. Evenly space them apart, with about 2-3 inches in between each ball.

8. Place cookie sheet directly on the grill grate and bake for 20-25 minutes until the cookies' outside is slightly browned.

9. Remove from grill and allow to rest for 10 minutes. Serve and enjoy!

Nutrition:

*   Calories: 120
*   Fat: 4
*   Cholesterol: 7.8 mg
*   Carbohydrate: 22.8 g
*   Fiber: 0.3 g
*   Sugar: 14.4 g
*   Protein: 1.4 g

242. Delicious Donuts on a Grill

Preparation Time: 5 Minutes

Cooking Time: 10 Minutes

Servings: 6

Ingredients:

- 1-1/2 cups sugar, powdered; 1/3 cup whole milk
- 1/2 teaspoon vanilla extract; 16 ounces of biscuit dough, prepared
- Oil spray, for greasing; 1cup chocolate sprinkles, for sprinkling

Directions:

1. Take a medium bowl and mix sugar, milk, and vanilla extract.
2. Combine well to create a glaze. Set the glaze aside for further use.
3. Place the dough onto the flat, clean surface.
4. Flat the dough with a rolling pin. Use a ring mold, about an inch, and cut the hole in each round dough's center.
5. Place the dough on a plate and refrigerate for 10 minutes.
6. Open the grill and install the grill grate inside it. Close the hood.
7. Now, select the grill from the menu, and set the temperature to medium. Set the time to 6 minutes. Select start and begin preheating.
8. Remove the dough from the refrigerator and coat it with cooking spray from both sides.
9. When the unit beeps, the grill is preheated; place the adjustable amount of dough on the grill grate.
10. Close the hood, and cook for 3 minutes. Remove donuts and place the remaining dough inside. Cook for 3 minutes.
11. Once all the donuts are ready, sprinkle chocolate sprinkles on top.

Nutrition: Calories: 400 | Fat: 11g | Cholesterol: 1mg | Sodium: 787mg
Total Carbohydrate: 71.3g | Fiber 0.9g | Total Sugars: 45.3g | Protein: 5.7g

243. Smoked Pumpkin Pie

Preparation Time: 10 Minutes

Cooking Time: 50 Minutes

Servings: 8

Ingredients:

- 1tbsp cinnamon; 15oz can pumpkin
- 1-1/2 tbsp pumpkin pie spice
- 14oz can sweetened condensed milk
- 2beaten eggs; 1unbaked pie shell
- Topping: whipped cream

Directions:

1. Preheat your smoker to 325 F.
2. Place a baking sheet, rimmed, on the smoker upside down, or use a cake pan.
3. Combine all your ingredients in a bowl, large, except the pie shell, then pour the mixture into a pie crust.
4. Place the pie on the baking sheet and smoke for about 50-60 minutes until a knife comes out clean when inserted. Make sure the center is set.
5. Remove and cool for about 2 hours or refrigerate overnight.
6. Serve with a whipped cream dollop and enjoy it!

Nutrition:

Calories: 292 | Total Fat: 11g | Fiber: 5g

Total Carbs: 42g | Protein: 7g

Sugars: 29g | Sodium: 168mg

244. Wood Pellet Smoked Nut Mix

Preparation Time: 15 Minutes

Cooking Time: 20 Minutes

Servings: 12

Ingredients:

- 3cups mixed nuts (pecans, peanuts, almonds, etc.)
- 1/2 tbsp brown sugar
- 1tbsp thyme, dried
- 1/4 tbsp mustard powder
- 1tbsp olive oil, extra-virgin

Directions:

1. Preheat your pellet grill to 250 F with the lid closed for about 15 minutes.

2. Combine all ingredients in a bowl, large, then transfer into a cookie sheet lined with parchment paper.

3. Place the cookie sheet on a grill and grill for about 20 minutes.

4. Remove the nuts from the grill and let cool.

5. Serve and enjoy.

Nutrition:

Calories: 249 | Total Fat: 21.5g | Saturated Fat: 3.5g

Total Carbs: 12.3g | Net Carbs: 10.1g | Protein: 5.7g

Sugars: 5.6g | Fiber: 2.1g | Sodium: 111mg

245. Grilled Peaches and Cream

Preparation Time: 15 Minutes

Cooking Time: 8 Minutes

Servings: 8

Ingredients:

- 4halved and pitted peaches
- 1tbsp vegetable oil
- 2tbsp clover honey
- 1cup cream cheese, soft with honey and nuts

Directions:

1. Preheat your pellet grill to medium-high heat.
2. Coat the peaches lightly with oil and place on the grill pit side down.
3. Grill for about 5 minutes until nice grill marks on the surfaces.
4. Turn over the peaches, then drizzle with honey.
5. Spread and cream cheese dollop where the pit was and grill for additional 2-3 minutes until the filling becomes warm.
6. Serve immediately.

Nutrition:

Calories: 139 | Total Fat: 10.2g

Total Carbs: 11.6g | Protein: 1.1g

Sugars: 12g | Sodium: 135mg

246. Berry Cobbler on a Pellet Grill

Preparation Time: 15 Minutes

Cooking Time: 35 Minutes

Servings: 8

Ingredients:

For fruit filling

- 3cups frozen mixed berries
- 1 lemon juice
- 1cup brown sugar
- 1tbsp vanilla extract
- 1bsp lemon zest, finely grated
- A pinch of salt

For cobbler topping

- 1-1/2 cups all-purpose flour
- 1-1/2 tbsp baking powder
- 3tbsp sugar, granulated
- 1/2 tbsp salt
- 8tbsp cold butter
- 1/2 cup sour cream
- 2tbsp raw sugar

Directions:

1. Set your pellet grill on "smoke" for about 4-5 minutes with the lid open until fire establishes, and your grill starts smoking.

2. Preheat your grill to 350 F for about 10-15 minutes with the grill lid closed.

3. Meanwhile, combine frozen mixed berries, Lemon juice, brown sugar, vanilla, lemon zest, and salt pinch. Transfer into a skillet and let the fruit sit and thaw.

4. Mix flour, baking powder, sugar, and salt in a bowl, medium. Cut cold butter into peas sizes using a pastry blender, then add to the mixture. Stir to mix everything.

5. Stir in sour cream until dough starts coming together.

6. Pinch small pieces of dough and place over the fruit until fully covered. Splash the top with raw sugar.

7. Now place the skillet directly on the grill grate, close the lid, cook for about 35 minutes until juices bubble, and a golden-brown dough topping.

8. Remove the skillet from the pellet grill and cool for several minutes.

9. Scoop and serve warm.

Nutrition:

Calories: 371 | Total Fat: 13g

Total Carbs: 60g | Protein: 3g

Sugars: 39g | Fiber: 2g | Sodium: 269mg

247. Pellet Grill Apple Crisp

Preparation Time: 20 Minutes

Cooking Time: 60 Minutes

Servings: 15

Ingredients:

- Apples; Ten large apples
- 1/2 cup flour; 1cup sugar, dark brown
- 1/2 tbsp cinnamon; 1/2 cup butter slices
- Crisp; 3cups oatmeal, old-fashioned
- 1-1/2 cups softened butter, salted
- 1-1/2 tbsp cinnamon; 2cups brown sugar

Directions:

1. Preheat your grill to 350 F.
2. Wash, peel, core, and dice the apples into cubes, medium-size
3. Mix flour, dark brown sugar, and cinnamon, then toss with your apple cubes.
4. Spray a baking pan, 10x13", with cooking spray, then place apples inside. Top with butter slices.
5. Mix all crisp ingredients in a medium bowl until well combined. Place the mixture over the apples.
6. Place on the grill and cook for about 1-hour checking after every 15-20 minutes to ensure cooking is even. Do not place it on the hottest grill part. Remove and let sit for about 20-25 minutes. It's very warm.

Nutrition:

Calories: 528 | Total Fat: 26g

Total Carbs: 75g | Protein: 4g

Sugars: 51g | Fiber: 5g | Sodium: 209mg

248. Fromage Macaroni and Cheese

Preparation Time: 30 Minutes

Cooking Time: 1 Hour

Servings: 8

Ingredients:

- ¼ c. all-purpose flour; ½ stick butter
- Butter, for greasing; One-pound cooked elbow macaroni
- One c. grated Parmesan; 8 ounces cream cheese
- Two c. shredded Monterey Jack; 3 t. garlic powder
- Two t. salt; One t. pepper; Three c. milk
- Two c. shredded Cheddar, divided

Directions:

1. Add the butter to a pot and melt. Mix in the flour. Stir constantly for a minute. Mix in the pepper, salt, garlic powder, and milk. Let it boil.

2. After lowering the heat, let it simmer for about 5 mins, or until it has thickened. Remove from the heat.

3. Mix in the cream cheese, parmesan, Monterey Jack, and 1 ½ c. of cheddar. Stir everything until melted. Fold in the pasta.

4. Add wood pellets to your smoker and keep your cooker's startup procedure. Preheat your smoker, with your lid closed, until it reaches 225.

5. Butter a 9" x 13" baking pan. Pour the macaroni mixture into the pan and lay on the grill. Cover and allow it to smoke for an hour, or until it has become bubbly. Top the macaroni with the rest of the cheddar during the last. Serve.

Nutrition:

Calories: 180 | Carbs: 19g | Fat: 8g | Protein: 8g

249. Spicy Barbecue Pecans

Preparation Time: 15 Minutes

Cooking Time: 1 Hour

Servings: 2

Ingredients:

- 2 ½ t. garlic powder
- 16 ounces raw pecan halves
- One t. onion powder
- One t. pepper; Two t. salt
- One t. dried thyme
- Butter, for greasing
- 3 T. melted butter

Directions:

1. Add wood pellets to your smoker and follow your cooker's startup method.
2. Preheat your smoker, with your lid closed, until it reaches 225.
3. Cover and smoke for an hour, flipping the nuts one. Make sure the nuts are toasted and heated. They should be removed from the grill.
4. Set aside to cool and dry.

Nutrition:

- Calories: 150
- Carbs: 16g
- Fat: 9g
- Protein: 1g

250. Traeger Blackberry Pie

Preparation Time: 10 Minutes

Cooking Time: 40 Minutes

Servings: 8

Ingredients:

- Butter, for greasing
- ½ c. all-purpose flour
- ½ c. milk
- Two pints blackberries
- Two c. sugar, divided
- One box of refrigerated piecrusts
- One stick melted butter
- One stick of butter
- Vanilla ice cream

Directions:

1. Add wood pellets to your smoker and follow your cooker's startup method.
2. Preheat your smoker, with your lid closed, until it reaches 375.
3. Unroll the second pie crust and lay it over the skillet.
4. Lower the lid, then smoke for 15 to 20 minutes or until it is browned and bubbly.
5. Serve the hot pie with some vanilla ice cream.

Nutrition:

Calories: 100 | Carbs: 10g

Fat: 0g | Protein: 15g

251. S'mores Dip

Preparation Time: 0 Minutes

Cooking Time: 15 Minutes

Servings: 6-8

Ingredients:

- 12 ounces semisweet chocolate chips
- ¼ c. milk
- Two T. melted salted butter
- 16 ounces marshmallows
- Apple wedges
- Graham crackers

Directions:

1. Add wood pellets to your smoker and get your cooker's startup procedure. Preheat your smoker, with your lid closed, until it reaches 450.

2. Put a cast-iron skillet on your grill and add in the milk and melted butter. Stir together for a minute.

3. Cover, and let it smoke for five to seven minutes. The marshmallows should be toasted lightly.

4. Take the skillet off the heat and serve with apple wedges and graham crackers.

Nutrition:

Calories: 90 | Carbs: 15g

Fat: 3g | Protein: 1g

252. Bacon Chocolate Chip Cookies

Preparation Time: 10 Minutes

Cooking Time: 30 Minutes

Servings: 24

Ingredients:

- Eight slices of cooked and crumbled bacon
- 2 ½ t. apple cider vinegar; One t. vanilla
- Two c. semisweet chocolate chips
- Two-room temp eggs; ½ t. baking soda
- One c. granulated sugar; ½ t. salt
- Two ¾ c. all-purpose flour
- One c. light brown sugar
- 1 ½ stick softened butter

Directions:

1. Mix the flour, baking soda, and salt. Cream the sugar and the butter together. Then lower the speed. Add in the eggs, vinegar, and vanilla.

2. Still on low, slowly add in the flour mixture, bacon pieces, and chocolate chips.

3. Add wood pellets to your smoker and follow your cooker's startup method. Preheat your smoker, with your lid closed, until it reaches 375.

4. Place some parchment on a baking sheet and drop a teaspoonful of cookie batter on the baking sheet. Let them cook on the grill,

5. Covered, for approximately 12 minutes or until they are browned.

Nutrition:

Calories: 167 | Carbs: 21g

Fat: 9g | Protein: 2g

253. Cinnamon Sugar Pumpkin Seeds

Preparation Time: 12 Minutes

Cooking Time: 30 Minutes

Servings: 8-12

Ingredients:

- Two T. sugar
- seeds from a pumpkin
- One t. cinnamon
- Two T. melted butter

Directions:

1. Add wood pellets to your smoker and follow your cooker's startup operation. Preheat your smoker, with your lid closed, until it reaches 350.

2. Clean the seeds and toss them in the melted butter. Add them to the sugar and cinnamon. Spread them out on a baking sheet, place on the grill, and smoke for 25 minutes.

3. Serve.

Nutrition:

Calories: 160 | Carbs: 5g

Fat: 12g | Protein: 7g

254. Apple Cobbler

Preparation Time: 20 Minutes
Cooking Time: 1 Hour and 30 Minutes
Servings: 8
Ingredients:

- 8 Granny Smith apples
- One c. sugar
- Two eggs
- Two t. baking powder
- Two c. plain flour
- 1 ½ c. sugar

Directions:

1. Peel and quarter apples, place into a bowl. Add in the cinnamon and one c. sugar. Stir well to coat and let it sit for one hour.

2. Add wood pellets to your smoker and follow your cooker's startup form. Preheat your smoker, with your lid closed, until it reaches 350.

3. Place apples into a Dutch oven. Add the crumble mixture on top and drizzle with melted butter.

4. Place on the grill and cook for 50 minutes.

Nutrition:

Calories: 152 | Carbs: 26g

Fat: 5g | Protein: 1g

255. Pineapple Cake

Preparation Time: 20 Minutes

Cooking Time: 60 Minutes

Servings: 8

Ingredients:

- One c. sugar; One T. baking powder
- One c. buttermilk; Two eggs
- ½ t. salt; ¾ c. brown sugar
- One jar maraschino cherry
- One stick butter, divided
- One can pineapple slice; ½ c. flour

Directions:

1. Add wood pellets to your smoker and observe your cooker's startup procedure. Preheat your smoker, with your lid closed, until it reaches 350.

2. Take a medium-sized cast-iron skillet and melt one half stick butter. Be sure to coat the entire skillet. Sprinkle brown sugar into a cast-iron skillet.

3. Lay the sliced pineapple on top of the brown sugar. Place a cherry into the middle of each pineapple ring.

4. Mix the salt, baking powder, flour, and sugar. Add in the eggs; one-half stick melted butter and buttermilk. Whisk to combine.

5. Put the cake on the grill and cook for an hour.

6. Take off from the grill and let it sit for ten minutes. Flip onto a serving platter.

Nutrition:

Calories: 165 | Carbs: 40g | Fat: 0g | Protein: 1g

256. Ice Cream Bread

Preparation Time: 10 Minutes

Cooking Time: 1 Hour

Servings: 12-16

Ingredients:

- 1 ½ quart full-fat butter pecan ice cream, softened
- One t. salt
- Two c. semisweet chocolate chips
- One c. sugar
- One stick melted butter
- Butter, for greasing
- 4 c. self-rising flour

Directions:

1. Add wood pellets to your smoker and follow your cooker's startup program. Preheat your smoker, with your lid closed, until it reaches 350.

2. Set the cake on the grill, cover, and smoke for 50 minutes to an hour. A toothpick should come out clean.

3. Take the pan off of the grill. For 10 mins., cool the bread.

Nutrition:

Calories: 135 | Carbs: 0g

Fat: 0g | Protein: 0g

257. Mediterranean Meatballs

Preparation Time: 15 Minutes

Cooking Time: 35 Minutes

Servings: 8

Ingredients:

- Pepper; Salt; One t. vinegar
- Two T. olive oil; Two eggs
- One chopped onion
- One soaked slice of bread
- ½ t. cumin; One T. chopped basil
- 1 ½ T. chopped parsley
- 2 ½ pounds ground beef

Directions:

1. Use your hands to combine everything until thoroughly combined. If needed, when forming meatballs, dip your hands into some water. Shape into 12 meatballs.

2. Add wood pellets to your smoker.

3. Preheat your smoker, with your lid closed, until it reaches 380.

4. Place the meatballs onto the grill and cook on all sides for eight minutes. Take off the grill and let sit for five minutes.

5. Serve with favorite condiments or a salad.

Nutrition:

Calories: 33 | Carbs: 6g

Fat: 0g | Protein: 1g

258. Greek Meatballs

Preparation Time: 10 Minutes

Cooking Time: 40 Minutes

Servings: 6

Ingredients:

- Pepper; Salt; Two eggs
- Two chopped green onions
- One T. almond flour
- ½ pound ground pork
- 2 ½ pound ground beef

Directions:

1. Mix all the ingredients using your hands until everything is incorporated evenly. Form mixture into meatballs until all meat is used.

2. Add wood pellets to your smoker and follow your cooker's startup procedure. Preheat your smoker, with your lid closed, until it reaches 380.

3. Brush the meatballs with olive oil and place onto the grill—Cook for ten minutes on all sides.

Nutrition:

Calories: 161 | Carbs: 10g

Fat: 6g | Protein: 17g

259. Banana Boats

Preparation Time: 30 minutes

Cooking time: 10 minutes

Servings: 4

Ingredients:

- Four green bananas
- Chocolate chips
- Miniature marshmallows
- Peanut butter chips
- Crushed cookies

Directions:

1. Split a banana lengthwise from end to end, leaving the peel intact on the opposite side.
2. Top with desired toppings.
3. Wrap the banana in heavy-duty aluminum foil.
4. Grilling:
5. Place the bananas on a 400F grill and close the dome for 10 minutes.
6. Unwrap and serve topped with vanilla ice cream, whipped cream, or by them.

Nutrition:

Calories: 310 | Fat: 17 g

Carbohydrates: 40 g | Protein: 4 g

260. Grilled Pineapple Sundaes

Preparation Time: 30 minutes

Cooking time: 5 minutes

Servings: 4

Ingredients:

- 4 fresh pineapple spears
- Vanilla Ice Cream
- Jarred Caramel Sauce
- Toasted Coconut

Directions:

1. Place pineapple spears on a 400F grill and close the dome for 2 minutes.
2. Turn the pineapple and close the dome for another 2 minutes.
3. Turn the pineapple once more and close the dome for another minute.
4. Serve pineapple topped with ice cream, caramel sauce, and toasted coconut.

Nutrition:

Calories: 112 | Fat: 1 g

Carbohydrates: 29 g | Protein: 0.4g

261. Blueberry Cobbler

Preparation time: 15 minutes

Cooking time: 30 minutes

Servings: 6

Ingredients:

- 4 cups fresh blueberries; 1 tsp. grated lemon zest
- 1 cup sugar, plus 2 tbsp; 1 cup all-purpose flour, plus 2 tbsp.
- Juice of 1 lemon; 2 tsp. baking powder
- ¼ teaspoon salt; Six tablespoons unsalted butter
- ¾ cup whole milk; 1/8 teaspoon ground cinnamon

Directions:

1. In a prepared medium bowl, combine the blueberries, lemon zest, two tablespoons of sugar, two tablespoons of flour, and lemon juice.

2. In a prepared medium bowl, combine the remaining 1 cup of flour and 1 cup of sugar, baking powder, and salt. Cut the butter into the flour mixture until it forms an even crumb texture. Stir in the milk until a dough form.

3. Select BAKE, set the temperature to 350 degrees F, and set the time to 30 minutes. Select START/STOP to begin preheating.

4. Meanwhile, pour the blueberry mixture into the Multi-Purpose Pan, spreading it evenly across the pan. Gently pour the batter over the blueberry mixture, and then sprinkle the cinnamon over the top.

5. If the unit beeps to signify it has preheated, place the pan directly in the pot. Close the hood and cook for 30 minutes, until lightly golden.

6. When cooking is complete, serve warm.

Nutrition:

Calories: 408 | Saturated fat: 8g | Carbohydrates: 72g | Protein: 5g

262. Rum-Soaked Grilled Pineapple Sundaes

Preparation time: 15 minutes

Cooking time: 8 minutes

Servings: 6

Ingredients:

- ½ cup dark rum; ½ cup packed brown sugar
- One teaspoon ground cinnamon, plus more for garnish
- One pineapple, cored and sliced; Vanilla ice cream, for serving

Directions:

1. In a large shallow bowl or storage container, combine the rum, sugar, and cinnamon. Add the pineapple slices and arrange them in a single layer. Coat with the mixture, then let soak for at least 5 minutes per side.

2. Insert the Grill Grate and cover the hood. Select GRILL, then set the temperature to MAX, and set the time to 8 minutes. Select START/STOP to begin preheating.

3. While the unit is preheating, strain the extra rum sauce from the pineapple.

4. When the unit beeps to it is a sign that it has preheated, place the fruit on the Grill Grate in a single layer (you may need to do this in multiple batches). Gently press the fruit down to maximize grill marks. Close the hood and grill for about 6 to 8 minutes without flipping. If working in batches, remove the pineapple, and repeat this step for the remaining pineapple slices.

5. When cooking is complete, remove, and top each pineapple ring with a scoop of ice cream. Sprinkle with cinnamon and serve immediately.

Nutrition:

Calories: 240 | Saturated fat: 2g | Carbohydrates: 43g | Protein: 2g

263. Charred Peaches with Bourbon Butter Sauce

Preparation time: 10 minutes

Cooking time: 12 minutes

Servings: 4

Ingredients:

- Four tablespoons salted butter; ¼ cup bourbon; ¼ cup candied pecans
- ½ cup brown sugar; Four ripe peaches halved and pitted

Directions

1. Insert the Grill Grate and cover the hood. Select GRILL, then set the temperature to MAX, and set the time to 12 minutes. Select START/STOP to begin preheating.

2. While the unit is preheating, in a saucepan over medium heat, melt the butter for about 5 minutes. Once the butter is browned, remove the pan from the heat and carefully add the bourbon.

3. Return the saucepan into medium-high heat and add the brown sugar. Bring to a boil and let the sugar dissolve for 5 minutes, stirring occasionally.

4. Pour the bourbon butter sauce into a medium shallow bowl and arrange the peaches cut side down to coat in the sauce.

5. When the unit beeps a sign that it has preheated, place the fruit on the Grill Grate in a single layer (you may need to do this in multiple batches). Gently press the fruit down to maximize grill marks. Close the hood and grill for 10 to 12 minutes without flipping. If working in batches, repeat this step for all the peaches.

6. When cooking is complete, remove the peaches and top each with the pecans. Drizzle with the remaining bourbon butter sauce and serve immediately.

Nutrition: Calories:309 | Saturated fat:8g | Carbohydrates:34g | Protein:2g

264. Chocolate-Hazelnut and Strawberry Grilled Dessert Pizza

Preparation time: 10 minutes

Total cooking time: 6 minutes

Servings: 4

Ingredients:

- 2 tbsp. all-purpose flour, plus more as needed
- ½ store-bought pizza dough (about 8 ounces)
- 1 tbsp. canola oil
- 1 cup sliced fresh strawberries
- 1 tbsp. sugar
- ½ cup chocolate-hazelnut spread

Directions:

1. Insert the Grill Grate and cover the hood. Select GRILL, then set the temperature to MAX, and set the time to 6 minutes. Select START/STOP to begin preheating.

2. While the unit is preheating, dust a clean work surface with the flour, place the dough on the floured surface and roll it out to a 9-inch round of even thickness. Sprinkle the roller and work surface with additional flour, as needed, to ensure the dough does not stick.

3. Brush the surface of the rolled-out dough evenly with half the oil. Flip the dough over, and brush with the remaining oil. Poke the dough with a fork 5 or 6 times across its surface to prevent air pockets from forming during cooking.

4. When the unit beeps to signify it has preheated, place the dough on the Grill Grate. Close the hood and cook for 3 minutes.

5. After 3 minutes, flip the dough. Close the hood and continue cooking for the remaining 3 minutes.

6. Meanwhile, in a medium mixing bowl, combine the strawberries and sugar.

7. Move the pizza to a cutting board and let cool. Top with the chocolate-hazelnut spread and strawberries. Cut into pieces and serve.

Nutrition:

Calories: 377 | Saturated fat: 4g

Sodium: 258mg | Carbo: 53g | Protein: 7g

265. Bacon and Chocolate Cookies

Preparation time: 20 minutes

Total cooking time: 10-12minutes

Servings: 2 ounces cookies

Ingredients:

- 2¾ cups all-purpose flour; 1½ teaspoons baking soda
- ½ teaspoon salt; 1 cup light brown sugar
- 12 tablespoons (1½ sticks) unsalted butter, softened
- 1 cup light brown sugar; 1 cup granulated sugar
- Two eggs, at room temperature; 2½ teaspoons apple cider vinegar
- 1 tsp. vanilla extract; 2 cups semisweet chocolate chips
- Eight slices bacon, cooked and crumbled

Directions:

1. In a prepared large bowl, combine the flour, baking soda, and salt, and mix well. In a separate large bowl, using an electric mixer on medium speed, cream the butter and sugars. Reduce the rate to low and mix in the eggs, vinegar, and vanilla.

2. With the mixer speed still on low, slowly incorporate the dry ingredients, chocolate chips, and bacon pieces.

3. Supply your smoker with wood pellets and follow the manufacturer's specific start-up procedure. Preheat, with the lid closed, to 375degrees F (191°C).

4. Line a large baking sheet drop a rounded teaspoonful of cookie batter onto the prepared baking sheet and place on the grill grate. Close the lid and smoke for 10 to 12 minutes, or until the cookies are browned around the edges.

Nutrition: Calories: 376 kcal | Protein: 5.88 g | Fat: 18.72 g | Carbo: 50.08 g

266. Fast S'Mores Dip Skillet

Preparation time: 5 minutes

Total cooking time: 6-8 minutes

Servings: 4-6

Ingredients:

- 2 tbsp. salted butter, melted; ¼ cup milk
- 12 ounces (340 g) semisweet chocolate chips
- 16 ounces (454 g) Jet-Puffed marshmallows
- Graham crackers and apple wedges, for serving

Directions:

1. Supply your smoker with wood pellets and follow the manufacturer's specific start-up procedure. Preheat, with the lid closed, to 450°F (232°C).

2. Place a cast-iron skillet on the preheated grill grate and pour in the melted butter and milk, stirring for about 1 minute.

3. Once the mixture starts to heat, top with the chocolate chips in an even layer and arrange the marshmallows standing up to cover all of the chocolate.

4. Close the lid and smoke for 5 to 7 minutes, or until the marshmallows are lightly toasted.

5. Remove from the heat and serve immediately with graham crackers and apple wedges for dipping.

Nutrition:

Energy (calories): 893 kcal | Protein: 7.1 g

Fat: 42.02 g | Carbohydrates: 143.07 g

267. Blackberry Pie

Preparation time: 15 minutes
Total cooking time: 20-25 minutes
Servings: 4-6
Ingredients:

- Nonstick cooking spray or butter, for greasing
- One box (2 sheets) refrigerated piecrusts
- 8 tbsp. (1 stick) unsalted butter, melted, plus eight tablespoons (1 stick) cut into pieces
- ½ cup all-purpose flour
- 2 cups sugar, divided
- 2 pints blackberries
- ½ cup milk
- Vanilla ice cream, for serving

Directions:

1. Supply your smoker with wood pellets and follow the manufacturer's specific start-up procedure. Preheat, with the lid closed, to 375degrees F (191°C).
2. Coat a cast-iron skillet with cooking spray.
3. Unroll one refrigerated piecrust and place it in the bottom and up the side of the skillet. Using a fork, poke holes in the crust in several places.
4. Set the skillet on the grill grate, close the lid, and smoke for 5 minutes, or until lightly browned. Remove from the grill and set aside.
5. In a large bowl, combine the stick of melted butter with the flour and 1½ cups of sugar.
6. Add the blackberries to the flour-sugar mixture and toss until well coated.

7. Spread the berry mixture evenly in the skillet and sprinkle the milk on top. Scatter half of the cut pieces of butter randomly over the mixture.

8. Unroll the remaining piecrust, place it over the top of the skillet, slice the dough into even strips, and weave it into a lattice. Scatter the remaining pieces of butter along the top of the crust.

9. Sprinkle the remaining ½ cup of sugar on top of the crust and return the skillet to the smoker.

10. Close the lid and smoke for 15 to 20 minutes, or until bubbly and brown on top. It may be necessary to use some aluminum foil around the edges near the end of the cooking time to prevent the crust from burning.

11. Serve the pie hot with some vanilla ice cream.

Nutrition:

Energy (calories): 295 kcal | Protein: 2.83 g

Fat: 11.41 g | Carbohydrates: 46.8 g

268. Frosted Carrot Cake

Preparation time: 20 minutes
Total cooking time: 60 minutes
Servings: 4-6

- Eight carrots, peeled and grated
- Four eggs, at room temperature
- 1 cup of vegetable oil; ½ cup milk
- 1 tsp. vanilla extract; 2 cups of sugar
- 2 cups self-rising or cake flour
- 2 tsp. baking soda; 1 tsp. salt
- 1 cup finely chopped pecans
- Nonstick cooking spray or butter, for greasing
- 8 ounces (227 g) cream cheese; 1 cup confectioners' sugar
- 8 tbsp. (1 stick) unsalted butter, at room temperature
- 1 tsp. vanilla extract; ½ teaspoon salt; 2 tbsp. to ¼ cup milk

Directions:

For the Cake

1. Supply your smoker with wood pellets and follow the manufacturer's specific start-up procedure. Preheat, with the lid closed, to 350°F (177°C).

2. In a prepared blender, combine the grated carrots, eggs, oil, milk, vanilla, and process until the carrots are finely minced.

3. In a large mixing bowl, combine the sugar, flour, baking soda, and salt.

4. Add the carrot mixture to the flour mixture and stir until well incorporated. Fold in the chopped pecans.

5. Glaze a 9-by-13-inch baking pan with cooking spray.

6. Spill the batter into the prepared pan and place on the grill grate. Close the lid and smoke for about 1 hour, or until a toothpick inserted in the center comes out clean.

7. Remove the cake from the grill and let cool completely.

For the Frosting

1. Using an electric mixer on low speed, beat the cream cheese, confectioners, sugar, butter, vanilla, and salt, adding two tablespoons to ¼ cup of milk to thin the frosting as needed.

2. Frost the cooled cake and slice to serve.

Nutrition:

Energy (calories): 1116 kcal | Protein: 13.37 g

Fat: 75.47 g | Carbohydrates: 102.02 g

269. Lemony Smokin' Bars

Preparation time: 30 minutes

Total cooking time: 60 minutes

Servings: 8-12

Ingredients:

- ¾ cup lemon juice; 1½ cup sugar; Two eggs
- Three egg yolk; 1½ teaspoon cornstarch
- Pinch sea salt; 4 tbsp. unsalted butter
- ¼ cup olive oil; ½ tablespoon lemon zest
- 1¼ cup flour; ¼ cup granulated sugar
- Three tablespoon confectioner's sugar
- 1 tsp. lemon zest; ¼ teaspoon sea salt, fine
- 10 tbsp. unsalted butter, cut into cubes

Directions:

1. When you're ready to cook, set grill temperature to 180°F (82°C) and preheat, lid closed for 15 minutes.

2. In a prepared small bowl, combine the lemon juice, sugar, eggs and yolks, cornstarch and acceptable sea salt. Pour into a baking sheet or cake pan and place on the grill. Smoke for 30 minutes, whisking the mixture halfway through cooking. Take from grill and set aside.

3. Pour mixture into a small saucepan. Place on a stovetop set to medium heat until boiling. Once boiling, boil for 60 seconds. Take from heat and strain through a mesh strainer into a bowl. Whisk in cold butter, olive oil, and lemon zest.

4. To make a crust, whisk together the flour, granulated sugar, powdered sugar, lemon zest, and salt in a food processor. Add the butter and blend until you get a crumbly dough. Press the dough into a prepared 9 "by 9" baking sheet lined with parchment paper that is long enough to hang on 2 of the sides. When ready to cook, set the pellet grill to 350°F (177°C) and preheat, lid closed for 15 minutes.

5. Bake or cook until crust is very lightly golden brown, about 30 to 35 minutes.

6. Remove from the grill and pour the lemon filling over the crust. Return to grill and continue to bake until filling is just set, about 15 to 20 minutes.

7. Allow to cool at room temperature, then refrigerate until chilled before slicing into bars. Sprinkle with confectioners' sugar and flaky sea salt right before serving. Enjoy!

Nutrition:

Energy (calories): 246 kcal | Protein: 2.91 g

Fat: 14.85 g | Carbohydrates: 26.05 g

270. Chocolate Chip Brownie Pie

Preparation time: 20 minutes

Total cooking time: 45 minutes

Servings: 8-12

Ingredients:

- ¾ cup lemon juice; 1½ cup sugar; Two eggs
- Three egg yolk; 1½ teaspoon cornstarch
- Pinch sea salt; 4 tbsp. unsalted butter
- ¼ cup olive oil; ½ tablespoon lemon zest
- 1¼ cup flour; ¼ cup granulated sugar
- Three tablespoon confectioner's sugar
- 1 tsp. lemon zest; ¼ teaspoon sea salt, fine
- 10 tbsp. unsalted butter, cut into cubes

Directions:

1. When ready to cook, set grill temperature to 180°F (82°C) and preheat, lid closed for 15 minutes.

2. In a small mixing bowl, whisk together lemon juice, sugar, eggs and yolks, cornstarch, and acceptable sea salt. Pour into a sheet tray or cake pan and place on the grill. Smoke for 30 minutes, whisking mixture halfway through smoking. Remove from grill and set aside.

3. Pour mixture into a small saucepan. Place on a stovetop set to medium heat until boiling. Once boiling, boil for 60 seconds. Remove from heat and strain through a mesh strainer into a bowl. Whisk in cold butter, olive oil, and lemon zest.

4. To make a crust, pulse together the flour, granulated sugar, confectioners 'sugar, lemon zest, and salt in a food processor. Add butter and pulse until just mixed into a crumbly dough. Press dough into a prepared 9" by 9" baking dish lined with parchment paper that is long enough to hang over 2 of the sides.

5. When ready to cook, turn the temperature to 350°F (177°C) and preheat, lid closed for 15 minutes.

6. Bake until crust is very lightly golden brown, about 30 to 35 minutes.

7. Remove from the grill and pour the lemon filling over the crust. Return to grill and continue to bake until filling is just set, about 15 to 20 minutes.

8. Allow to cool at room temperature, then refrigerate until chilled before slicing into bars. Sprinkle with confectioners' sugar and flaky sea salt right before serving. Enjoy!

Nutrition:

Energy (calories): 368 kcal | Protein: 4.37 g

Fat: 22.27 g | Carbohydrates: 39.08 g

271. Bourbon Maple Pumpkin Pie

Preparation time: 20 minutes

Total cooking time: 45 minutes

Servings: 8-12•

Ingredients:

- ½ cup semisweet chocolate chips; 1 cup butter
- 1 cup brown sugar; 1 cup of sugar; Four whole eggs
- 2 tsp. vanilla extract; 2 cup all-purpose flour
- 2/3cup cocoa powder, unsweetened; 1 tsp. baking soda
- 1 tsp. salt; 1 cup semisweet chocolate chips
- ¾ cup white chocolate chips; ¾ cup nuts (optional)
- 1 (8-ounce / 227-g) whole hot fudge sauce
- Two tablespoon Guinness beer

Directions:

1. Coat the inside of a 10-inch pie plate with non-stick cooking spray.

2. When ready to cook, set the grill temperature to 350°F (177°C) and preheat, lid closed for 15 minutes.

3. Melt ½ cup (100 g) of the semi-sweet chocolate chips in the microwave—cream together butter, brown sugar, and granulated sugar. Beat in the eggs, adding one at a time and mixing after each egg, and the vanilla. Add in the melted chocolate chips.

4. On a large piece of wax paper, sift together the cocoa powder, flour, baking soda, and salt. Lift the corners of the form and pour slowly into the butter mixture.

5. Beat until the dry ingredients are just incorporated. Stir in the remaining semi-sweet chocolate chips, white chocolate chips, and nuts. Press the dough into the prepared pie pan.

6. Place the brownie pie on the grill and bake for 45-50 minutes or until the pastry is set in the middle. Rotate the pan halfway through cooking. If the top or edges begin to brown, cover the top with a piece of aluminum foil.

7. In a microwave-safe measuring cup, heat the fudge sauce in the microwave. Stir in the Guinness.

8. Once the brownie pie is done, allow sitting for 20 minutes. Slice into wedges and top with the fudge sauce. Enjoy.

Nutrition:

Energy (calories): 838 kcal | Protein: 9.23 g

Fat: 49.83 g | Carbohydrates: 99.74 g

CHAPTER 13:
Extra Recipes

272. Sweet & Spicy Chicken Thighs

Preparation Time: 15 minutes
Cooking Time: 15 minutes
Servings: 4
Ingredients:

- 2 garlic cloves, minced
- ¼ cup honey
- 2 tablespoons soy sauce
- ¼ teaspoon red pepper flakes, crushed
- 4 (5-ounce) skinless, boneless chicken thighs
- 2 tablespoons olive oil
- 2 teaspoons sweet rub
- ¼ teaspoon red chili powder
- Ground black pepper, as required

Directions

1. Preheat the Traeger grill & Smoker on grill setting to 400 degrees F.

2. In a small bowl, add garlic, honey, soy sauce and red pepper flakes and with a wire whisk, beat until well combined.

3. Coat chicken thighs with oil and season with sweet rub, chili powder and black pepper generously.

4. Arrange the chicken drumsticks onto the grill and cook for about 15 minutes per

5. In the last 4-5 minutes of cooking, coat drumsticks with garlic mixture.

6. Serve immediately.

Nutrition:

- Calories 309
- Total Fat 12.1 g
- Saturated Fat 2.9 g
- Cholesterol 82 mg
- Sodium 504 mg
- Total Carbs 18.7 g
- Fiber 0.2 g
- Sugar 17.6 g
- Protein 32.3 g

273. Bacon Wrapped Chicken Breasts

Preparation Time: 0 minute

Cooking Time: 3 hours

Servings: 6

Ingredients:

For Brine:

- ¼ cup brown sugar; ¼ cup kosher salt;
- 4 cups water; For Chicken:
- skinless, boneless chicken breasts ¼ cup chicken rub;
- 18 bacon slices; 1½ cups BBQ sauce

Directions:

1. For brine: in a large pitcher, dissolve sugar and salt in water. Place the chicken breasts in brine and refrigerate for about 2 hours, flipping once in the middle way.

2. Preheat the Traeger grill & Smoker on grill setting to 230 degrees F. Remove chicken breasts from brine and rinse under cold running water. Season chicken breasts with rub generously.

3. Arrange 3 bacon strips of bacon onto a cutting board, against each other. Place 1 chicken breast across the bacon, leaving enough bacon on the left side to wrap it over just a little.

4. Wrap the bacon strips around chicken breast and secure with toothpicks. Repeat with remaining breasts and bacon slices.

5. Arrange the chicken breasts into Traeger grill and cook for about 2½ hours. Coat the breasts with BBQ sauce and cook for about 30 minutes more. Serve immediately.

Nutrition: Calories 481 | Total Fat 12.3g | Saturated Fat 4.2g | Fiber 0.4g Cholesterol 41mg | Sodium 3000mg | Carbs 32g | Sugar 22.2g | Protein55.9g

274. Glazed Chicken Wings

Preparation Time: 15 minutes

Cooking Time: 2 hours

Servings: 6

Ingredients:

- 2 pounds' chicken wings; 2 garlic cloves, crushed
- 3 tablespoons hoisin sauce; 2 tablespoons soy sauce
- 1 teaspoon dark sesame oil; 1 tablespoon honey
- ½ teaspoon ginger powder
- 1 tablespoon sesame seeds, toasted lightly

Directions:

1. Preheat the Traeger grill & Smoker on grill setting to 225 degrees F.
2. Arrange the wings onto the lower rack of grill and cook for about 1½ hours.
3. Meanwhile, in a large bowl, mix together remaining all ingredients.
4. Remove wings from grill and place in the bowl of garlic mixture.
5. Coat wings with garlic mixture generously.
6. Now, set the grill to 375 degrees F.
7. Arrange the coated wings onto a foil-lined baking sheet and sprinkle with sesame seeds.
8. Place the pan onto the lower rack of Traeger grill and cook for about 25-30 minutes.
9. Serve immediately.

Nutrition:

Calories 336 | Total Fat 13 g | Saturated Fat 3.3 g | Cholesterol 135 mg
Sodium 560 mg | Total Carbs 7.6 g | Fiber 0.5 g | Sugar 5.2 g | Protein 44.7 g

275. Chicken Casserole

Preparation Time: 15 minutes

Cooking Time: 55 minutes

Servings: 8

Ingredients:

- 2 (15-ounce) cans cream of chicken soup
- 2 cups milk; 2 tablespoons unsalted butter
- ¼ cup all-purpose flour; ½ cup hatch chiles, chopped
- 1-pound skinless, boneless chicken thighs, chopped
- 2 medium onions, chopped; 1 tablespoon fresh thyme, chopped
- Salt and ground black pepper, as required; 1 cup tater tots
- 1 cup cooked bacon, chopped

Directions:

1. Preheat the Traeger grill & Smoker on grill setting to 400 degrees F.
2. In a large bowl, mix together chicken soup and milk.
3. In a skillet, melt butter over medium heat. Slowly, add flour and cook for about 1-2 minutes or until smooth, stirring continuously.
4. Slowly, add soup mixture, beating continuously until smooth.
5. Cook until mixture starts to thicken, stirring continuously. Stir in remaining ingredients except bacon and simmer for about 10-15 minutes.
6. Stir in bacon and transfer mixture into a 2½-quart casserole dish.
7. Place tater tots on top of casserole evenly. Arrange the pan onto the grill and cook for about 30-35 minutes. Serve hot.

Nutrition: Calories 440 | Fat 25.8g | Saturated Fat 9.3g | Protein 28.9g
Cholesterol 86mg | Sodium 1565mg | Carbs 22.2g | Sugar 4.6g | Fiber 1.5g

276. Buttered Turkey

Preparation Time: 15 minutes

Cooking Time: 4 hours

Servings: 16

Ingredients:

- ½ pound butter, softened
- 2 tablespoons fresh thyme, chopped
- 2 fresh rosemary, chopped
- garlic cloves, crushed
- 1 (20-pound) whole turkey, neck and giblets removed
- Salt and ground black pepper, as required

Directions:

1. Preheat the Traeger grill & Smoker on smoke setting to 300 degrees F, using charcoal.
2. In a bowl, place butter, fresh herbs, garlic, salt and black pepper and mix well.
3. With your fingers, separate the turkey skin from breast to create a pocket.
4. Stuff the breast pocket with ¼-inch thick layer of butter mixture.
5. Season the turkey with salt and black pepper evenly.
6. Arrange the turkey onto the grill and cook for 3-4 hours.
7. Remove turkey from pallet grill and place onto a cutting board for about 15-20 minutes before carving.
8. With a sharp knife, cut the turkey into desired-sized pieces and serve.

Nutrition: Calories 965 | Total Fat 52 g | Saturated Fat 19.9 g | Fiber 0.2 g Cholesterol 385mg | Sodium 1916mg | Carbs 0.6g | Sugar 0g | Protein 106.5g

277. Glazed Turkey Breast

Preparation Time: 15 minutes

Cooking Time: 4 hours

Servings: 6

Ingredients:

- ½ cup honey; ¼ cup dry sherry
- 1 tablespoon butter; Salt, as required
- 2 tablespoons fresh lemon juice
- 1 (3-3½-pound) skinless, boneless turkey breast

Directions:

1. In a small pan, place honey, sherry and butter over low heat and cook until the mixture becomes smooth, stirring continuously.
2. Remove from heat and stir in lemon juice and salt. Set aside to cool.
3. Transfer the honey mixture and turkey breast in a sealable bag.
4. Seal the bag and shake to coat well.
5. Refrigerate for about 6-10 hours.
6. Preheat the Traeger grill & Smoker on grill setting to 225-250 degrees F.
7. Place the turkey breast onto the grill and cook for about 2½-4 hours or until desired doneness.
8. Remove turkey breast from pallet grill and place onto a cutting board for about 15-20 minutes before slicing.
9. With a sharp knife, cut the turkey breast into desired-sized slices and serve.

Nutrition:

Calories 443 | Total Fat 11.4g | Saturated Fat 4.8g | Cholesterol 159mg

Sodium 138mg | Total Carbs 23.7g | Fiber 0.1g | Sugar 23.4g | Protein 59.2g

278. Crispy Duck

Preparation Time: 15 minutes

Cooking Time: 4 hours 5 minutes

Servings: 6

Ingredients:

- ¾ cup honey; ¾ cup soy sauce
- ¾ cup red wine; 1 teaspoon paprika
- 1½ tablespoons garlic salt
- Ground black pepper, as required
- 1 (5-pound) whole duck, giblets removed and trimmed

Directions:

1. Preheat the Traeger grill & Smoker on grill setting to 225-250 degrees F.
2. In a bowl, add all ingredients except for duck and mix until well combined.
3. With a fork, poke holes in the skin of the duck.
4. Coat the duck with honey mixture generously.
5. Arrange duck in Traeger gill, breast side down and cook for about 4 hours, coating with honey mixture one after 2 hours.
6. Remove the duck from grill and place onto a cutting board for about 15 minutes before carving.
7. With a sharp knife, cut the duck into desired-sized pieces and serve.

Nutrition:

Calories 878 | Total Fat 52.1g | Saturated Fat 13.9g | Cholesterol 3341mg

Sodium 2300mg | Total Carbs 45.4g | Fiber 0.7g | Sugar 39.6g | Protein 51g

279. Jerked Up Tilapia

Preparation Time: 20 minutes

Cooking Time: 45 minutes

Serving: 8

Ingredients:

- cloves of garlic; 1 small sized onion
- 3 Jalapeno Chiles; 3 teaspoon of ground ginger
- 3 tablespoons of light brown sugar
- 3 teaspoons of dried thyme; 2 teaspoons of salt
- 2 teaspoons of ground cinnamon
- 1 teaspoon of black pepper; 1 teaspoon of ground allspice
- ¼ teaspoon of cayenne pepper; 4 -6 ounce of tilapia fillets
- ¼ cup of olive oil; 1 cup of sliced up carrots
- 1 bunch of whole green onions; 2 tablespoons of whole allspice

Directions:

1. Take a blending bowl and combine the first 11 of the listed ingredients and puree them nicely using your blender or food processor
2. Add the fish pieces in a large-sized zip bag and toss in the pureed mixture alongside olive oil
3. Seal it up and press to make sure that the fish is coated well
4. Let it marinate in your fridge for at least 30 minutes to 1 hour
5. Take your drip pan and add water, cover with aluminum foil. Pre-heat your smoker to 225 degrees F
6. Use water fill water pan halfway through and place it over drip pan. Add wood chips to the side tray

7. Take a medium-sized bowl and toss in some pecan wood chips and soak them underwater alongside whole allspice

8. Prepare an excellent 9x 13-inch foil pan by poking a dozen holes and spraying it with non-stick cooking spray

9. Spread out the carrots, green onions across the bottom of the pan

10. Arrange the fishes on top of them

11. Place the container in your smoker

12. Smoke for about 45 minutes making sure to add more chips after every 15 minutes until the internal temperature of the fish rises to 145 degrees Fahrenheit

13. Serve hot

Nutrition:

Calories: 347 | Fats: 19g

Carbs: 18g | Fiber: 1g

280. Premium Salmon Nuggets

Preparation Time: 20 minutes +marinate time

Cooking Time: 1-2 hours

Servings: 8

Ingredients:

- 3 cups of packed brown sugar
- 1 cup of salt; 1 garlic clove, minced
- 1 tablespoon of onion, minced
- 2 teaspoons of chipotle seasoning
- 2 teaspoons of fresh ground black pepper
- 1-2 pound of salmon fillets, cut up into bite-sized portions

Directions:

1. Take a large-sized bowl and stir in brown sugar, salt, chipotle seasoning, onion, garlic and pepper
2. Transfer salmon to a large shallow marinating dish
3. Pour dry marinade over fish and cover, refrigerate overnight
4. Take your drip pan and add water, cover with aluminum foil. Pre-heat your smoker to 180 degrees F
5. Use water fill water pan halfway through and place it over drip pan. Add wood chips to the side tray
6. Rinse the salmon chunks thoroughly and remove salt
7. Transfer them to grill rack and smoke for 1-2 hours
8. Remove the heat and enjoy it!

Nutrition:

Calories: 120 | Fats: 18g

Carbs: 3g | Fiber: 2g

281. Creative Sablefish

Preparation Time: 15 minutes

Cooking Time: 3 hours

Servings: 8

Ingredients:

- 2-3 pounds of sablefish fillets
- 1 cup of kosher salts
- ¼ cup of sugar
- 2 tablespoon of garlic powder
- Honey for glazing
- Sweet paprika for dusting

Directions:

1. Take a bowl and mix salt, garlic powder, and sugar
2. Pour on a healthy layer of your mix into a lidded plastic tub, large enough to hold the fish
3. Cut up the fillet into pieces
4. Gently massage the salt mix into your fish meat and place them with the skin side down on to the salt mix in the plastic tub
5. Cover up the container and keep it in your fridge for as many hours as the fish weighs
6. Remove the sablefish from the tub and place it under cold water for a while
7. Pat, it dries using a kitchen towel and puts it back to the fridge, keep it uncovered overnight
8. Take your drip pan and add water, cover with aluminum foil. Pre-heat your smoker to 225 degrees F

9. Use water fill water pan halfway through and place it over drip pan. Add wood chips to the side tray

10. Smoke for 2-3 hours

11. After the first hour of smoking, make sure to baste the fish with honey and keep repeating this after every hour

12. One done, move the fish to a cooling rack and baste it with honey one last time

13. Let it cool for about an hour

14. Use tweezers to pull out the bone pins

15. Dust the top with some paprika and wait for 30 minutes to let the paprika sink in

16. Put the fish in your fridge

17. Serve hot or chilled!

Nutrition:

Calories: 171 | Fats: 10g

Carbs: 13g | Fiber: 1g

282. Halibut Delight

Preparation Time: 4-6 hours

Cooking Time: 15 minutes

Servings: 4-6

Ingredients:

- ½ a cup of salt
- ½ a cup of brown sugar
- 1 teaspoon of smoked paprika
- 1 teaspoon of ground cumin
- 2 pounds of halibut
- 1/3 cup of mayonnaise

Directions:

1. Take a small bowl and add salt, brown sugar, cumin, and paprika
2. Coat the halibut well and cover, refrigerate for 4-6 hours
3. Take your drip pan and add water, cover with aluminum foil. Pre-heat your smoker to 200 degrees F
4. Use water fill water pan halfway through and place it over drip pan. Add wood chips to the side tray
5. Remove the fish from refrigerator and rinse it well, pat it dry
6. Rub the mayonnaise on the fish
7. Transfer the halibut to smoker and smoke for 2 hours until the internal temperature reaches 120 degrees Fahrenheit

Nutrition:

Calories: 375 | Fats: 21g

Carbs: 10g | Fiber: 2g

283. Roast Rack of Lamb

Preparation Time: 10 minutes

Cooking Time: 1 hour

Servings: 6-8

Ingredients:

- Traeger Flavor: Alder
- 1 (2-pound) rack of lamb
- 1 batch Rosemary-Garlic Lamb Seasoning

Directions:

1. Supply your smoker with Traeger's and follow the manufacturer's specific start-up procedure. Preheat the grill to 450°F.

2. Using a boning knife, score the bottom fat portion of the rib meat.

3. Using your hands, rub the rack of lamb with the lamb seasoning, making sure it penetrates into the scored fat.

4. Place the rack directly on the grill grate and smoke until its internal temperature reaches 145F.

5. Take off the rack from the grill and let it rest for 20 to 30 minutes, before slicing into individual ribs to serve.

Nutrition:

- Calories: 50
- Carbs: 4g
- Fiber: 2g
- Fat: 2.5g
- Protein: 2g

284. Ultimate Lamb Burgers

Preparation Time: 20 minutes

Cooking Time: 30 minutes

Servings: 4

Ingredients:

Burger:

- 2 lbs. ground lamb; 1 jalapeño
- scallions, diced;2 tablespoons mint
- 2 tablespoons dill, minced
- 3 cloves garlic, minced
- Salt and pepper; 4 brioche buns
- 4 slices manchego cheese

Sauce:

- 1 cup mayonnaise
- 2 cloves garlic
- 2 teaspoons lemon juice
- 1 bell pepper, diced;
- salt and pepper

Directions

1. When ready to cook, turn your smoker to 400F and preheat.
2. Add the mint, scallions, salt, garlic, dill, jalapeño, lamb, and pepper to the mixing bowl.
3. Form the lamb mixture into eight patties.
4. Lay the pepper on the grill and cook for 20 minutes.
5. Take the pepper from the grill and place it in a bag, and seal. After ten minutes, remove pepper from the bag, remove seeds and peel the skin.

6. Add the garlic, lemon juice, mayo, roasted red pepper, salt, and pepper and process until smooth. Serve alongside the burger.

7. Lay the lamb burgers on the grill, and cook for five minutes per side, then place in the buns with a slice of cheese, and serve with the homemade sauce.

Nutrition:

- Calories: 50
- Carbs: 4g
- Fiber: 2g
- Fat: 2.5g
- Protein: 2g

285. Citrus- Smoked Trout

Preparation Time: 10 minutes

Cooking Time: 1 to 2 hours

Servings: 6 to 8

Ingredients:

- 6 to 8 skin-on rainbow trout, cleaned and scaled
- 1-gallon orange juice; ¼ cup salt; 1 lemon, sliced
- ½ cup packed light brown sugar
- 1 tablespoon freshly ground black pepper
- Nonstick spray, oil, or butter, for greasing
- 1 tablespoon chopped fresh parsley

Directions:

1. Fillet the fish and pat dry with paper towels
2. Pour the orange juice into a large container with a lid and stir in the brown sugar, salt, and pepper
3. Place the trout in the brine, cover, and refrigerate for 1 hour
4. Cover the grill grate with heavy-duty aluminum foil. Poke holes in the foil and spray with cooking spray
5. Supply your smoker with Traeger's and follow the manufacturer's specific start-up procedure. Preheat, with the lid closed, to 225°F
6. Remove the trout from the brine and pat dry. Arrange the fish on the foil-covered grill grate, close the lid, and smoke for 1 hour 30 minutes to 2 hours, or until flaky
7. Remove the fish from the heat. Serve garnished with the fresh parsley and lemon slices.

Nutrition:

Calories: 220 | Protein: 33 g | Fat: 4 g | Carbohydrates: 17 g

286. Sunday Supper Salmon with Olive Tapenade

Preparation Time: 1 hour and 20 minutes

Cooking Time: 1 to 2 hours

Servings: 10 to 12

Ingredients:

- 2 cups packed light brown sugar
- ½ cup salt; ¼ cup maple syrup
- 1/3 cup crab boil seasoning
- 1 (3- to 5-pound) whole salmon fillet, skin removed
- ¼ cup extra-virgin olive oil; 1 tablespoon dried oregano
- 1 (15-ounce) can pitted green olives, drained
- 1 (15-ounce) can pitted black olives, drained
- 3 tablespoons jarred sun-dried tomatoes, drained
- 3 tablespoons chopped fresh basil
- 2 tablespoons freshly squeezed lemon juice
- 2 tablespoons jarred capers, drained
- 2 tablespoons chopped fresh parsley, plus more for sprinkling

Directions:

1. In a medium bowl, combine the brown sugar, salt, maple syrup, and crab boil seasoning.

2. Rub the paste all over the salmon and place the fish in a shallow dish. Cover and marinate in the refrigerator for at least 8 hours or overnight.

3. Remove the salmon from dish, rinse, and pat dry, and let stand for 1 hour to take off the chill.

4. Meanwhile, in a food processor, pulse the olive oil, green olives, black olives, sun-dried tomatoes, basil, oregano, lemon juice, capers, and parsley to a chunky consistency. Refrigerate the tapenade until ready to serve.

5. Supply your smoker with Traeger's and follow the manufacturer's specific start-up procedure. Preheat, with the lid closed, to 250°F.

6. Place the salmon on the grill grate (or on a cedar plank on the grill grate), close the lid, and smoke for 1 to 2 hours, or until the internal temperature reaches 140°F to 145°F. When the fish flakes easily with a fork, it's done.

7. Remove the salmon from the heat and sprinkle with parsley. Serve with the olive tapenade.

Nutrition:

- Calories: 240;
- Proteins: 23g;
- Carbs: 3g;
- Fat: 16g

287. Grilled Tuna

Preparation Time: 20 minutes

Cooking Time: 4 hours

Servings: 6

Ingredients:

- Albacore tuna fillets – 6, each about 8 ounces
- Salt – 1 cup; Brown sugar – 1 cup
- Orange, zested – 1; Lemon, zested – 1

Directions:

1. Before preheating the grill, brine the tuna, and for this, prepare brine stirring together all of its ingredients until mixed.

2. Take a large container, layer tuna fillets in it, covering each fillet with it, and then let them sit in the refrigerator for 6 hours.

3. Then remove tuna fillets from the brine, rinse well, pat dry and cool in the refrigerator for 30 minutes.

4. When the grill has preheated, place tuna fillets on the grilling rack and let smoke for 3 hours, turning halfway.

5. Check the fire after one hour of smoking and add more wood pallets if required.

6. Then switch temperature of the grill to 225 degrees F and continue grilling for another 1 hour until tuna has turned nicely golden and fork-tender.

7. Serve immediately.

Nutrition:

Calories: 311 | Fiber: 3 g | Saturated Fat: 1.2 g

Protein: 45 g | Carbs: 11 g | Fat: 8.8 g | Sugar: 1.3 g

288. Grilled Swordfish

Preparation Time: 10 minutes
Cooking Time: 18 minutes
Servings: 4
Ingredients:

- Swordfish fillets – 4; Salt – 1 tablespoon
- Ground black pepper – ¾ tablespoon
- Olive oil – 2 tablespoons; Ears of corn – 4
- Cherry tomatoes – 1 pint; Lime, juiced – 1
- Cilantro, chopped – 1/3 cup
- Medium red onion, peeled, diced – 1
- Serrano pepper, minced – 1; Salt – ½ teaspoon
- Ground black pepper – ¼ teaspoon

Directions:

1. In the meantime, prepare fillets and for this, brush them with oil and then season with salt and black pepper.

2. Prepare the corn, and for this, brush with olive oil and season with ¼ teaspoon each of salt and black pepper.

3. When the grill has preheated, place fillets on the grilling rack along with corns and grill corn for 15 minutes until light brown and fillets for 18 minutes until fork tender.

4. When corn has grilled, cut kernels from it, place them into a medium bowl, add remaining ingredients for the salsa and stir until mixed.

5. When fillets have grilled, divide them evenly among plates, top with corn salsa and then serve.

Nutrition: Calories: 311 | Total Fat: 8.8 g | Saturated Fat: 1.2 g
Fiber: 3 g | Protein: 45 g | Sugar: 1.3 g | Carbs: 11 g

289. Lamb Kebabs

Preparation Time: 15 minutes

Cooking Time: 10 minutes

Servings: 4

Ingredients:

Traeger's: Mesquite

- 1/2 tablespoon salt; 2 tablespoons fresh mint
- 3 lbs. leg of lamb; 1/2 cup lemon juice
- 1 tablespoon lemon zest; 15 apricots, pitted
- 1/2 tablespoon cilantro; 2 teaspoons black pepper
- 1/2 cup olive oil;1 teaspoon cumin; 2 red onion

Directions:

1. Combine the olive oil, pepper, lemon juice, mint, salt, lemon zest, cumin, and cilantro. Add lamb leg, then place in the refrigerator overnight.
2. Remove the lamb from the marinade, cube them, and then thread onto the skewer with the apricots and onions.
3. When ready to cook, turn your smoker to 400F and preheat.
4. Lay the skewers on the grill and cook for ten minutes.
5. Remove from the grill and serve.

Nutrition:

- Calories: 50
- Carbs: 4g
- Fiber: 2g
- Fat: 2.5g
- Protein: 2g

290. Special Occasion's Dinner Cornish Hen

Preparation Time: 15 Minutes

Cooking Time: 1 Hour

Servings: 4

Ingredients:

- 4 Cornish game hens
- Four fresh rosemary sprigs
- 4 tbsp. butter, melted
- 4 tsp. chicken rub

Directions:

1. Set the temperature of Traeger Grill to 375 degrees F and preheat with a closed lid for 15 mins.

2. With paper towels, pat dries the hens.

3. Tuck the wings behind the backs, and with kitchen strings, tie the legs together.

4. Coat the outside of each hen with melted butter and sprinkle with rub evenly.

5. Stuff the cavity of each hen with a rosemary sprig.

6. Place the hens onto the grill and cook for about 50-60 mins.

7. Remove the hens from the grill and place onto a platter for about 10 mins.

8. Cut each hen into desired-sized pieces and serve.

Nutrition:

Calories per serving: 430 | Carbohydrates: 2.1g

Protein: 25.4g | Fat: 33g | Sodium: 331mg | Fiber: 0.7g

291. Crispy and Juicy Chicken

Preparation Time: 15 Minutes

Cooking Time: 5 Hours

Servings: 6

Ingredients:

- ¾ C. dark brown sugar
- ½ C. ground espresso beans
- 1 tbsp. ground cumin
- 1 tbsp. ground cinnamon
- 1 tbsp. garlic powder
- 1 tbsp. cayenne pepper
- Salt and freshly ground black pepper
- 1 (4-lb.) whole chicken, neck and giblets removed

Directions:

1. Set the temperature of Traeger Grill to 200-225 degrees F and preheat with a closed lid for 15 mins.
2. In a bowl, mix brown sugar, ground espresso, spices, salt, and black pepper.
3. Rub the chicken with spice mixture generously.
4. Put the chicken onto the grill and cook for about 3-5 hours.
5. Remove chicken from grill and place onto a cutting board for about 10 mins before carving.
6. With a sharp knife, cut the chicken into desired sized pieces and serve.

Nutrition:

Calories per serving: 540 | Carbohydrates: 20.7g | Protein: 88.3g

Fat: 9.6g | Sugar: 18.1g | Sodium: 226mg | Fiber: 1.2g

292. Ultimate Tasty Chicken

Preparation Time: 15 Minutes

Cooking Time: 3 Hours

Servings: 5

Ingredients:

For Brine:

- 1 C. brown sugar
- ½ C. kosher salt
- 16 C. water

For Chicken:

- 1 (3-lb.) whole chicken
- 1 tbsp. garlic, crushed
- 1 tsp. onion powder
- Salt and freshly ground black pepper
- One medium yellow onion, quartered
- Three whole garlic cloves, peeled
- One lemon, quartered
- 4-5 fresh thyme sprigs

Directions:

1. For the brine: in a bucket, dissolve brown sugar and kosher salt in water.
2. Place the chicken in brine and refrigerate overnight.
3. Set the temperature of Traeger Grill to 225 degrees F.
4. Preheat with closed lid for 15 mins.
5. Remove the chicken from the brine, and with paper towels, pat it dry.

6. In a small bowl, mix crushed garlic, onion powder, salt, and black pepper.

7. Rub the chicken with garlic mixture evenly.

8. Stuff the cavity of the chicken with onion, garlic cloves, lemon, and thyme.

9. With kitchen strings, tie the legs together.

10. Place the chicken onto grill and cook, covered for about 2½-3 hours.

11. Remove chicken from pallet grill and transfer onto a cutting board for about 10 mins before carving.

12. Cut the chicken into desired sized pieces and serve.

Nutrition:

- Calories per serving: 641
- Carbohydrates: 31.7g
- Protein: 79.2g
- Fat: 20.2g
- Sugar: 29.3g
- Sodium: 11500mg
- Fiber: 0.6g

293. South-East-Asian Chicken Drumsticks

Preparation Time: 15 Minutes

Cooking Time: 2 Hours

Servings: 6

Ingredients:

- 1 C. fresh orange juice
- ¼ C. honey; 1 tsp. Sriracha
- 2 tbsp. sweet chili sauce
- 2 tbsp. hoisin sauce
- 2 tbsp. fresh ginger, grated finely
- 2 tbsp. garlic, minced
- ½ tsp. sesame oil
- Six chicken drumsticks

Directions:

1. Set the condition of Traeger Grill to 225 degrees F.
2. Preheat with closed lid for 15 mins.
3. In a bowl, place all fixings except for chicken drumsticks and mix until well combined.
4. Reserve half of the honey mixture in a small bowl.
5. In the bowl of the remaining sauce, add drumsticks and mix well.
6. Arrange the chicken drumsticks onto the grill and cook for about 3 hours, basting with remaining sauce occasionally.
7. Serve hot.

Nutrition:

Calories per serving: 385 | Carbohydrates: 22.7g | Protein: 47.6g

Fat: 10.5g | Sugar: 18.6g | Sodium: 270mg | Fiber: 0.6g

294. Glazed Chicken Thighs

Preparation Time: 15 Minutes

Cooking Time: 30 Minutes

Servings: 4

Ingredients:

- Two garlic cloves, minced; ¼ C. honey
- 2 tbsp soy sauce; 2 tbsp. olive oil
- ¼ tsp. red pepper flakes, crushed
- 4 (5-oz.) skinless, boneless chicken thighs
- 2 tsp. Sweet rub; ¼ tsp. red chili powder
- Freshly ground black pepper, to taste

Directions:

1. Set the temperature of Traeger Grill to 400 degrees F and preheat with a closed lid for 15 mins.
2. In a small bowl, add garlic, honey, soy sauce, and red pepper flakes, and with a wire whisk, beat until well combined.
3. Coat chicken thighs with oil and season with sweet rub, chili powder, and black pepper generously.
4. Arrange the chicken drumsticks onto the grill and cook for about 15 mins per side.
5. In the last 4-5 mins of cooking, coat the thighs with garlic mixture.
6. Serve immediately.

Nutrition:

Calories per serving: 309 | Carbohydrates: 18.7g | Protein: 32.3g

Fat: 12.1g | Sugar: 17.6g | Sodium: 504mg | Fiber: 0.2g

295. Cajun Chicken Breasts

Preparation Time: 10 Minutes

Cooking Time: 6 Hours

Servings: 6

Ingredients:

- 2 lb. skinless, boneless chicken breasts
- 2 tbsp. Cajun seasoning
- 1 C. BBQ sauce

Directions:

1. Set the temperature of Traeger Grill to 225 degrees F and preheat with a closed lid for 15 mins.
2. Rub the chicken breasts with Cajun seasoning generously.
3. Put the chicken breasts onto the grill and cook for about 4-6 hours.
4. During the last hour of cooking, coat the breasts with BBQ sauce twice.
5. Serve hot.

Nutrition:

- Calories per serving: 252
- Carbohydrates: 15.1g
- Protein: 33.8g
- Fat: 5.5g
- Sugar: 10.9g
- Sodium: 570mg
- Fiber: 0.3g

296. BBQ Sauce Smothered Chicken Breasts

Preparation Time: 15 Minutes

Cooking Time: 30 Minutes

Servings: 4

Ingredients:

- 1 tsp. garlic, crushed; ¼ C. olive oil
- 2 tbsp. spicy BBQ sauce
- 1 tbsp. sweet mesquite seasoning
- 1 tbsp. Worcestershire sauce
- Four chicken breasts
- 2 tbsp. regular BBQ sauce
- 2 tbsp. honey bourbon BBQ sauce

Directions:

1. Set the temperature of Traeger Grill to 450 degrees F and preheat with a closed lid for 15 mins.
2. In a large bowl, mix garlic, oil, Worcestershire sauce, and mesquite seasoning.
3. Brush chicken breasts with seasoning mixture evenly.
4. Place the chicken breasts onto the grill and cook for about 20-30 mins.
5. In the meantime, in a bowl, mix all 3 BBQ sauces.
6. In the last 4-5 mins of cooking, coat the breast with BBQ sauce mixture.
7. Serve hot.

Nutrition:

Calories per serving: 421 | Carbohydrates: 10.1g | Protein: 41.2g

Fat: 23.3g | Sugar: 6.9g | Sodium: 763mg | Fiber: 0.2g

297. Thanksgiving Dinner Turkey

Preparation Time: 15 Minutes

Cooking Time: 4 Hours

Servings: 16

Ingredients:

- ½ lb. butter, softened
- 2 tbsp. fresh thyme, chopped
- 2 tbsp. fresh rosemary, chopped
- Six garlic cloves, crushed
- 1 (20-lb.) whole turkey, neck, and giblets removed
- Salt and freshly ground black pepper

Directions:

1. Set the temperature of Traeger Grill to 300 degrees F and preheat with closed lid for 15 mins, using charcoal.
2. Place butter, fresh herbs, garlic, salt, and black pepper and mix well in a bowl.
3. With your fingers, separate the turkey skin from the breast to create a pocket.
4. Stuff the breast pocket with a ¼-inch thick layer of the butter mixture.
5. Season the turkey with salt and black pepper evenly.
6. Arrange the turkey onto the grill and cook for 3-4 hours.
7. Remove the turkey from the grill and place onto a cutting board for about 15-20 mins before carving.
8. With a sharp knife, cut the turkey into desired-sized pieces and serve.

Nutrition: Calories per serving: 965 | Carbohydrates: 0.6g | Protein: 106.5g Fat: 52g | Sugar: 0g | Sodium: 1916mg | Fiber: 0.2g

298. Perfectly Smoked Turkey Legs

Preparation Time: 15 Minutes

Cooking Time: 4 Hours

Servings: 6

Ingredients:

For Turkey:

- 3 tbsp. Worcestershire sauce
- 1 tbsp. canola oil
- Six turkey legs

For Rub:

- ¼ C. chipotle seasoning
- 1 tbsp. brown sugar
- 1 tbsp. paprika

For Sauce:

- 1 C. white vinegar
- 1 tbsp. canola oil
- 1 tbsp. chipotle BBQ sauce

Directions:

1. For turkey in a bowl, add the Worcestershire sauce and canola oil and mix well.
2. With your fingers, loosen the skin of legs.
3. With your fingers, coat the legs under the skin with an oil mixture.
4. In another bowl, mix rub ingredients.
5. Rub the spice mixture under and the outer surface of turkey legs generously.

6. Transfer the legs into a large sealable bag and refrigerate for about 2-4 hours.

7. Remove the refrigerator's turkey legs and set aside at room temperature for at least 30 mins before cooking.

8. Set the temperature of Traeger Grill to 200-220 degrees F and preheat with a closed lid for 15 mins.

9. In a small pan, mix all sauce ingredients on low heat and cook until warmed thoroughly, stirring continuously.

10. Place the turkey legs onto the grill cook for about 3½-4 hours, coating with sauce after every 45 mins.

11. Serve hot.

Nutrition:

- Calories per serving: 430
- Carbohydrates: 4.9g
- Protein: 51.2g
- Fat: 19.5g
- Sugar: 3.9g
- Sodium: 1474mg
- Fiber: 0.5g

299. Texas-Style Brisket Rub

Preparation Time: 5 Minutes
Cooking Time: 10 Minutes
Servings: 1
Ingredients:

- 2 tsp Sugar
- 2 Tbsp Kosher salt
- 2 tsp Chili powder
- 2 Tbsp Black pepper
- 2 Tbsp Cayenne pepper
- 2 Tbsp Powdered garlic
- 2 tsp Grounded cumin
- 2 Tbsp Powdered onion
- 1/4 cup paprika, smoked

Directions:

1. Mix all the ingredients in a small bowl until it is well blended.
2. Transfer to an airtight jar or container. Store in a cool place.

Nutrition:

- Calories: 18kcal
- Carbs: 2g
- Fat: 1g
- Protein: 0.6g

300. Pork Dry Rub

Preparation Time: 5 Minutes
Cooking Time: 10 Minutes
Servings: 1 Cup
Ingredients:

- 1 Tbsp Kosher salt
- 2 Tbsp Powered onions
- 1 Tbsp Cayenne pepper
- 1 tsp Dried mustard
- 1/4 cup brown sugar
- 1 Tbsp Powdered garlic
- 1 Tbsp Powdered chili pepper
- 1/4 cup smoked paprika
- 2 Tbsp Black pepper

Directions:

1. Combine all the ingredients in a small bowl.
2. Transfer to an airtight jar or container.
3. Keep stored in a cool, dry place.

Nutrition:

- Calories: 16kcal
- Carbs: 3g
- Fat:0.9g
- Protein: 0.8g

301. Texas Barbeque Rub

Preparation Time: 5 Minutes

Cooking Time: 10 Minutes

Servings: ½ cup

Ingredients:

- 1 tsp Sugar
- 1 Tbsp Seasoned salt
- 1 Tbsp Black pepper
- 1 tsp Chili powder
- 1 Tbsp Powdered onions
- 1 Tbsp Smoked paprika
- 1 tsp Sugar
- 1 Tbsp Powdered garlic

Directions:

1. Pour all the ingredients into a small bowl and mix thoroughly.
2. Keep stored in an airtight jar or container.

Nutrition:

- Calories: 22kcal
- Carbs: 2g
- Fat: 0.2g
- Protein: 0.6g

302. Barbeque Sauce

Preparation Time: 5 Minutes

Cooking Time: 10 Minutes

Servings: 2 Cups

Ingredients:

- 1/4 cup of water
- 1/4 cup red wine vinegar
- 1 Tbsp Worcestershire sauce
- 1 tsp Paprika
- 1 tsp Salt
- Tbsp Dried mustard
- 1 tsp black pepper
- 1 cup ketchup
- 1 cup brown sugar

Directions:

1. Pour all the ingredients into a food processor, one after the other.
2. Process until they are evenly mixed.
3. Transfer sauce to a close lid jar. Store in the refrigerator.

Nutrition:

- Calories: 43kcal
- Carbs: 10g
- Fat: 0.3g
- Protein: 0.9g

303. Steak Sauce

Preparation Time: 5 Minutes

Cooking Time: 20 Minutes

Servings: ½ Cup

Ingredients:

- 1 Tbsp Malt vinegar
- 1/2 tsp Salt
- 1/2 tsp black pepper
- 1 Tbsp Tomato sauce
- 2 Tbsp brown sugar
- 1 tsp hot pepper sauce
- 2 Tbsp Worcestershire sauce
- 2 Tbsp Raspberry jam.

Directions:

1. Preheat your grill for indirect cooking at 150°F
2. Place a saucepan over grates, add all your ingredients, and allow to boil.
3. Reduce the temperature to Smoke and allow the sauce to simmer for 10 minutes or until sauce is thick.

Nutrition:

- Calories: 62.1kcal
- Carbs: 15.9g
- Fat: 0.3g
- Protein:0.1g

304. Bourbon Whiskey Sauce

Preparation Time: 20 Minutes

Cooking Time: 25 Minutes

Servings: 3 Cups

Ingredients:

- 2 cups ketchup; 1/2 Tbsp Salt
- 1/4 cup Worcestershire sauce
- 3/4 cup bourbon whiskey
- 1/3 cup apple cider vinegar
- 1/2 onions, minced
- 1/4 cup of tomato paste
- 2 cloves of garlic, minced
- 1/2 tsp Black pepper
- 1/2 cup brown sugar
- Hot pepper sauce to taste
- 1 Tbsp Liquid smoke flavoring

Directions:

1. Preheat your grill for indirect cooking at 150°F
2. Place a saucepan over grates, then add the whiskey, garlic, and onions.
3. Simmer until the onion is translucent. Then add the other ingredients and adjust the temperature to Smoke. Simmer for 20 minutes. For a smooth sauce, sieve.

Nutrition:

Calories: 107kcal | Carbs:16.6g

Fat: 1.8g | Protein:0.8g

305. Chicken Marinade

Preparation Time: 5 Minutes

Cooking Time: 30 Minutes

Servings: 3 Cups

Ingredients:

- halved chicken breast (bone and skin removed)
- 1 Tbsp Spicy brown mustard
- 2/3 cup of soy sauce; 1 tsp Powdered garlic
- 2 Tbsp Liquid smoke flavoring
- 2/3 cup extra virgin olive oil
- 2/3 cup lemon juice; 2 tsp Black pepper

Directions:

1. Mix all the ingredients in a large bowl.
2. Pour the chicken into the bowl and allow it to marinate for about 3-4hours in the refrigerator. Remove the chicken, then smoke, grill, or roast the chicken.

Nutrition:

- Calories: 507kcal
- Carbs:46.6g
- Fat: 41.8g
- Protein: 28g

306. Carne Asada Marinade

Preparation Time: 30 Minutes

Cooking Time: 1 Hour and 30 Minutes

Servings: 5 Cups

Ingredients:

- 2 cloves garlic, chopped
- 1 tsp Lemon juice
- 1/2 cup extra virgin olive oil
- 1/2 tsp Salt
- 1/2 tsp Pepper

Directions:

1. Mix all your ingredients in a bowl.
2. Pour the beef into the bowl and allow to marinate for 2-3hours before grilling.

Nutrition:

- Calories: 465kcal
- Carbs: 26g
- Fat: 15g
- Protein: 28g

307. Grapefruit Juice Marinade

Preparation Time: 25 Minutes

Cooking Time: 35 Minutes

Servings: 3 Cups

Ingredients:

- 1/2 reduced-sodium soy sauce
- 3 cups grapefruit juice, unsweetened
- 1-1/2 lb. Chicken, bone and skin removed
- 1/4 brown sugar

Directions:

1. Thoroughly mix all your ingredients in a large bowl.
2. Add the chicken and allow it to marinate for 2-3 hours before grilling.

Nutrition:

- Calories: 489kcal
- Carbs: 21.3g
- Fat: 12g
- Protein: 24g

308. Steak Marinade

Preparation Time: 5 Minutes

Cooking Time: 10 Minutes

Servings: 2 Cups

Ingredients:

- 1 Tbsp Worcestershire sauce
- 2 Tbsp Red wine vinegar
- 1/2 cup barbeque sauce
- 3 Tbsp soy sauce
- 1/4 cup steak sauce
- 1 clove garlic (minced)
- 1 tsp Mustard
- Pepper and salt to taste

Directions:

1. Pour all the ingredients in a bowl and mix thoroughly.
2. Use immediately or keep refrigerated.

Nutrition:

- Calories: 303kcal
- Carbs: 42g
- Fat: 10g
- Protein:2.4g

309. Dry Rub for Ribs

Preparation Time: 10 Minutes

Cooking Time: 0 Minutes

Servings: 8

Ingredients:

- three tablespoons brown sugar
- One and a half tablespoons paprika
- One and a half tablespoons salt
- one teaspoon garlic powder
- One and a half tablespoons ground black pepper

Directions:

1. Combine black pepper, brown sugar, salt, paprika, and garlic powder. Now, rub into the pork ribs. Let ribs to marinate whole night and then grill as you want.

Nutrition:

- Calories: 16kcal
- Carbs: 3g
- Fat:0.9g
- Protein: 0.8g

310. Special BBQ Sauce

Preparation Time: 10 Minutes

Cooking Time: 0 Minutes

Servings: 32

Ingredients:

- One and half cups brown sugar
- One and a half cups ketchup
- one tablespoon Worcestershire sauce
- Two and a half tablespoons dry mustard
- Two teaspoons paprika
- Two teaspoons salt
- Half cup red wine vinegar
- Half cup waters
- One and a half teaspoons black pepper
- Two dashes hot pepper sauce

Directions:

1. Take a blender; merge Worcestershire sauce, vinegar, brown sugar, water, and ketchup. Now, season with hot pepper sauce, paprika, mustard, pepper, and salt. Mix until it gets smooth.

Nutrition:

- Calories: 43kcal
- Carbs: 10g
- Fat: 0.3g
- Protein: 0.9g

311. Special Teriyaki Marinade

Preparation Time: 10 Minutes

Cooking Time: 0 Minutes

Servings: 24

Ingredients:

- one cup soy sauce
- one cup water
- ¾ cup white sugar
- ¼ cup Worcestershire sauce
- othree tablespoons distilled white vinegar
- three tablespoons vegetable oil
- one teaspoon grated fresh ginger
- 1/3 cup dried onion flakes
- two teaspoons garlic powder

Directions:

1. Take an intermediate bowl and combine sugar, onions, ginger, water, Worcestershire sauce, soy sauce, garlic powder, vinegar, and oil. Now, stir well until sugar dissolves completely

Nutrition:

- Calories: 465kcal
- Carbs: 26g
- Fat: 15g
- Protein: 28g

Conclusion

Traeger grills are revolutionary and may forever change the way we cook.

These days, anyone can own a Traeger grill since manufacturers meet the demand of clients from various backgrounds.

Modern Traeger grills make grilling simple and enjoyable.

The ability to remotely track and change your temperatures, as well as the easy-to-follow recipes, removes the guesswork.

A Traeger grill can quickly become one of the most valuable appliances you can own to help you make flavorful meals with far less effort, whether you're an inexperienced home cook hosting a backyard cookout or a pitmaster at a barbecue competition.

Despite the fact that Traeger's grill isn't everyone's favorite, it's obvious that it's a must-have outdoor kitchen gadget. Traeger grills are obviously versatile and have you covered whether you enjoy smoking, grilling, roasting, barbecuing, or direct cooking of food.

When you cook on a Traeger grill, you can choose the Traeger flavor you want to create the perfect smoke flavor for your cooking. Each Traeger has its own personality and preferences. The best thing is that you can use a single flavor or mix and match flavors to create your own unique blend.

Traegers, like any other cooking appliance, have some disadvantages, but the advantages outweigh them. As a result, it is certainly worth a shot.

Smoking is a common form of cooking these days, and many enthusiasts use it. If modern cooking methods are used, proteins such as various types of beef, poultry, and fish can spoil easily. Smoking, on the other hand, is a lengthy and low-temperature process that thoroughly cooks the meat. The flavor of almost any food item is greatly enhanced by smoke, especially white smoke. Smoking, on the other hand, seals and retains the nutrients in the food. Smoking is a versatile method of food preparation and one of the oldest.

Smoking was once considered an art form. Any enthusiast can quickly learn the basics and advanced techniques with just a short time of continuous effort. It is also said that once you learn and develop your smoking skills, you can no longer consider mastering other cooking techniques. However, since there are so many different smoking methods, you must find one that fits your disposition and style. You may do so by experimenting with various smoking methods and different types of woodland. Using a heat source that is not directly on the beef, cook meat items for many hours. However, you must ensure that the smoke has enough space to soak your meat and that it has a way out.

Isn't it lovely to imagine having a nice time with loved ones, neighbors, and friends while enjoying a backyard barbeque? When you have guests, having a smoker-grill and some grilled and smoked recipes is ideal because you can provide both delicious food and a magical moment, such as on a summer night. There are hundreds of delicious recipes to try with a Traeger smoker-grill! It's up to you to experiment, develop, or create your own recipes. It's simple and quick to do. However, if you want to be safe, stick to the tried and true options. These recipes have a reputation for being just right in terms of taste and reliability. Your edge would come from a mix of making the right impression the first time and every time, as well as enjoying delicious food along the way.

Another benefit of these recipes is that they are simple to prepare and do not necessitate culinary wizardry. These recipes can be used to make delicious food in no time by simply following a few simple steps and getting the right ingredients on hand. So, give these recipes a try and tell your friends about them! I'm certain that this Traeger smoker-grill recipe book would be a fantastic gift for your loved ones as well!

Finally, while any Traeger grill model can provide excellent smoking and grilling opportunities, the models vary significantly. As a result, they have a variety of facilities and are appropriate for a variety of users. With the new Traeger grill series being released every year, you'll want to shop wisely to ensure that you get a grill that suits you perfectly and meets all of your requirements.

If you're thinking of buying a grill for yourself, you should first learn about the different types of grills available and which ones would work better for you. You must understand how they function, how they compare, and the ones that are common. The Traeger grill is the best on the market and has a lot of benefits over the traditional cooking grill that everyone has. New technology is constantly releasing better and better goods, and if you do not update your purchase and continue to buy the same old things, you will fall behind.

The Traeger grill offers a perfect barbecuing experience for all, improving the taste of food and making cooking simpler.

You won't have to scour the internet for your favorite Traeger smoker-grill recipes anymore. This book is a one-stop-shop for all of your Traeger smoker-grill recipe needs for yourself and your loved ones.

Made in the USA
Columbia, SC
01 July 2021

41249887R00220